EARLY CHILDHOOD SPECIAL EDUCATION

EARLY CHILDHOOD SPECIAL EDUCATION

Program Development and Administration

Toni W. Linder, Ed.D.
Associate Professor
School of Education
University of Denver

·P·A·U·L·H·
BROOKES
PUBLISHING C°

Baltimore • London

Paul H. Brookes Publishing Co.
Post Office Box 10624
Baltimore, MD 21204

Portions of this publication were developed under USOE Grant No.
G007902569 awarded to the Colorado Department of Education, Denver, Colorado.

Typeset by Brushwood Graphics, Baltimore, Maryland.
Manufactured in the United States of America by
Universal Lithographers, Cockeysville, Maryland.

Library of Congress Cataloging in Publication Data

Linder, Toni W., 1946–
    Early childhood special education.

    Bibliography: p.
    Includes index.
    1. Handicapped children—Education (Preschool).   I. Title.
LC4019.2.L56   371.9   82-4496
ISBN 0-933716-28-1   AACR2

Contents

Foreword

The documentation of the success of early childhood programs for handicapped children has been substantial. Not only do these programs alleviate some of the effects of stress associated with prematurity and low birthweight, but they also result in marked improvement in the lives of sensory-impaired infants. It is well known that early treatment and training of deaf and blind children before 2 years of age can assist these children in living normal lives, and it is suspected that similar results can be realized with other developmentally disabled children.

Further, the impact of early childhood programs on children who reside in poverty alters the typical negative course of their lives. Strong effects of early intervention have been found in studies in Michigan, Florida, New York, Wisconsin, and other areas of the world. Two programs, Homestart and Head Start, have demonstrated that the child who lives on a poverty level has the genetic potential to meet the requirements of the culture and to function within it. One of the keys to the success of these programs is the attention given to strengthening the families of these children so that facilitative childrearing and stimulation strategies are put into practice.

The focus of recent efforts of early childhood programs for handicapped children has been to involve the family and thereby serve the child through the family. Unfortunately, many public schools have not focused on early childhood programs and the involvement of parents to strengthen the family. This trend should change as schools become aware that impaired school-age children who have experienced an early intervention program have many strengths and skills not possessed by those impaired children who have not had the benefit of such a program.

However, early childhood programs, particularly those for impaired children, are a new experience for many school districts. School personnel are presented with new dilemmas involving what criteria to evoke in making the decisions necessary for setting up a preschool program. They are confronted with problems in the areas of selecting curriculum, determining what type of staff to hire, providing inservice training for their staff, establishing a parent program, finding the means to finance the classes, choosing what management organization to use, and discovering which evaluation strategies and evaluation procedures have been proven effective. In the 1960s, early childhood programs for children who reside in poverty (Head Start and others) and for children who were sensory-impaired had to invent means to organize and manage classrooms and to construct curriculum, assessment devices, and evaluation strategies. In the process, much was learned and much was developed. What is needed now is a comprehensive look at the various facets of program development, implementation, operation, and management to enable others to establish their own programs, to avoid the pitfalls predecessors have discovered, and to move forward on the strengths of the past achievements of the pioneers in the field.

Such a comprehensive look at early childhood programs for handicapped children is what Dr. Toni Linder has provided in this book. She presents a cogent rationale as to why early childhood and parent involvement programs are needed and then proceeds to examine in detail all aspects of program operation. The strength of the text is Dr. Linder's attention to the large organizational issues related to program success, such as the need for a consistent philosophy, as well as to the practical concerns, such as how to write a proposal when seeking funds. The book should help many in establishing programs that will provide the early experience, stimulation, and training necessary to improve the life chances and life outcome of handicapped children and their families.

Nicholas J. Anastasiow, Ph.D.
Professor
Hunter College, City University of New York

Preface

This text has been written to aid persons in planning, developing, implementing, and evaluating an early childhood special education program. Its intent is to offer guidelines to assist in obtaining funding for programs and also to provide a foundation for developing quality-effective early intervention programs. It should also serve as a reference with respect to various aspects of program maintenance and modification.

The growth of early childhood programs for handicapped children in the past 10 to 15 years has resulted in the development of a variety of training efforts. Projects funded under the Handicapped Children's Early Education Program have developed "outreach" efforts that train staff of new and existing programs in their particular model and intervention techniques. Universities across the country have initiated preservice training programs at the graduate and undergraduate levels. Many existing direct service programs have implemented ongoing inservice training efforts. The majority of these training programs are directed at teachers; thus, the content is primarily related to child development, handicapping conditions, assessment, and intervention strategies. A very small proportion of teacher training is related to the administration of early childhood special education programs. Program staff, however, must frequently assume administrative positions or functions. Consequently, training in administration and program development has proven to be lacking in preservice training. This book is intended to partially fill that gap. In addition, it is intended to provide administrators who are unfamiliar with early childhood special education programs with the basic understanding of programmatic differences between school-age and early childhood programs.

Early Childhood Special Education: Program Development and Administration is thus directed at three specific audiences: 1) graduate students in preservice training programs preparing to work in early childhood special education programs, 2) early childhood special educators who are directing or coordinating a program for handicapped infants or preschool children, and 3) administrators of early intervention programs who lack background and training related to early childhood special education. In addition, the book should be helpful to early childhood administrators in general who are interested in developing quality, individualized programs. Educational administrators of all levels should also find sections of the book a practical aid to program development.

The format of the text leads the reader from a basic understanding of the current state of the art in early childhood special education through practical considerations in program development and administration. The book culminates with suggestions for funding alternatives and guidelines for proposal writing. The reader who has integrated information from the first nine chapters should be able to conceptualize and plan the implementation and evaluation of an early childhood special education program. The last two chapters are intended to stimulate creative problem solving in relation to financing of new and existing programs.

Chapter 1, Something Old, Something New, reviews the historical perspective of the development of early childhood programs. The classic and current research on the early years of life, legislation having an impact on early intervention, and some important issues presently affecting the field are delineated.

Chapter 2, Conceptualizing and Developing a Program, provides a framework and process model for the development of a service delivery system for young handicapped children. Guidelines for determining an appropriate program model are also presented with consideration being given to staffing patterns, theoretical approach, curriculum and evaluation instruments, and site. The nature of the interaction among the child, the staff, the parents, and the environment is also examined in relation to program philosophy.

Chapter 3, Leadership and Administration, specifies the characteristics and functions of the early childhood administrator. Planning functions are emphasized, including coordination with other agencies and establishment of policies and procedures. Management and supervision responsibilities are also introduced.

Chapter 4, Coordinating Community Resources, explains the rationale for interagency coordination, barriers to this coordination, and a model for the planning and implementation of a local coordination effort. A step-by-step process is presented with sample forms to illustrate procedures.

Chapter 5, Screening and Assessment, differentiates the screening process from the assessment process. A detailed assessment process is suggested, outlining the five phases of assessment planning, assessment, interpretation, program planning, and classroom assessment. Guidelines for screening, formal and informal assessment, and conducting staffings are offered.

Chapter 6, Selecting and Using Curricula, describes various approaches to curricula in early childhood, and modifications in content, sequencing, and usage. The major developmental areas that need to be incorporated into the program are outlined with emphasis on the importance of interrelatedness. Guidelines are presented for selecting curricula and modifying methodology to reflect the nature of the target population.

Chapter 7, Parent Involvement, begins with the rationale for parent involvement. The impact of a handicapped child on the family system is discussed along with the programmatic implications that need to be considered to meet the needs of families of handicapped children. Delivery of services to parents is addressed in staffings, in conferences, and through individual and group counseling. Alternatives for parent involvement in the early childhood program are detailed along with suggestions for incorporating parent education options.

Chapter 8, Staff Development, demonstrates a process model for developing inservice training programs that derive from the necessity of competent staff and are directly related to program evaluation. The chapter delineates important competencies, assessment of staff needs, planning for individualized professional development, implementing staff development alternatives, and evaluating growth.

Chapter 9, Evaluation, demonstrates the parallel between program evaluation and child evaluation in both formative and summative methods. The chapter outlines components to evaluate and types of data that are needed. A sample evaluation plan is included.

Chapter 10, Funding Alternatives, examines historical federal, state, and local funding patterns. Change that are occurring in funding patterns are addressed along with implications for early childhood special education programs. Alternatives for developing funding options are discussed.

Chapter 11, Proposal Writing, outlines a format for the synthesis of the previously discussed material into an early childhood special education proposal. Suggestions are made for identification of funding sources and guidelines are given for writing a proposal that is relevant to that funding source.

The book may be studied in sequence in order to obtain an overview of administrative concerns or may be broken up into sections to meet specific training objectives. For example, in a course on proposal writing or program development, the first two chapters on the state of the art and conceptualizing a program plus the last two chapters on funding and proposal writing might be studied initially to give the reader a format for the inclusion of the proposal content, which is covered in Chapters 3 through 9.

The text might also be used as a reference for specific areas of study such as evaluation. In this instance, child evaluation, program evaluation, and staff evaluation would need to be related to the philosophy, objectives, policies and procedures, and funding issues covered in the various chapters.

Early Childhood Special Education is intended both as a preservice training text and as a reference for program administrators. It is hoped that the contents will assist in the development of an increased number of quality early childhood programs serving young handicapped children and their families.

Acknowledgments

Of the many people who facilitated the writing of this book, I would like especially to acknowledge the contribution of Brian McNulty, Consultant in Early Childhood Special Education, Colorado Department of Education, Denver, Colorado. His recognition of the need for guidelines to implement programs for young handicapped children led him to write a grant that funded the development of a manual for early childhood special education for the state of Colorado. His initial conceptualization was the seed of this book. In addition, his editorial assistance has been invaluable, and his continued personal support has been a mainstay throughout the work on the manuscript. He has been a wonderful friend and colleague.

I am also grateful to Dr. Nicholas Anastasiow, at Hunter College, and Dr. Norris Haring, at the University of Washington, for their review of early versions of many of the chapters. Their comments and recommendations have made an important contribution. I also appreciate their professional encouragement. I would, in addition, like to thank Dr. James Davis and Dr. Kenneth Seeley at the University of Denver, who have frequently provided both the professional and emotional bolster to enable me to sustain my efforts.

Two graduate research assistants, Pam Aglar and Connie Dalke, have rendered invaluable assistance. Their reaction from a ''consumer'' point of view also furnished helpful perspective.

I would like to thank Sanndi Glasheen and Linda McCarthy for many hours of secretarial work and for typing sections of the manuscript. A special thanks to Connie Dalke whose caring and perseverance resulted in the final typed manuscript. I am grateful to my editor, Melissa Behm, for her editorial acumen and also to Betsy Duffner and Dr. John Runkel for their editorial assistance in the final stages of the work.

Finally, an additional expression of gratitude to Dr. John Runkel, who gave up dinners, nights out, and companionship on evenings and weekends so that I might keep writing. Without his patience and support, this work would not have been completed.

To all of the above, thank you. I hope that this final product of all of your efforts will help in some way to better the lives of handicapped children and their families.

*To my mother and father
in appreciation of their love
and continuous support of
a rather unconventional
daughter.*

EARLY
CHILDHOOD
SPECIAL
EDUCATION

chapter

1

Something Old, Something New

Early childhood special education derives much from past research and present knowledge, but it is also a rapidly expanding field in its own right. The marriage of early childhood and special education has yielded modified theories, innovative models and techniques, and impressive research. The goal of early childhood special education is to intervene during the critical development years from birth to age 6, in order to prevent or ameliorate the effects of a handicapping condition or problems that have a high probability of manifesting themselves as developmental or school-related difficulties in later childhood. Early intervention can prevent concomitant problems from compounding existing deviations or delays. Another goal of intervention programs is to provide support and guidance to parents of handicapped children to enable them to better cope with and facilitate their child's development.

THE STATE OF THE ART

In the past 15 years the number of early intervention programs serving handicapped infants and preschool children has grown tremendously. Several factors have contributed to this proliferation. Research demonstrating the importance of the early years has influenced educators' thinking in regard to the early experiences of at-risk, disadvantaged, and handicapped children. Theorizing that intervention and special techniques to enrich early experiences could correct or reduce developmental and environmental deficits, practitioners sought funding to test their hypotheses. Research institutes, model research and demonstration projects, Head Start programs, longitudinal studies, and public and private infant and preschool projects were initiated. After years of such study, the evidence is now

1

conclusive that early intervention is, in fact, effective. Much more research and many more programs are needed, however, to examine the specific techniques and approaches that are most appropriate for individual children.

This chapter provides a brief overview of the current state of the art in early education services for children with handicaps. Research relating to the importance of the early years is summarized. The evidence of the impact of early intervention programs on children, families, and society is discussed, along with the current status of programs for children. Some of the research findings that have been generated from these programs are also addressed, in addition to current issues and questions needing further research.

THE IMPORTANCE OF THE EARLY YEARS

Evidence of the critical importance of the early years of life has been mounting steadily. Empirical research findings demonstrating the effects of early life experience on animals have been used as a basis for inferences regarding the importance of the early years to human infants. Studies on children reared in "deprived" environments have also revealed the long-term impact of early environmental conditions. In addition, research in motor, cognitive, language, social, and emotional development has contributed to our understanding of the interactive nature of these areas of development. Researchers and theorists are developing conceptual frameworks to analyze learning and apply developmental principles. This expanding knowledge base has encouraged trends, both social and political, supporting early intervention for handicapped infants and preschoolers.

In animal research, the classic studies of Lorenz (1971), Harlow (1974), Denenberg (1969), and others have demonstrated that the procedures used in raising an animal from infancy have profound effects upon behavior and physiology in maturity. The effects of environmental conditions such as light (Hebb, 1937; Riesen, 1961), tactile, kinesthetic, and manipulative experiences (Levine, 1969; Nissen, Chow, & Semmens, 1951), nutrition (Hall, 1956), amount and type of stimulation (Berkson & Mason, 1964; Rosenzweig, 1966) have all been shown to affect later cognitive functioning in animals.

Research on human babies has examined similar factors. Early studies revealed the negative impact of maternal deprivation (Bowlby, 1973; Dennis, 1960, Spitz & Wolff, 1946). In recent studies the importance of tactile and vestibular stimulation (Clark, Kreutzberg, & Chee, 1977; Weeks, 1979) to later development continues to be demonstrated, along with the significance of the parent-child attachment process (Ainsworth, 1973; Mahler, 1972; Rheingold, 1970).

However, the outlook for children who are "deprived" during their early years is not totally bleak. Both animal and human studies have revealed the early plasticity of the brain and the possible reversibility of negative environmental events. Novak and Harlow (1975), Denenberg and Thoman (1976), and others have demonstrated the reversibility of damage to animals. Dennis (1960) and the now classic Skeels and Dye (1939) study and its follow-up (Skeels, 1966) have shown that early damage to infants as a result of environmental deprivation can be ameliorated.

These studies and others, as well as reviews of the literature on the effects of experience on intelligence (Bloom, 1964; Hunt, 1979), have led experts to conclude that intervention in the early years is important to maximize later potential. The research supports the contention that the best time to attack a child's mental, physical, or emotional handicap is in the years from birth through early childhood (Jensen, 1966; La Cross & Lee, 1970; Lillie, 1975; Northern & Downs, 1974; Roos, 1974).

On the other hand, *failure* to provide remedial programs for disadvantaged and handicapped children at an early age can have negative results. A ''cumulative developmental deficit'' has been noted (Bloom, 1964; Bruner, 1972). The areas of development (for example, language, cognition) are interrelated, and thus a problem in one developmental area may have an effect on one or more other areas. For instance, a physical handicap in the motor area can limit the child's mobility within his or her environment and restrict the child's opportunities to interact with objects, events, and people. This limited interaction may lead to reduced understanding of relationships (both physical and cognitive) between objects, events, and people, with a resultant diminished capacity for problem solving. Thus cognitive, language, and social development may also be impaired or delayed. Any handicap may have deleterious consequences on all areas of development. Failure to intervene may allow the effects of the handicap to be compounded. (See Chapter 6 for a further discussion of the interrelated nature of developmental areas.)

RESULTING LEGISLATION

As a result of the above cited research (as well as extensive research that space does not make it possible to cite), there has developed a growing interest in and demand for increased services for young handicapped children and their families. The federal government has played a major role in responding to this interest and demand. Initial federal support came with the passage of the Handicapped Children's Early Education Assistance Act of 1968 (Public Law 90-538). This law established experimental programs to serve as models to demonstrate and disseminate exemplary practices and materials for working with young handicapped children.

The Education of the Handicapped Amendments of 1974 (PL 93-380) added the stipulation that states needed to set a goal for serving all handicapped children from birth to 21 years of age. The timetable for meeting this goal was to be included in the state plan submitted to the Bureau of Education for the Handicapped (now entitled Special Education Programs [SEP]). Although philosophically a federal commitment, the states could evade the issue by tying their time-lines to funding constraints. PL 93-380 also required the establishment of "child find" efforts for handicapped children from birth through 21. Young children were to be identified, and, even if they were not served, the service system would at least have information for future planning. This, of course, led to conflicts over the ethics of identifying children without supporting their needs.

Also included in the Handicapped Children's Early Education Assistance Act was authorization for State Implementation Grants, enabling states to set up comprehensive plans to serve their young handicapped population. These grants have aided states in system development and coordination with human service agencies, needs assessment, planning, program management, coordination of resources, personnel training, parent involvement, and technical assistance to programs (Carter, Imhoff, Lacoste, McNulty, & Peterson, 1980).

In 1975, Public Law 94-142, the Education for All Handicapped Children Act, was passed. This monumental piece of legislation, in addition to mandating a free appropriate education for all handicapped school-age children, also included a mandate (of sorts) for a free appropriate public education for handicapped preschoolers:

> A free appropriate public education will be available for all handicapped children between the ages of three and eighteen within the State not later than September 1, 1978, and for all handicapped children between the ages of three and twenty-one within the State not later than September 1, 1980, except that with respect to handicapped children aged three to five and aged eighteen to twenty-one, inclusive, the requirements of this clause shall not be applied in any State if the application of such requirements would be inconsistent with State law or practice, or the order of any court, respecting public education with such age groups in the State. [Public Law 94-142, 1975, Section 612(2)(B)]

Obviously, the law leaves a gaping loophole to enable states to avoid serving handicapped preschool children. Certain conditions were included, however, that are equivalent to a mandate:

1) if State law or court order requires the State to provide education to any category of handicapped preschooler, then an education must be provided to all who have that disability;
2) if a public agency provides education to non-handicapped then it must provide services to at least a proportional number of handicapped children of the same age;
3) if a public agency provides education to 50 percent or more of its handicapped children in any disability category, it must make a free appropriate education available to all handicapped children of the same disability and age. [Education for All Handicapped Children, 1977 45 CFR Part 121a., 300(b)(i), (2), and (3)]

These conditions of the law have had both positive and negative effects on the services delivered to handicapped children; these effects are addressed later in this chapter in relation to current issues.

In addition to the above aspects of the law, Section 619 of the act established the Preschool Incentive Grant Program to stimulate the development of services for 3-, 4-, and 5-year-olds. Up to $300 per child was authorized to states with an approved plan who chose to serve preschool children. DeWeerd (1981) notes that in fiscal year 1980, the average allotment of funds under PL 94-142 was $159 per child. An additional $80 was provided for children ages 3 to 5 under the Preschool Incentive Grant Program.

An additional assurance of services for young handicapped children is provided through Section 504 of the Rehabilitation Act of 1973 (PL 93-112), which is a civil rights provision dealing with discrimination against handicapped persons. Section 504 requires that any state that offers services to nonhandicapped preschool children must offer services to handicapped children also. In order to continue to receive federal funds, programs must be in compliance.

Head Start, another federal program, was established in 1964 through the Economic Opportunity Act to serve disadvantaged preschoolers. Head Start has also been required to serve no less than 10% handicapped children as a result of the Economic Opportunity and Community Partnership Act of 1974 (PL 93-644). Cooperative activities and training of Head Start staff are authorized through 14 regional access projects funded by the Administration for Children, Youth, and Families.

As is clear from this brief overview of legislation, the federal government has recognized the importance of early intervention on a philosophical level. However, much remains to be done. The present political climate may not be conducive to further expansion of programs through federal support. Thus, future funding of early intervention programs is open to question (see Chapter 10).

ADVANCES IN THE FIELD

As a result of the previously mentioned legislation, a variety of benefits have been documented. For example, there are an increasing number of educational programs based on theory and research in the growth and development of young, handicapped children. Research and evaluation activities have evolved for assessing program effectiveness. More discrete child measurement activities have been developed to ascertain child functioning and progress. Research is demonstrating complex issues relating to individual development and the handicapped child (Hamilton & Swan, 1981). The importance of supportive interactions between parents and professionals has been shown, resulting in increased attention to the family's in the handicapped child's education (Cartwright, 1981; Foster, Berger, & McLean, 1981).

Deweerd (1981) notes the following changes in services to young handicapped children in the past three decades:

Public school provision of services for children under 6 is increasing.
Ten percent of students enrolled by Head Start are handicapped.

Early intervention programs are now found in private agencies, clinics, hospitals, universities, nursery schools, residential programs, and some day-care facilities.

Hospital-based programs are providing services for newborn handicapped and high-risk babies.

Models

A variety of models for educating young, handicapped children have been developed. The models vary in theoretical approach, the children they serve, the site of service delivery, staffing patterns, methodology, use of materials, and evaluation techniques (Jordan, Hayden, Karnes, & Wood, 1977). Numerous models have been replicated throughout the United States and are now being adopted in other countries. Although many of the original models were developed with federal support, Swan (1980) discovered that 86% of the first group of federal Handicapped Children's Early Education Program (HCEEP) demonstration projects maintained outside continuation funding 7 years after their initiation. Once initiated, the programs have proven both programmatically effective and cost efficient. For a helpful resource on models, the reader is referred to *Educational Programs That Work—The National Diffusion Network Catalog* (Far West Laboratory, 1980). The group of programs it describes was judged exemplary by the Joint Dissemination Review Panel of the U.S. Department of Education. (See Chapters 2 and 6 for a further discussion of models.)

Assessment

Another area in which strides are being made is in individual screening and assessment. The Child Find program has had varying degrees of success. Although many new screening tests have been developed, issues such as cultural differences, race, and poverty confound efforts to identify handicapped children. Many children are still not identified until school age. Anastasiow (1981) discusses recent screening-related efforts such as *The Baby Book* in Colorado. The book, now being field tested, is designed as a photograph album and is given to new parents just after delivery. In addition to providing spaces for photos of the child as he or she gets older, the book contains pictures of children demonstrating age-related (at the 95 percentile) development competencies. Descriptions of each competency are offered in English and Spanish, and a telephone number and a stamped postcard are included to aid parents in contacting an appropriate source should they have concerns about their child's development. It is hoped that this type of effort will help identify more children at earlier ages.

Regarding assessment after a child has been screened, a number of new instruments have been developed (Katoff & Reuter, 1979). These instruments are important, as traditional tests developed for the older child may not be appropriate for the young or severely handicapped child. Professionals have also addressed adaptive processes in assessing young, severely handicapped children (Bagnato,

1981; Dubose, 1981; Dubose, Langley, & Stagg, 1979). Alternative approaches to measurement, including case report systems and daily in-class data collection to document skills acquisition over time, are being incorporated into assessment procedures. Competency assessment profiles (Brooks-Gunn & Lewis, 1981) examine children across competency areas and explore interactions within developmental areas. Although many problems are yet unsolved in accurately screening and assessing young handicapped children, many advances have been made.

Curriculum and Materials

Numerous materials have been developed recently to help those who are planning, implementing, or evaluating early intervention services. Curricula, textbooks, guidebooks, videotapes, films, and a wealth of other resources are now available. *Early Childhood Curriculum Materials: An Annotated Bibliography* (Harbin, Cross, & Mears, 1976) and *Educational Products for the Exceptional Child* (1980) are two resource guides to available materials.

Parent Involvement

Much research has been done on the effects on the family of a handicapped child (Cunningham & Sloper, 1977; McAndrew, 1976; Olshansky, 1962; Solnit & Stark, 1961). Early intervention programs have consequently devoted increasing attention to parents. Depending on their needs and interests, parents have assumed a variety of program roles—including observer, learner, teacher, therapist, aide, and policymaker. They have been involved to varying degrees, in planning, implementing, and evaluating their child's program. The documented benefits of early intervention programs to families are many. Intervention program staff (Bronfenbrenner, 1975; Cartwright, 1981; Lazar, Hubbell, Murray, Rosche, & Royce, 1977; Levitt & Cohen, 1975; Lillie, Trohanis, & Goin, 1976; Mallory, 1981) have:

1. Offered emotional support to families in times of difficulty or crisis
2. Helped parents understand the handicapping conditions, the strengths and weaknesses, and program needs of their child
3. Offered suggestions, demonstrations, and have taught parents how to intervene on behalf of their child
4. Offered educational programs to increase parents' knowledge and skills in areas relating to the parents' or child's needs
5. Aided parents in obtaining needed services and resources to allow the family to maintain the child in the home and to provide for his/her needs
6. Facilitated the development of positive attitudes toward the school system

Personnel Preparation

As the number of programs serving young handicapped children has increased, the need for trained personnel has also grown. Persons trained to work with older handicapped children have been found to lack the skills to work with the very young, and those trained to work with young normal children lack the skills to work with handicapped children. In addition, many programs serve children with multiple problems thus necessitating that staff have a broad knowledge base. Infant and preschool programs also require close coordination with parents, who may also have multiple needs. In response to these needs, preservice and inservice training programs have been developed across the country. As with the early intervention programs, these programs espouse a variety of theoretical approaches and methodologies. An emerging trend is a noncategorical approach with interdisciplinary or transdisciplinary training (Bluhm, Egan, & Perry, 1981; Buktenica, 1981; Golin & Ducanis, 1981), emphasizing skills for working with parents (Anastasiow, 1981) and incorporating research and methodology from developmental and behavioral schools of thought. Development of training programs is furthermore being encouraged by the increase in state certification requirements (Hirshoren & Umansky, 1977). In addition to teacher training, heightened attention is also being paid to training pediatricians in the benefits of early intervention, the needs of families, and how to work with teams from other disciplines (Guralnick & Richardson, 1980; Guralnick, 1981).

PROGRAM EFFECTIVENESS

In addition to examining the programmatic changes that have resulted from increased intervention efforts, it is important to investigate the efficacy of these programs. In perhaps one of the most comprehensive studies of the effects of early intervention, Lazar et al. (1977) summarized the findings of the Developmental Continuity Consortium, a collaborative effort of 12 research groups conducting longitudinal studies on the outcome of early education programs for low-income infants and preschool children. Three important results were reported: 1) early education significantly reduced the number of children assigned to special classes, 2) early education reduced the number of children held back one or more grades, and 3) children surpassed their control group on IQ tests. Following are some results of specific projects.

In the Milwaukee Project (Heber, Garber, Harrington, Hoffman, & Falendar, 1975), families of selected low-income children with mothers of subnormal IQ were provided intensive support from the child's birth to school age. The families were helped to develop survival skills, while also being taught good parenting skills. The results showed that children participating in the project had at least normal intelligence, with the group average being at least one standard deviation above the mean. This type of evidence supports the premise that environmental stimulation and parent education can be tremendously beneficial to children at risk for developmental and/or school-related problems.

Alice Hayden and her colleagues at the Model Preschool Center for Handicapped Children at the Experimental Education Unit in Seattle have demonstrated that Down syndrome children who were formerly thought to be "trainable" or institutional candidates could, with intensive early intervention, function at a low-average level of intelligence. They were mainstreamed successfully with normal peers, and learned academic tasks such as reading (Hayden & McGinness, 1977). Thirty-four percent functioned well in regular classrooms; another 22% needed support services, but were able to function cognitively on a level equal to those in regular classes (Hayden, Morris, & Bailey, 1977).

The Perry Preschool Project accumulated longitudinal data on children who participated in the program (Schweinhart & Weikart, 1980). The results showed significant gains by age 15. Children with preschool experience demonstrated better achievement in reading, arithmetic, and language at all grades. They also demonstrated better motivation than those who did not attend preschool. Overall, they had a 50% reduction in the need for special education.

DeWeerd (1981) summarizes several project findings, including that of the Battelle Institute (1976) that studied 129 children from 29 early intervention projects. The findings indicated that many children gained from 1.5 to 2 times more from pre- to posttests than would have been expected without intervention. As with the Lazar et al. study, a high percentage (64%) of children progressed to regular classes. Moore, Anderson, Fredericks, Baldwin, and Moore (1979) have documented that the more years retarded children spend in preschool programs, the greater the gain.

Many programs have proven so effective that they are in demand for use by other school systems, agencies, and groups. The Joint Dissemination Review Panel of the U.S. Department of Education has approved 19 federal projects for dissemination. All met stringent requirements and demonstrated both program and cost effectiveness. (For further information on specific programs, the reader is referred to the December 1981 *Journal of the Division of Early Childhood*, which is devoted entirely to results of efficacy studies in early intervention programs.)

Cost Effectiveness

Education programs for handicapped children cost money. The more segregated and restrictive the programs, the more they cost. Therefore, it makes fiscal (as well as philosophical) sense to provide services to handicapped children in the least restrictive environment possible. In the Perry Preschool Project study, Schweinhart and Weikart (1980) support Lazar et al.'s (1977) previous finding that early intervention may make it possible for a child to move into regular educational programs earlier than the child who receives no "early" assistance. Lazar et al. (1977) conclude in their review of program effectiveness:

> Infant and preschool services improve ability of low income children to meet minimal requirements of the school they enter. This effect can be manifested in either a reduced probability of being assigned to special classes or a reduced probability of being held back a grade. Either reduction constitutes a substantial cost reduction for the school system (p. 19).

Hodges, McCandless, and Spicker (1967) reported similar results with disadvantaged mentally retarded children.

The Perry Preschool Project longitudinal study (Schweinhart & Weikart, 1980) demonstrated significant cost benefits. The approximate cost of $3,000 per child for one preschool year was recovered over the long term through: $3,353 saved per child because of the need for fewer years in special education and fewer years of grade retention; $10,798 in projected additional lifetime earnings for the handicapped person; and $668 from the mother's released time. The cost of 2 years of preschool was $5,984 per child, with benefits totaling $14,819.

The cost of providing special education at various age levels was calculated by Wood (1980). The total cost per child to age 18 for four entry ages was as follows:

1. Intervention at birth: $37,273
2. Intervention at age 2: $37,600
3. Intervention at age 6: $46,816
4. Intervention at age 6 with no eventual movement to regular education: $53,340

The cumulative cost is thus demonstrated to be lower the earlier intervention begins.

Cost benefits to the education system of early intervention are significant, but even more striking are the long-range societal advantages. *Closer Look* (1976), in analyzing the pay-off of education, found that handicapped people who are given an appropriate education repay the costs of that education in actual taxes within 5 years, and that they continue paying taxes and producing products or services over their lifetimes, instead of becoming dependents of society.

In 1973, Conley estimated the lifetime costs of maintaining a person in a state institution at $500,000; with current rates of inflation and the high cost of living, this figure is now much greater. Certainly whatever can be done to reduce the need for more restrictive and more specialized placements for handicapped children is of benefit to society. Early childhood special education takes advantage of the crucial learning years to reduce cumulative negative effects of a handicap and to increase independence. By supporting family maintenance of the child, early intervention results in cost benefits to society.

Number of Children Served

In analyzing the present status of early childhood special education, it is important to determine the number of children who could benefit from early intervention and how many of these are actually receiving services. Hayden (1979) discusses the problems involved in obtaining this information. Major difficulty relates to the definition of *handicapped*, which varies from program to program and state to state.

The federal definition of handicapped children in the regulations implementing PL 94–142 states:

> Handicapped children are those children evaluated as being mentally retarded, hard-of-hearing, deaf, speech impaired, visually handicapped, seriously emotionally disturbed, orthopedically impaired, other health impaired, deaf-blind, multi-handicapped, or having specific learning disabilities, who because of these impairments need special education and related services. [Sec. 121a.5 (42 Fed. Reg. 12478)]

Behr and Gallagher (1981) propose a definition that more accurately takes into account the special neurological, physiological, and developmental nature of the child from birth to 3 years old:

> A handicapped infant is a child who, from the time of birth (0) to the completion of the third year of life (3), has a high probability of manifesting, in later childhood, a sensory motor deficit and/or mental handicap which may be the result of a birth defect, disease process, trauma, or environmental conditions present during the prenatal and/or postnatal periods. Due to these factors, the infant may be unable to achieve the important developmental milestones necessary for future learning and socialization. These deficits and/or handicaps may be consistent with all the classifications set forth in PL 94-142 (Sec. 1219.5), Sec. 504, and PL 94-103, but may not allow for confirmation through medical/educational assessment or categorical classification until a later age (p. 114).

Estimates of the potential population for early intervention can be made based on epidemiological studies, but these estimates will vary, depending on whether one counts only "diagnosed" problems (as in the federal definition) or whether "high risk" children (as in the Behr and Gallagher definition) are also included. Estimates of the percentage of U.S. children from birth through 5 who would qualify range from a low of 3% to a high of 17% (Garland, Stone, Swanson, & Woodruff, 1980; Hayden, 1979)—the latter figure including medical or environmental factors that would indicate a high risk for possible handicapping conditions. Using the 1977 U.S. census figure of 15,339,000 children from birth through 5 years, the 3% estimate represented about 460,000 handicapped children and the 17% estimate, about 1.8 million handicapped children. As of 1982, using either definition, we have no accurate count of how many handicapped children there are between the ages of birth and 6.

As far as the numbers of children being served, the average percentage of children ages 3 to 21 receiving service during the 1979–1980 school year was 9.54%. The percentage of children aged 3 to 5 who were served in the same year was only 2.59%. Public schools served 11,800 children from birth to 2 years in the 1976–1977 school year. (Of the few school districts that have elected to serve children down to birth, Madison, Wisconsin, has, notably, developed a zero reject model, with 50% of the children moving into regular education without further special education.) In addition, the Bureau of Developmental Disabilities network is now serving children in the birth to 2 age range (DeWeerd, 1981).

Smith (1980) has summarized state legislation in relation to education of the handicapped infant and preschooler: 46 states have some provision for educating handicapped children below 6 years of age; 23 states mandate services to some portion of the birth to 5 years population; 16 states have permissive services; 9 states have conflicting policies; and 8 states appear to authorize services from birth. In the analysis of 50 states and the District of Columbia, it was noted that since 1973 (prior to PL 94-142), 7 states have lowered the age for preschool services and 12 states have raised the age.

The actual number of handicapped infants and preschoolers receiving services is impossible to determine without accurate accounting measures. The service delivery system for such children is fragmented, with services spread among many different agencies. The types of services available also differ greatly: While few programs offer comprehensive services, most include some aspect of diagnosis, treatment, education, counseling, and financial assistance.

Cost

The average cost of early intervention for handicapped children is likewise difficult to determine, and depends on various factors, including: age of population, staffing patterns, types of services offered, amount of program time, use of volunteers, costs of meeting individual needs associated with specific handicaps, and building costs. Smith and Greenberg (1981) cite several reports summarizing cost data and note that average annual per pupil expenditure for projects in the Handicapped Children's Early Education Program (HCEEP) was approximately $2,000 to $2,500, with a wide range ($1,080 to $4,822). The median cost of seven projects serving moderately to severely handicapped populations was $1,995. As discussed above, these costs appear to be repaid in the form of savings in later education and increased earnings.

Administrative Alternatives

One of the reasons that it is difficult to document the numbers of young handicapped children being served is the multiplicity of different agencies providing a great variety of services. There is a need to develop a more unified, coordinated service delivery system to meet the needs of handicapped children and their families. A controversy currently exists over which kind of agency or agencies should have the major policymaking responsibility for early intervention programs and services. Two major service systems, education and social services, seem to parallel each other, but while they often overlap in services, major gaps frequently exist.

Behr and Gallagher (1981) surveyed 57 state directors of special education; 24 early childhood state coordinators; 13 directors of state implementation grants for preschool handicapped children; 52 state directors of mental retardation programs administered in health and social service departments; 54 directors of state protection and advocacy agencies; and 27 directors of national voluntary organizations for the handicapped. Respondents were asked to rank the following 10 alternatives as to which would be the most appropriate to assume responsibility for infant intervention:

1. Department of Human Resources
2. Handicapped Children's Early Education Program
3. Public schools as service providers
4. Head Start
5. New federal agency
6. Public schools as access agencies
7. Developmental Disabilities agency
8. Vouchers
9. Local government
10. Title XX

The results indicated that

> the public schools were considered to be the most appropriate agency to be responsible for administering programs and services for handicapped infants.... This was the majority opinion, not only of the state officials in the educational establishment, but also of officials in state departments of social services and of those professionals and lay persons active in advocacy systems (Behr & Gallagher, 1981, p. 121).

This study offers one evaluation of how services for young handicapped children could be coordinated. Whatever alternative is finally decided upon, there will be a need for further state and federal legislation. In addition, ongoing interagency coordination will be necessary, and supplemental study is needed to determine how such coordination can be facilitated.

Legislation and Regulation

As a result of the increased number of handicapped children being identified, assessed, and placed in special services, attention is being focused on gaps in service delivery systems. Advocates are calling for a continuum of services (Goldgraber, 1981) to allow children to be placed in the setting most appropriate for their needs. In order to develop such a continuum, new legislation, regulations, and interagency agreements will be imperative.

Smith (1980) notes that PL 94-142, although meant to stimulate services for the young handicapped child, may in fact serve as a disincentive by permitting states that have no preschool mandate to serve preschoolers voluntarily. (The act does, however, serve as a mandate for states that have their own mandatory policies.) Moreover, the inadequate federal appropriation for preschool handicapped children through the Preschool Incentive Grant Program has created a situation in which many states have actually revoked their early education legislation by raising the age level for mandatory education. As previously mentioned, although 7 states lowered the age eligibility for services, 12 states *raised* the age eligiblity (Smith, 1980)—demonstrating an overall negative trend. Certainly, educators and lawmakers are studying this situation carefully. The need to address the problems associated with current policies cannot be delayed.

Mainstreaming

The requirement of PL 94-142 to place children in the "least restrictive environment" to meet their needs has resulted in increased emphasis on mainstreaming children. Recent studies indicate that effective mainstreaming is a complicated process; in some instances, mainstreaming may even have detrimental effects (Smith & Greenberg, 1981). In order to mainstream children successfully, it has been found that teachers must plan and facilitate social interaction, teach imitation and reward modeling, and ensure a smooth transition between programs (Allen, 1980; Guralnick, 1978). Teacher attitudes (Phillip & Vandivier, 1981), teacher training (Dickerson & Davis, 1979), and parent involvement (Wynne, Brown, Dakof, & Ulfelder, 1975) are also critical variables in effective mainstreaming. Although mainstreaming can be accomplished in many different preschool models, the process requires careful orchestration. More research is needed on which children might benefit from mainstreaming and what classroom techniques are most promising. Research is also crucial to guide professionals in helping children make transitions to mainstreamed settings.

Noncategorical Services and Training

As stated earlier, there has been a growing trend toward providing noncategorical services, especially in the areas of educable mental retardation, learning disabilities, and emotional disturbance (Reynolds, 1973). This change will affect both state certification standards and personnel preparation and training (Blackhurst, 1981). Many early childhood programs are already serving young handicapped children using a noncategorical model. Early childhood special education programs can, in fact, serve as a model for school-age programs in the transition to noncategorical service. Noncategorical programs will necessitate cross-disciplinary training and intervention. Teachers will need to develop consultation skills in order to work effectively with parents, other teachers, and professionals from other disciplines (Idol-Maestas, Lloyd, & Lilly, 1981). They will also need skills to enable them to work with a variety of problems in relation to developmental and learning theories. These competency areas can be expected to be reflected in the new certification requirements being developed in early childhood special education.

Research

Research in normal child development, developmental psychology, special education, and various other areas is contributing to a growing body of knowledge leading to advances in early childhood special education. For example, important investigations are taking place in relation to parent-child interactions; the development of cognitive, language, and social processes; screening and assessment procedures; mainstreaming techniques and transitional methods; educational and therapeutic approaches; and program accountability.

Researchers are gaining greater understanding of the nature of the development of socialization in the child and the importance of parent-child interactions to emotional development. Several researchers have investigated differences in early interactions through eye-contact (Hittelman & Dickes, 1979; Lasky & Klein, 1979). Early emotional development (Sroufre, 1979) and its relationship to parent-child attachment in normal and handicapped children are being examined (Lewis & Rosenblum, 1974; Murdock, 1979; Stone & Chesney, 1978). Findings in the latter area have already had an impact on intervention models and techniques (Bromwich, 1981), and will probably continue to influence approaches to handicapped children and their parents.

Research continues on instructional strategies. In addition to the previously discussed effectiveness studies, which have looked at benefits of various models, a great deal of research has emerged that examines specific techniques or intervention practices. Studies on the effects of vestibular and proprioceptive stimulation (Sandler & Coren, 1981; Weeks, 1979), analyses of various antecedent, response and consequence events in treatment in education (Gaylord-Ross, Weeks, & Lipner, 1980), use of reinforced modeling (Cooke, Apolloni, & Cooke, 1977; Guralnick, 1978), and facilitation of play behaviors (Peterson & Haralick, 1977) are providing information on relevant practices. In addition, professionals are developing and modifying existing symbol systems to enable severely handicapped persons to communicate; and hardware technology in prostheses is becoming more sophisticated. The interface between teachers and support staff is expanding (Allen, Holm, & Schiefelbusch, 1978); and professionals are becoming more adept at developing instructional activities for young handicapped children that foster generalization of skills and incorporate multiple developmental areas (Kaczmarek & Dell, 1981).

Issues that have evolved from the research include:

How to meaningfully involve fathers in their children's program
How to work more effectively with regular education personnel
How to conduct more accurate and functional assessments of young handicapped children
How to improve interdisciplinary services
How to utilize telecommunications in programs for children
How to effectively provide for accountability
How to expand services for handicapped infants and preschoolers
How to individualize programs in relation to temperament and learning style

Many questions remain to be answered and much research must still be performed in order to expand our knowledge base in early childhood special education. Impressive advances have been made in serving young handicapped children, but we still have "miles to go."

SUMMARY

During the past decade, there has been a dramatic upswing in society's attitudes toward services for its handicapped members. All branches of our government—executive, judicial, and legislative—have supported the worth of education for handicapped citizens. There is now substantial evidence to indicate that the earlier education is initiated, the more significant the gains for the child, the family, and society. Although a great deal of effort has been contributed to developing early intervention programs, still only a small number of children are receiving needed services. Educational trends are highly influenced by the prevailing political climate. With the current emphasis on cutbacks and private support, it will be necessary to rally early childhood special education advocates, not only to avoid losing what we have gained, but to investigate a variety of alternatives for increasing services to handicapped infants and preschoolers.

REFERENCES

Ainsworth, M.D.S. The development of infant-mother attachment. In: B.M. Caldwell & H.N. Ricciutti (eds.), *Review of child development research*, Vol. 3. Chicago: University of Chicago Press, 1973.

Allen, K.E. Mainstreaming: What have we learned? *Young Children*, 1980, *35*(5), 54–62.

Allen, K.E., Holm, V.A., & Schiefelbusch, R.L. (eds.). *Early intervention: A team approach*. Baltimore: University Park Press, 1978.

Anastasiow, N.J. The needs of early childhood education for the handicapped: A song for the 80's. *Journal of the Division of Early Childhood*, 1981, *2*, 1–7.

Bagnato, S.J. Developmental diagnostic reports: Reliable and effective alternatives to guide individualized intervention. *Journal of Special Education*, 1981, *15*(1), 65–76.

Battelle Institute of Columbus, Ohio. *A summary of the evaluation of the Handicapped Children's Early Education Program*. Columbus: Battelle Institute, 1976.

Behr, S., & Gallagher, J.J. Alternative administrative strategies for young handicapped children: A policy analysis. *Journal of the Division of Early Childhood*, 1981, *2*, 113–122.

Berkson, G., & Mason, W.A. Stereotyped behaviors of chimpanzees: Relation to general arousal level and alternative activities. *Perceptual and Motor Skills*, 1964, *19*, 635–652.

Blackhurst, A.E. Noncategorical teacher preparation: Problems and promises. *Exceptional Children*, 1981, *48*(3), 197–205.

Bloom, B. *Stability and change in human characteristics*. New York: John Wiley & Sons, 1964.

Bluhm, H.P., Egan, M.W., & Perry, M.L. The training and evaluation of preservice multidisciplinary teams. *Teacher Education and Special Education*, 1981, *4*(1), 18–23.

Bowlby, J. *Attachment and loss, Vol. 2: Separation*. New York: Basic Books, 1973.

Bromwich, R. *Working with parents and infants*. Baltimore: University Park Press, 1981.

Bronfenbrenner, U. Is early intervention effective? In: J. Hellmuth (ed.), *Exceptional infants*, Vol. 3. New York: Brunner/Mazel, 1975.

Brooks-Gunn, J., & Lewis, M. Assessing young handicapped children: Issues and solutions. *Journal of the Division for Early Childhood*, 1981, *2*, 84–94.

Bruner, J. Poverty in childhood. In: R. Parker (ed.), *The preschool in action*. Boston: Allyn and Bacon, 1972.

Buktenica, N.A. Multidisciplinary training teams: A transactional approach to training and service. *Teacher Education and Special Education*, 1981, *4*(1), 31.

Carter, J.A., Imhoff, C., Lacoste, R., McNulty, B., & Peterson, P. The implementation of statewide early education plans: A two-year report. *Education and Training of the Mentally Retarded*, 1980, *15*(1), 58–64.

Cartwright, C.A. Effective programs for parents of young handicapped children. *Topics in Early Childhood Special Education*, 1981, *1*(3), 1–9.

Clark, D.L., Kreutzberg, J.R., & Chee, F.K.W. Vestibular stimulation influence on motor development in infants. *Science*, 1977, *196*(4295), 1228–1229.

Closer look. A position paper for the national media on special education in the United States. Washington, DC: Bureau of Education for the Handicapped (DHEW/OEO), 1976.

Conley, R.W. *The economics of mental retardation*. Baltimore: The Johns Hopkins University Press, 1973.

Cooke, T.P., Apolloni, T., & Cooke, S.A. Normal preschool children as behavioral models for retarded peers. *Exceptional Children*, 1977, *43*(8), 531–532.

Cunningham, C.C., & Sloper, T. Parents of Down's syndrome babies: Their early needs. *Child: Care, Health, and Development*, 1977, *3*, 325–347.

Denenberg, V.H. The effects of early experience. In: E.S.E. Hafez (ed.), *The behavior of domestic animals* (2nd ed.). London: Bailliere, Tindall and Cox, 1969.

Denenberg, V.H. & Thoman, E.B. From animal to infant research. In: T. Tjossem (ed.), *Intervention strategies for high risk infants and young children*. Baltimore: University Park Press, 1976.

Dennis, W. Causes of retardation among institutional children: Iran. *Journal of Genetic Psychology*, 1960, *96*, 47–59.

DeWeerd, J. Early education services for children with handicaps—Where have we been, where are we now, and where are we going? *Journal of the Division of Early Childhood*, 1981, *2*, 15–24.

Dickerson, M.G., & Davis, M.D. Implications of PL 94-142 for developmental early childhood programs. *Young Children*, 1979, *34*(2), 28–31.

Dubose, R.F. Assessment of severely impaired young children: Problems and recommendations. *Topics in Early Childhood Special Education*, 1981, *1*(2), 9–21.

Dubose, R.F., Langley, M.B., & Stagg, V. Assessing severely handicapped children. In: E.L. Meyen, G.A. Vergason, & R.L. Whelan (eds.), *Instructional planning for exceptional children*. Denver: Love Publishing Co., 1979.

Education of Handicapped Children, Implementation of Part B of the Education of the Handicapped Act, *Federal Register*, August 23, 1977, *42*(163), 42178.

Educational products for the exceptional child. Phoenix: The Oryx Press, 1980.

Far West Laboratory for Educational Research and Development. *Educational programs that work—The national diffusion network catalog*. Prepared for the U.S. Office of Education, Department of Health, Education, and Welfare. San Francisco: Far West Laboratory, 1980.

Foster, M., Berger, M., & McLean, M. Rethinking a good idea: A reassessment of parent involvement. *Topics in Early Childhood Special Education*, 1981, *1*(3), 55–65.

Garland, C., Stone, N., Swanson, J., & Woodruff, G. (eds.). Early intervention for children with special needs and their families: Findings and recommendations. *Interact* (Newsletter of the National Committee for Very Young Children and Their Families), 1980.

Gaylord-Ross, R.J., Weeks, M., & Lipner, C. An analysis of antecedent, response and consequence events in treatment of self-injurious behavior. *Education and Training of the Mentally Retarded*, 1980, *15*(1), 35–42.

Goldgraber, V. Educating severely handicapped children in the least restrictive environment. *Journal for Special Educators*, 1981, *17*(4), 401–410.

Golin, A.K., & Ducanis, A.J. Preparation for team work. *Teacher Education and Special Education*, 1981, *4*(1), 25–30.

Guralnick, M.J. (ed.). *Early intervention and the integration of handicapped and non-handicapped children.* Baltimore: University Park Press, 1978.

Guralnick, M.J. Early intervention and pediatrics: Current status and future directions. *Journal of the Division of Early Childhood,* 1981, *2,* 52–60.

Guralnick, M.J., & Richardson, H.B., Jr. *Pediatric education and the needs of exceptional children.* Baltimore: University Park Press, 1980.

Hall, J.F. The relationship between external stimulation, food deprivation and activity. *Journal of Comparative and Physiological Psychology,* 1956, *49,* 339–341.

Hamilton, J.L., & Swan, W.W. Measurement references in the assessment of preschool handicapped children. *Topics in Early Childhood Special Education,* 1981, *1*(2), 41–48.

Harbin, G., Cross, L., & Mears, C. (eds.). *Early childhood curriculum materials: An annotated bibliography.* New York: Walker and Co., 1976.

Harlow, H.F. Syndromes resulting from maternal deprivation. In: J.H. Cullen (ed.), *Experimental behavior: A basis for the study of mental disturbance.* New York: John Wiley & Sons, 1974.

Hayden, A. Handicapped children, birth to age 3. *Exceptional Children,* 1979, *45*(7), 510–516.

Hayden, A., & McGinness, G. Bases for early intervention. In: E. Sontag (ed.), *Educational programming for the severely and profoundly handicapped.* Reston, VA: The Council for Exceptional Children, 1977.

Hayden, A.H., Morris, K., & Bailey, D. *Effectiveness of early education for handicapped children.* Financial Report of a 1976–77 project, submitted to the Bureau of Education for the Handicapped, U.S. Office of Education, September, 1977.

Hebb, D.O. The innate organization of visual activity: Perception of figure in rats raised in total darkness. *Journal of Genetic Psychology,* 1937, *51,* 101–126.

Heber, R., Garber, H., Harrington, C., Hoffman, C., & Falendar, C. *Rehabilitation of families at risk for mental retardation. The Milwaukee Project.* Madison: University of Wisconsin, 1975.

Hirshoren, A., & Umansky, W. Certification for teachers of preschool handicapped children. *Exceptional Children,* 1977, *44*(3), 191–193.

Hittelman, J.H., & Dickes, R. Sex differences in neonatal eye contact time. *Merrill-Palmer Quarterly,* 1979, *25*(3), 171–184.

Hodges, W.L., McCandless, B.R., & Spicker, H.H. *The development and evaluation of a diagnostically based curriculum for psychologically deprived preschool children.* Washington, D.C.: U.S. Department of Health, Education and Welfare, Office of Education, 1967.

Hunt, J.M. Psychological development: Early experience. In: M.R. Rosenzweig & L.W. Porter (eds.), *Annual Review of Psychology,* 1979, *30,* 103–143. Palo Alto, CA: Annual Reviews, Inc.

Idol-Maestas, L., Lloyd, S., & Lilly, M.S. A noncategorical approach to direct service and teacher education. *Exceptional Children,* 1981, *48*(3), 213–220.

Jensen, A.R. Cumulative deficit compensatory education. *Journal of School Psychology,* 1966, *4,* 37–47.

Jordan, J.B., Hayden, A.H., Karnes, M.B., & Wood, M.M. (eds.). *Early education for exceptional children: A handbook of exemplary ideas and practices.* Reston, VA: The Council for Exceptional Children, 1977.

Kaczmarek, L.A., & Dell, A.G. Designing instructional activities for young children. *Journal of the Division of Early Childhood,* 1981, *2,* 74–83.

Katoff, L.S., & Reuter, J. Review of infant tests. In: *Journal Supplement Abstract Service (JSAS) catalog of selected documents in psychology.* Washington, DC: American Psychological Association, 1979.

La Cross, E.R., & Lee, P.C. (eds.). The first six years of life: A report on current research and educational practice. *Genetic Psychology Monographs*, 1970, *82*, 161–266.

Lasky, R., & Klein, R.E. Reactions of five-month-old infants to eye contact. *Merrill-Palmer Quarterly*, 1979, *25*(3), 163–170.

Lazar, I., Hubbell, V.R., Murray, H., Rosche, M., & Royce, J. *The persistence of preschool effects*. Washington, DC: U.S. Department of Health, Education and Welfare Publications, (OHDS) 78-30129, 1977.

Levine, S. Infantile stimulation: A perspective. In: J.A. Ambrose (ed.), *Stimulation in early infancy*. New York: Academic Press, 1969.

Levitt, E., & Cohen, S. An analysis of selected parent-intervention programs for handicapped and disadvantaged children. *Journal of Special Education*. 1975, *9*, 345–365.

Lewis, M., and Rosenblum, L.A. (eds.). *The effect of the infant on its caregiver*. New York: John Wiley & Sons, 1974.

Lillie, D.L. *Early childhood curriculum: An individualized approach*. Chicago: Science Research Associates, 1975.

Lillie, D.L., Trohanis, P.L., & Goin, K.W. (eds.). *Teaching parents to teach: A guide for working with the special child*. New York: Walker and Co., 1976.

Lorenz, K. *Studies in animal and human behavior*, Vol. 2. Cambridge, MA: Harvard University Press, 1971.

McAndrew, I. Children with a handicap and their families. *Child: Care, Health and Development*, 1976, *2*, 213–237.

Mahler, M.S. On the first three subphases of the separation-individuation process. *International Journal of Psychoanalysis*, 1972, *53*, 333–338.

Mallory, B.L. The impact of public policies on families of young handicapped children. *Topics in Early Childhood Special Education*, 1981, *1*(3), 77–86.

Moore, M.G., Anderson, R.A., Fredericks, H.D., Baldwin, V.L., & Moore, W.G. (eds.). *The longitudinal impact of preschool programs on trainable mentally retarded children*. Monmouth, OR: Exceptional Child Department, Teaching Research Division, Oregon State System of Higher Education, 1979.

Murdock, J.B. The separation-individuation process and developmental disabilities. *Exceptional Children*, 1979, *46*(3), 176–184.

Nissen, H.W., Chow, K.L., & Semmens, J. Effects of restricted opportunity for tactual, kinesthetic, and manipulative experiences on the behavior of a chimpanzee. *American Journal of Psychology*, 1951, *64*, 485–507.

Northern, J., & Downs, M. *Hearing in children*. Baltimore: Williams & Wilkins Co., 1974.

Novak, M., & Harlow, H. Social recovery of monkeys isolated for the first year of life: Rehabilitation and therapy. *Developmental Psychology*, 1975, *11*, 453–465.

Olshansky, S. Chronic sorrow: A response to having a mentally defective child. *Social Casework*, 1962, *43*, 190–193.

Peterson, N.L., & Haralick, V.G. Integration of handicapped and nonhandicapped preschoolers: An analysis of play behavior and social interaction. *Education and Training of the Mentally Retarded*, 1977, *12*(3), 235–245.

Phillip, L., & Vandivier, S.C. Teacher attitudes toward mainstreaming exceptional students. *The Journal for Special Educators*, 1981, *17*(4), 381–388.

Public Law 90-538, Handicapped Children's Early Education Assistance Act, September 30, 1968.

Public Law 93-112, Rehabilitation Act of 1973, Section 504, July 26, 1973.

Public Law 93-380, Education of the Handicapped Amendments of 1974, August 21, 1974.

Public Law 94-142, Education for All Handicapped Children Act of 1975, November 29, 1975.

Reynolds, M.C. *Delphi survey: A report of rounds I and II*. Reston, VA: The Council for Exceptional Children, 1973.

Rheingold, H.L. The effect of environmental stimulation upon social and exploratory behavior in the human infant. In: B.M. Foss (ed.), *Determinants of infant behavior*, Vol. 1. London: Metheun, 1970.

Riesen, A.H. Stimulation as a requirement for growth and function in behavioral development. In: D.W. Fiske & S.R. Maddi (eds.), *Functions of varied experience*. Homewood, IL: The Dorsey Press, 1961.

Roos, P. Trends and issues in special education for the mentally retarded. In: S.A. Kirk & F.E. Lord (eds.), *Exceptional children: Educational resources and perspectives*. Boston: Houghton Mifflin Co., 1974.

Rosenzweig, M. Environmental complexity, cerebral change and behavior. *American Psychologist*, 1966, *21*, 321–332.

Sandler, A., & Coren, A., Vestibular stimulation in early childhood: A review. *Journal for the Division of Early Childhood*, 1981, *3*, 48–55.

Schweinhart, L., & Weikart, D. *Young children grow up: The effects of the Perry Preschool Program on youths through age 15*. Ypsilanti, MI: High/Scope Educational Research Foundation, 1980.

Skeels, H.M. Adult status of children with contrasting early life experiences. *Monographs of the Society for Research in Child Development*, Serial No. 105, 1966, *31*(3). Chicago: University of Chicago for the Society for Research in Child Development.

Skeels, H.M., & Dye, H.B. A study of the effects of differential stimulation on mentally retarded children. In: *Proceedings and addresses of the American Association on Mental Deficiency*, Philadelphia, 1939, *44*, 114–136.

Smith, B.V. *Policy issues related to the provision of appropriate early intervention services for very young exceptional children and their families*. Unpublished paper prepared for The Council for Exceptional Children, Reston, VA, 1980.

Smith, C., & Greenberg, M. Step-by-step integration of handicapped preschool children in a day-care center for nonhandicapped children. *Journal of the Division of Early Childhood*, 1981, *2*, 96–101.

Solnit, A.J., & Stark, M.H. Mourning and the birth of a defective child. *Psychoanalytical Study of the Child*, 1961, *16*, 523–527.

Spitz, R.A., & Wolff, K.M. Anaclitic depression: An inquiry into the genesis of psychiatric conditions in early childhood. In: A. Freud et al. (eds.), *The psychoanalytic study of the child*, Vol. 2. New York: International Universities Press, 1946.

Sroufre, L.A. The coherence of individual development: Early care, attachment and subsequent developmental issues. *American Psychologist*, 1979, *34*(10), 834–841.

Stone, N.W., & Chesney, B.H. Attachment behaviors in handicapped infants. *Mental Retardation*, 1978, *16*, 8–12.

Swan, W.W. The Handicapped Children's Early Education Program. *Exceptional Children*, 1980, *47*(1), 12–16.

Weeks, Z.R. Effects of the vestibular system on human development Part 1. *The American Journal of Occupational Therapy*, 1979, *33*, 376–381.

Wood, P. Cost of services. In: C. Garland, N. Stone, J. Swanson, & G. Woodruff (eds.), *Early intervention for children with special needs and their families: Findings and recommendations*. *Interact* (Newsletter of the National Committee for Very Young Children and Their Families), 1980.

Wynne, S., Brown, J.K., Dakof, G., & Ulfelder, L.S. *Mainstreaming and early childhood education for handicapped children: A guide for teachers and parents: Final Report*. Washington, DC: Bureau of Education for the Handicapped, U.S. Office of Education, 1975. (ERIC Document Reproduction Service, No. ED. 119 455.)

chapter

2

Conceptualizing and Developing a Program

IMPORTANCE OF PHILOSOPHY

Webster's Dictionary (1967) defines philosophy as "an analysis of the grounds of and concepts expressing fundamental beliefs," and also "a theory underlying or regarding a sphere of activity or thought." In order to adequately serve handicapped children and their families, we need to examine our "fundamental beliefs" about how children learn and our theories concerning how best to facilitate children's growth and development.

Service delivery models developed in the past have had their roots in particular philosophies or theoretical models. Many of the philosophies stem from beliefs regarding the etiology of handicapping conditions, while others are based on specific theories of learning or development.

The perception of how the environment contributes to learning is one element of a program philosophy. The roles and responsibilities of various staff members, the teacher, and parents within the program are other elements reflecting "fundamental beliefs" about education and learning. A final element of a program philosophy is the content or targets chosen to comprise the curriculum. These considerations—etiology of handicap, learning/developmental theories, role of the environment, role of the staff, role of the parents, and program content or targets of training—are major aspects to be considered carefully in developing a philosophy and later designing a program model for an early intervention program.

The model selected for an infant or preschool program should reflect the philosophy of the agency, its staff, and consumers. The philosophy should be evident in program policies, procedures, and staffing patterns as well as in program goals, objectives, activities, and evaluation methods.

ADVANTAGES OF PHILOSOPHICAL UNITY

The advantages of a common philosophy are many. Staff may perceive their mutually held values as a unifying element—a foundation from which to begin program development, a base of reference for formative discussions on program implementation and modification, and a framework for determining summative evaluation concerns. In addition, staff who understand and operate from a common theoretical and philosophical base will utilize consistent terminology and "jargon," thus enhancing staff communication. A unified philosophy also reduces the possibility of conflict over selection of assessment instruments, curricula, and strategies and techniques of intervention.

PROCESS MODEL FOR DETERMINATION
OF SERVICE DELIVERY SYSTEM

Determining the nature of the philosophy and the service delivery system is not as easy as might be imagined. Often projects choose an assessment instrument, curriculum, or program model for dogmatic reasons, without taking into account all the relevant factors. Perhaps the instrument or curriculum is a widely accepted one, or the staff have attended a workshop on it, or it has been endorsed by a respected professional. Considerations such as these, however, should not be the deciding factors in choosing or designing any of the program components.

The nature of the population to be served, the services needed, the overall program philosophy—including model, curriculum, staffing patterns, and site of services—all have an impact on the interactions between staff-child-parent-environment. Each of these factors also contributes to final decisions about program design. Figure 1 outlines a process model that can facilitate decision making. Each component is discussed below to illustrate its effect on program planning.

Funding

The nature of the program is necessarily influenced by the type of funding available. Depending on the funding source—local, state, or federal—different requirements may apply in relation to such aspects as the population to be served, staff utilization, or accountability.

> Funding
> —sources
> —level

The level of funding available will obviously also influence the nature of the program and the degree of services that may be offered.

Determination of the Nature of the Population

Handicapping Conditions When examining information on the population to be served, staff need to determine the types and range of handicapping con-

> Types of Handicaps
> —single
> —multiple
>
> Number of Children

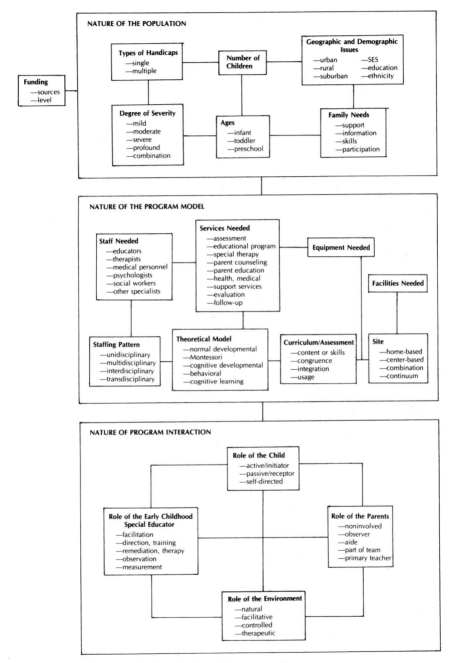

Figure 1. Process model for determination of the service delivery system.

ditions identified. Is the population relatively homogeneous in terms of handicapping condition (for example, language impairment, visual impairment, hearing loss), age, functioning level, and so on? If a single type of handicap is being served, this has implications for the type of services, staff, and curriculum needed. For instance, if blind preschool children are to be served, qualified vision specialists or teachers trained as educators of the blind will be needed. Mobility training may become part of the curriculum, and special materials or equipment, such as "twin vision" books and multisensory toys, may be necessary. If, on the other hand, a heterogeneous group—containing children with a variety of handicapping conditions—is being served, other considerations are important. For example, if cerebral palsied, mentally retarded, and emotionally disturbed children are to be served in one program, decisions about the staff, staffing patterns, inservice training, curricula, scheduling, and the philosophical model will all be affected. A physical therapist, for example, may be needed by the children with cerebral palsy or mental retardation. The teacher may need skills training in positioning techniques, in behavior management, and in the development of language and cognition. Some children may be able to explore their environment actively, while others may need facilitation or direct guidance. A curriculum emphasizing social and emotional development may be more appropriate for the emotionally disturbed child.

If, so as to reduce the negative effects of labeling, a noncategorical approach is used to identify children, children's *needs* rather than "handicapping conditions" should be determined. Program design should, accordingly, reflect the diverse needs of children to be served.

The number of handicapped children with specific handicaps or needs is also important, as this will influence the staff size and perhaps the service delivery mode. A home-based program, for example, may be appropriate for a multiply handicapped child who is unable to benefit from a center-based program that uses a cognitively oriented curriculum and serves predominantly mildly handicapped children.

Degree of Severity   The degree of severity of a handicapping condition affects services needed, both for the child and the family. A child who is profoundly retarded and severely physically handicapped may place great stress on the family. The family may need

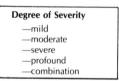

Degree of Severity
—mild
—moderate
—severe
—profound
—combination

financial and/or emotional support in order to maintain the child at home; they may need to develop special skills to be able to work with the child, including understanding the developmental skills and interaction patterns of the child so that they may interact positively with the child; the child may also need specialized therapy and a highly structured environment to foster learning. While home-based programs may meet some family needs, a center-based setting might afford some relief to the family and allow the child to receive assistance from a number of therapists.

Ages Determining the age range of the children to be served is also important. Although age as a factor by itself may not prove crucial to the type of setting, theoretical model, or staffing pattern employed, when

Ages
—infant
—toddler
—preschool

combined with other factors such as type of handicap, the number of children, and degree of severity, age can become critical. For instance, if 12 moderately retarded 4-year-olds were in need of service, a center-based program (regardless of the model) would enable the children to participate in vital social interactions. Age can also affect the amount of time a child can attend to the activities presented. The attention span of an infant, for example, may preclude lengthy 2½-hour-programs.

Family Needs In addition to assessing the needs of children, the needs of families should also be evaluated. Positive growth in the child may, in fact, depend on how well the program serves the family (Bronfenbrenner, 1975). Parents whose emotional and sur-

Family Needs
—support
—information
—skills
—participation

vival needs are met have more energy to expend on behalf of their handicapped child. Lillie and Trohanis (1976) discuss parents' needs in the areas of emotional support, exchange of information, facilitation of positive parent-child interactions, and participation in the program. Depending on the needs and interests of the parents, the child's program may vary. For example, parents who are deeply grieving the birth of the handicapped child may be emotionally unable to address the child's needs or to implement a home-based program. By placing the child in a center-based program while the parents are involved in support groups, counseling, or educational activities, the parents may be able to come to terms with their feelings, acquire new understanding of the strengths and limitations of the child, and gain new skills for coping with the problems of raising a handicapped child.

Geographic and Demographic Issues The geographic size of the area served, as well as the demographics of the population, has a direct bearing on fam-

Geographic and Demographic Issues	
—urban	—SES
—rural	—education
—suburban	—ethnicity

ilies' needs. If the area served is rural and covers many square miles, or is small but with mountainous or rugged terrain, transportation may be difficult. Parents may not be able to participate regularly in a center-based program. If buses are involved, the number of hours children must spend on a bus, especially if they are young children, may make center-based programs impractical. (There is little value in trying to administer a 2 hour stimulating, therapeutic, and educational program to an exhausted, cranky 2-year-old who has just spent 1½ hours on the bus. And the parents who "collect" the child at the end of the long trip home may be equally unconvinced of the program's worth.)

Demographics such as socioeconomic status (SES), education, and ethnic background may have major implications for the child's program and the family's needs. Parents of low socioeconomic status may need to expend considerable energy simply to survive. For them, the most pressing issues may relate to employment, food, and housing. What kind of toys the child has or how the child is physically positioned may seem frivolous and unimportant. Until basic needs are met, educational goals are understandably postponed or ignored. Socioeconomic status may also influence staffing patterns. Parents of low SES may relate better to trained laypersons or paraprofessionals from their own neighborhood, whether it be urban or rural (Heber, Garber, Harrington, Hoffman, & Falendar, 1975; Shearer & Shearer, 1972).

The parent's educational level is also a primary factor to be considered. If a parent cannot read, it is inappropriate and often insulting to send home written program plans for the parent to follow. Books, pamphlets, letters will go unheeded or misunderstood. Such parents may respond much more readily to alternate means of communication. Many parents, on the other hand, are eager from the start to learn everything they can (and in whatever way they can) about their child and his or her handicap. They will devour any information made available to them. They want and *need* to know, and the program can be their most valuable information resource.

Ethnic differences among families also can affect staff hiring and service delivery modes. Minority and/or bilingual personnel may be necessary if a significant percentage of the target population are minority or if English is not the primary language. Cultural considerations may make home visits undesirable or parent involvement in school-based programs unrealistic.

The above-mentioned geographic and demographic issues relate directly to the family's—and thus the child's—needs. Development of the delivery system should involve analysis of families' needs, with alternatives for meeting these needs reflected in the services available.

Determination of the Nature of the Program Model

Services Needed   Once the nature of the population has been determined, it is possible to ascertain the services needed. These may include: assessment, educational programming for the children, specialized therapy (speech therapy, occupational therapy, physical therapy, and so on), program planning for the parents (including counseling, education, training, and program participation alternatives), health, nutrition, medical consultation, family support systems (including interagency services), ongoing evaluation, and follow-up consultation.

Services Needed
—assessment
—educational program
—special therapy
—parent counseling
—parent education
—health, medical
—support services
—evaluation
—follow-up

Determining the specific ways in which services will be delivered in each of these areas depends largely on the operating philosophy in each of four components: 1) staff and staffing patterns, 2) theoretical approach, 3) curriculum and evaluation instruments, and 4) the site of service delivery. Each of these components should be in philosophical accord to ensure program consistency and evaluation validity.

Staff and Staffing Patterns With decisions made on the types of services needed, the next step is to determine who will provide these services. If moderately language-delayed or speech-impaired children are being served, the children will probably need both language experiences and training from an educator experienced in encouraging language growth in conjunction with other developmental areas. A speech and language therapist may also be needed to do indepth evaluations, provide individual and group therapy, and consult with the educator and/or parents on specific methods or techniques of

training. Severely multiply handicapped children will require specialized assessments and interventions in all developmental areas; thus, depending on individual and family needs, occupational and/or physical therapists, speech and language therapists, vision specialists, medical consultation, social workers, and other specialists may be appropriate.

Equally as critical as the question of *who* will provide the services, is the question of *how* staff will provide services. A major mistake made by many new programs is the failure to carefully delineate roles and responsibilities of staff members, both *individually* and as a *team* (B. McNulty, personal communication, 1980). It is fundamentally important that staff members agree philosophically as to which staffing pattern will most efficiently and effectively serve the handicapped children and their families. Lack of agreement can lead to duplication or gaps in services, misunderstandings and breakdown in communication, and staff tension and dissension. The following discussion of various staff patterns illustrates the philosophical implications of each.

Unidisciplinary Approach Agencies that provide categorical centers or mental health clinics may tend to specialize in the disabilities they serve and in the type of treatment offered. A child who is referred to the physical therapy department of the local hospital will receive treatment from physical therapists who are concerned primarily with improving skills related to motor coordination. They may make suggestions on improving speech or feeding skills as they relate to the oral motor mechanisms, but speech and language therapists will not be part of their team. Such a unidisciplinary approach is appropriate for highly specific problems, but for more varied problems the child's and family's total needs will probably not be met with unilateral service.

Many day care and nursery school programs operate on a unidisciplinary staffing pattern, primarily due to funding limitations. The discipline most frequently represented is that of early childhood education. Staff usually have been trained in normal development and normal developmental teaching models, and consequently, they may have difficulty modifying the regular curriculum or standard teaching techniques to meet the needs of children with deviating developmental patterns.

A unidisciplinary approach, in general, places a tremendous burden on staff who work with handicapped children, for they need knowledge and expertise in all areas of child development, an understanding of delays and deviations, and the ability to facilitate growth and change in important skill areas. Moreover, staff must be able to work closely with families on a variety of levels. Clearly, it would be difficult to provide a comprehensive program with a unidisciplinary approach.

Multidisciplinary Team The multidisciplinary approach is frequently found in public school programs. Professionals from several disciplines are available to provide services to children and their families. Most commonly included are: a psychologist, social worker, school nurse, speech and language pathologist, occupational therapist, and special educator. The team usually functions in one of two ways. The usual pattern is that the various specialists see the child for the initial assessment and determination of appropriate placement. Specialists such as the speech and language therapist or the occupational therapist see specific children on a "pull-out" basis; that is, they remove the child from the classroom, implement the child's therapy program, and take the child back to his or her classroom. In such instances, pull-out time becomes "magic" (K. Cessna, personal communication, 1980) time, as no one else knows what methods or techniques are used to remediate the child's problem. What is worse, the techniques used by the various disciplines may actually conflict; for example, the teacher typically conducts the educational program without much interaction with the therapists. The team meets periodically to review individualized education programs (IEPs) and to establish new goals and objectives. The social worker may be involved if a family is having problems with the child, or if the school is having "problems" with the family. This particular staff pattern makes a clear differentiation among the various specialists and the expertise they offer.

A similar but less common multidisciplinary pattern is one in which all disciplines are involved to a varying degree with each child. Personnel may work side by side, but their areas of responsibility are clearly defined (Holm & McCartin, 1978). For example, an infant program may have "centers" established for speech and language, gross motor, fine motor, cognitive, and social-emotional activities. Each of these areas may be supervised by a professional from a different discipline. Children are rotated through each center, working with an expert in each area of development. During this time, the social worker may meet with parents individually or in a group. The team may meet on a regular basis to discuss their goals and objectives for each child. Only a limited amount of time is spent in consultation among team members.

The limitation of a multidisciplinary team approach is that "this mode of sharing . . . does not take full advantage of the range of skills each person brings to the team" (Holm & McCartin, 1978). The result is that the child is treated in "pieces" rather than holistically.

Interdisciplinary Team   The interdisciplinary team emphasizes interaction among a variety of disciplines. Regular consultations take place among personnel from the various disciplines for the purpose of sharing information. For example, the occupational therapist who has been working on oral motor control may come to the classroom during snack time and work on feeding with a child, while at the same time demonstrating to the teacher what techniques are being used and providing a rationale for each. The teacher can then use these techniques when the therapist is not present. The child still receives therapy from the specialist, but skills generalization and practice are extended as a result of team communication. Team meetings are held frequently to discuss children's progress and effective methodology. Holm and McCartin (1978) describe interdisciplinary teams as able to "rely on each other to build on and complement the skills and expertise of the whole team."

One drawback of the interdisciplinary approach is that the quality and quantity of team interaction may be restricted due to heavy case loads. Individual staff may also tend to be more protective of professional "turf." For reasons such as these, time for cross-sharing may be limited unless it is specifically and frequently structured into the program.

Transdisciplinary Team   The difference between the interdisciplinary and transdisciplinary team is primarily one of degree. Members of a transdisciplinary team actually educate one another and practice the skills of the various disciplines. Holm and McCartin, in discussing this team approach, state that it "connotes crossing of discipline borders, assimilation of knowledge from other professions, and the incorporation of skills developed in other fields into one's practice" (p. 103). In a home-based program, for instance, often a single staff member visits the home. (It would be cost-prohibitive to have the entire team visit each child in the program.) Thus, the home visitor needs skills from all the other disciplines. The transdisciplinary team would, through inservice training, ongoing consultation, and team meetings, assist each other in acquiring necessary intervention skills. For example, the physical or occupational therapist would teach the other team members techniques related to facilitation and inhibition; the special educator might demonstrate cognitive sequences and how to enhance play behaviors; and the speech and language therapist might discuss approximations or parallel talking. In team meetings, objectives and activities are discussed and information exchange continues across disciplines. The teacher, however, is not expected to *become* a physical therapist or speech and language pathologist, or vice versa. The goal is that each staff member has a maximum amount of information and experience at his or her disposal in working with a child.

Ongoing information exchange and mutual support are vital aspects of the transdisciplinary team concept. The advantage of this approach is that each team member works with the whole child, rather than a specific aspect of the handicapping condition. The approach is not intended to do away with the need for a specialist, however. In fact, the child who does not receive needed individual therapy from a specialist is at a disadvantage. Optimally, the transdisciplinary approach should combine individual therapy, when appropriate, with generalization of that therapy through the other disciplines. Rather than always providing direct therapy to each child, the therapist adopts the role of resource person, using the classroom staff and parents as the primary implementers of the rehabilitative program (Sternat, Messina, Nietupski, Lyon, & Brown, 1977). Iacino and Bricker (1978) describe the ideal interventionist as a "generative teacher" who must have skill as a synthesizer. The teacher must be able to seek out and evaluate information from other professionals, as well as apply his or her own expertise to the child's program.

The problems of young handicapped children are multifaceted. Often one approach or one discipline is insufficient to deal with the child's and family's needs. A coordinated, multidimensional approach is therefore most effective. Children are complex organisms, and deviations or delays in any one area of development greatly affect the other areas. Any program philosophy should address how staff can most successfully deal with the totality of needs with a minimum of duplication, fragmentation, or contradiction of services.

It should also be remembered that staffing patterns influence the staff-child ratio. The number of children with whom each staff member works, or the actual number of contact hours spent with individual children or groups of children, should not be the only criteria for determining the type and amount of services received by children and families. Many children may also be served through consultation and discussion and planning in team meetings. It is important for administrators to recognize that the transdisciplinary communication concerning specific children that takes place in team meetings is time spent serving the child and family. By viewing team meetings as "service" time rather than staff time, more comprehensive programs can be delivered.

Theoretical Models How do children learn? What is the relationship between genetic, maturational, and environmental factors? How can developmental growth and learning best be facilitated in the handicapped child? What is the role of the child in

Theoretical Models
—normal developmental
—Montessori
—cognitive developmental
—behavioral
—cognitive learning

his or her own learning? What are the roles of the teacher, the therapist, the parents? Depending on what answers are accepted, one arrives at a different theoretical model for education.

Throughout history theories of learning have been generated. In recent centuries, medical, psychological, and sociological research have all made an impact. The problem of how best to educate the young handicapped child, however, is a relatively recent concern. Originators of early intervention programs at first looked to regular educational models, particularly those preschools and kindergartens based on developmental readiness. Projects of the Handicapped Children's Early Education Program (HCEEP), however, which were implemented with federal funding in the 1960s and 1970s, were intended to be "model" programs that were unique and could serve to "demonstrate" the effectiveness of various approaches for working with young handicapped children. The majority of these early intervention programs have their theoretical roots in developmental or learning theories and in varying views of the etiology of handicapping conditions.

Studies have frequently compared various early childhood educational models (Ackerman & Moore, 1976; Anastasiow, 1978; Boegehold, Cuffaro, Hooks, & Klopp, 1977). Regardless of the models compared, most can be described as falling on a continuum, with the differentiating elements being curriculum content, structure, and methodology. The extremes at either end of the continuum (from left to right, below) under each of these elements include:

A. Curriculum content
   1. Based on interests-------------------------------------Based on deficits
   2. Developmental areas ---------------------------------Skill areas
   3. Developmental sequences ---------------------------Skill sequences
B. Structure
         Informal---Formal
   1. Role of the environment
         Facilitative interaction-----------------------Shaping through lessons
   2. Role of the staff
         Facilitator--Trainer
   3. Role of the child
         Active transactor ----------------------------Passive receptor
C. Methodology
   1. Child-initiated--Teacher-initiated
   2. Child-child interaction ----------------------------Teacher-child interaction
   3. Natural reinforcers ---------------------------------Sequence of reinforcers
   4. Generalization and application ---------------------Criterion accomplishment
      of skills   of skills
   5. Developmental growth observed -------------------Skills growth measured

An examination of specific models reveals further distinctions. Different authors may refer to the same model by discrepant names, but analysis reveals the underlying theoretical congruence.

Child Development or Normal Developmental Model Ackerman and Moore (1976) identify the "child development model" as falling at the "informal" end of the continuum. Anastasiow (1978) refers to this as the "normal developmental model." This model emphasizes age-appropriate skills, with skills measured in relation to developmental norms. The curriculum content, the environmental structure, and the teaching methodology stress social and emotional development. Multiple activity areas are available, and children explore each of these "enrichment" centers, usually at their own discretion. Child-to-child interaction is encouraged. Activities such as creating art and science projects, building with blocks, and playing house allow social interaction, growth of developmental skills, and discovery learning. The teacher's role is to facilitate concept acquisition through informal exchange, modeling, and imitation. "Units" may be planned around specific topic areas, with children learning through observation, manipulation, and discussion of presented material and concepts. Specific learning targets are not identified or taught directly, because it is believed that the child will learn when developmentally ready.

Montessori or Sensory Cognitive Model   Maria Montessori's (1964) model for educating young children is based on the premise that children learn spontaneously, provided they are given a well-organized environment, tasks suited to their developmental level, and freedom to learn at their own pace. In contrast to the normal developmental model, the total environment and the materials are carefully sequenced and ordered. Lewis (1977) describes the Montessori curriculum as emphasizing sensory education, motor education, and language education, with academic learning added after age 4. Refinement of the senses through exercises of attention, comparison, and judgment is stressed. Functional activities of daily life are taught in a specific sequence. Language development is encouraged through drill. The teacher plays the role of observer, resource person, and facilitator of developmentally appropriate skill acquisition. Learning occurs as a result of the relationship between child and materials, with the teacher determining, through observation, what materials and concepts are appropriate for the child. As with the normal developmental model, the child paces him- or herself. The child's autonomous functioning and individuality are of primary importance. The child is expected to make choices, take the initiative, risk failure, and grow socially and emotionally through this autonomous process.

Cognitive Interactional or Cognitive Developmental Model   Variously named the "verbal cognitive model" (Ackerman & Moore, 1976), the "cognitive developmental model" (Anastasiow, 1978), and the "cognitive interactional model" (Boegehold et al., 1977), the principles embodied in this approach derive from education and psychology. The theories and practices of educators such as John Dewey, Susan Isaacs, and Constance Kamii; psychologists such as Anna Freud and Erik Erikson; and developmental psychologists Jean Piaget and Emmy Werner have contributed greatly to this increasingly popular model. Development is viewed as an outgrowth of the interaction between child and environment and the progressive differentiation of cognitive structures. The child's genetic and biological makeup and maturation are important considerations. Development proceeds through stages that are invariant, sequential, and hierarchical, though the rate of development varies.

In the cognitive developmental model, learning results from the interaction between the child and the physical and social environment, in conjunction with maturation. As a consequence of this interaction, cognitive structures or schema develop and continually become more complex and differentiated. This reorganization of mental structures occurs when a person spontaneously acts on the environment and thus "assimilates" new information and accommodates or adjusts his or her schema to make sense of the environment. Within Piaget's well-known stages of development, the first stage, sensorimotor development, and the second, preoperational, are most relevant for infant and preschool programs. The concrete operational and formal operational stages are applicable for school-age children. Regardless of the stage at which a child is functioning, however, the child's own *active* involvement is critical for learning to occur (Phillips, 1975).

The child is encouraged to invent interesting ideas, problems, and questions and to observe relationships, similarities, and differences. The emotional goal is for the child to develop independence, initiative, and self-confidence, while at the same time learning to appreciate the feelings and rights of others (Kamii & DeVries, 1977).

In terms of curriculum, the cognitive developmental model regards competence as more than the total number of skills demonstrated by a child. How the child *uses* skills and knowledge to solve problems in his or her environment is key. The goal is meaningful integration of concepts into the child's total cognitive structure. Cognitive development is emphasized, but in relation to motor, language, and social-emotional development.

The environment in the cognitive developmental model is arranged in centers similar to those in the normal developmental model, the difference being the way the teacher helps to facilitate learning. The activities or "key experiences" (Hohman, Banet, & Weikart, 1979) of the child are important. In the home or at school the parent or teacher may present specific objects, model their use, encourage the child to explore them, question him or her about their properties, or ask provocative questions to encourage higher-level problem solving (Anastasiow, 1978). Opportunities for practice and generalization of skills and concepts are provided through a variety of manipulative activities and constant verbal exchange. The role of play is also seen as essential and basic to maturation and development.

A major methodological difference between the cognitive interactionist and the behavioral points of view (see also below) is the role of failure in learning. The behavioral model views constant success as important, while the cognitive interactionist model perceives failure as critical to learning. When the child experiences something that does not conform to his or her existing world view, it becomes necessary to modify cognitive structures to obtain a new understanding. Thus, failure (on a task that is slightly novel and is developmentally appropriate) creates the incentive for learning (Furth & Wachs, 1975). The teacher can promote this growth by arranging appropriately challenging tasks and asking questions that inspire problem solving. Biber, Wickens, and Shapiro (1971) note that some of the philosophical goals of a developmental-interactionist program include: 1) promoting the child's ability to impact on the environment, 2) promoting the child's ability to order experience, 3) promoting the child's functional knowledge of the environment, 4) promoting internalized impulse control and ability to cope with conflicts, and 5) promoting mutually supportive patterns of interaction.

Behavior Modification or Precision Teaching   The behavioral approach to educating handicapped young children is based on the premise that learning takes place most quickly when the environment is controlled. The teacher's role is to shape or influence the child's adoption of specific behaviors. All behaviors are perceived as learned, observable, desirable or undesirable, and culturally determined (Anastasiow, 1978).

Behavioral programs rely heavily on continuous data collection, as it is necessary to specify objectively the target, or terminal, behaviors to be reached. It is important to: 1) identify and name the desired behavior, 2) define the conditions under which the behavior is to occur, and 3) define the criteria of acceptable performance (Mikulas, 1978). The teacher's responsibility is to specify the targets, conditions, and criteria, and to measure and plan growth.

The methodology employed relies heavily on task analysis, that is, the breakdown of skills into their component parts. Each child's instruction begins at the step or level appropriate to increase the probability of the child's success, and proceeds sequentially through all the steps and targets designated in the child's program. This method gives the teacher explicit direction in determining skill content through structure and order. Evaluation of progress is aided by specific criteria for determining successful performance. The precise delineation of such targets, conditions, and criteria affords easier replication of the child's instructional program by other staff or parents (Fallen, 1978).

One technique of the behavioral approach is to administer rewards contingent upon correct responses (various types and schedules of reinforcement are used). Cueing, prompting, shaping, modeling, and fading are all used to train a specific target skill. Elimination of maladaptive behaviors may also be a program goal, and training may sometimes use reductive procedures such as punishment, timeout, extinction, counterconditioning, aversive conditions, and flooding, in addition to the above methods. Behavioral approaches have been used successfully with all types of children, but have been particularly successful with severely and profoundly handicapped children.

Developmental Learning or Cognitive Learning Model The developmental learning or cognitive learning model attempts to combine the best aspects of the cognitive developmental and behavioral models. The principles of Piaget and other developmentalists are integrated with measurable behavioral objectives. An attempt is made to categorize sensorimotor or preoperational experiences into developmental sequences that can be trained. The role of play is important to augment the formal program and to encourage generalization of skills through functional practice. Thus, the concepts of ''assimilation'' and ''accommodation'' are combined with ''task analysis'' and ''reinforcement'' in a structured yet facilitative environment. Experimentation with this approach is relatively recent, and programs vary in the amount and degree of ''training'' versus ''facilitation'' that takes place. The goals however, are to maximize skill development, spontaneous environmental interaction, and generalization of functional application of skills.

Curriculum/Assessment Curriculum in its broadest sense is the *content* of what is taught in the program. Assessment entails determining what skills and abilities a child demonstrates at any given point. Both curriculum and assessment are discussed in detail

Curriculum/Assessment
—content or skills
—congruence
—integration
—usage

in subsequent chapters, and are therefore considered only briefly here as they relate to program philosophy. Basic consideration should be given to the content, philosophical congruence of assessment/curricular instruments, integration of curricular areas, and appropriate curriculum usage.

Content Curricula differ in the content or skills to be taught, the order or sequence of content presentation, the recommended teaching methods, and the manner in which progress is recorded. (Varying approaches to each of these areas are described in Chapter 6.) Content should be analyzed to determine if it is appropriate to the age, level, and handicapping conditions of those for whom it is intended. For example, an infant curriculum would need to address feeding problems; a curriculum for mildly handicapped children would need to include a preacademic area; and a curriculum for blind preschoolers should address mobility skills.

Congruence The curriculum that is chosen or developed should relate synergistically to the philosophical model selected, as well as to the consequent assessment measures utilized. Often programs profess to espouse a specific philosophical model, but the curriculum and assessment measures they select are inconsistent. For example, program staff may decide children learn best through a cognitive developmental approach, yet they may choose the Portage curriculum (Bluma, Shearer, Frohman, & Hilliard, 1976) and the Behavioral Characteristics Progression (1973) as an evaluation tool (both behaviorally oriented instruments). It is possible to combine elements of various models into a workable program design, but staff need to understand the underlying philosophical differences of each model and ensure that necessary modifications are made. For example, concepts considered important in the cognitive developmental curriculum may not be adequately addressed or appropriately developmentally sequenced in a behaviorally oriented tool. If specific concepts or skills are to be included as important learning targets, more than one type of evaluation instrument and/or curriculum may be in order.

Curricular Integration A program could incorporate a cognitive interaction time, developmental skills taught through structured behavioral principles, and precision teaching for vital skills that require specific intervention. The curriculum chosen for these diverse program elements will be distinctive, and staff should understand thoroughly how to apply each for maximum benefit. For example, a multiply handicapped child who is blind, severely mentally retarded, and hemiplegic may not be able to interact in a block area if left alone. However, cognitive interaction through play can be effectively facilitated by the teacher. This child may also benefit from more structured teaching of toileting skills in addition to precision teaching of speech sounds.

Appropriate Usage No one curriculum is appropriate or "most" appropriate for all handicapped children. The severity of the handicap and the developmental level of the children are important. Some curricula have been designed for mildly involved or disadvantaged children. The types of activities in these curricula often require a higher level of cognition and language than can be expected from more severely involved children. The assessment checklists that accompany such curricula often have wide developmental gaps between items, and are frequently misused by staff working with lower functioning children, so that a "minus" score on a checklist item often becomes the child's objective. If there are large gaps between developmental milestones on the assessment tool, the "next" objective may be too high for the child. Nevertheless, the teacher may persist in working on an inappropriate objective, with the consequence that the child does not progress. There is also the possibility that curriculum items may not be developmentally sequenced or may contain totally unrelated items. Clearly, a knowledge of normal development and task analysis would be beneficial for optimal use of such a curriculum. However, switching to a more appropriate assessment instrument and curriculum would greatly reduce staff planning time and allow consistent evaluation across staff.

Site Early intervention programs are most commonly home-based, center-based, or a combination home-and-center-based. As with other components of the program model, the setting must reflect the program philosophy. Inherent in the decision to offer a program at home or in a center are certain basic beliefs about the role of family, staff, and learning environments.

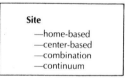

Site
—home-based
—center-based
—combination
—continuum

Shearer and Shearer (1972) have delineated the reasons for delivering services to handicapped children in their homes:

1. Learning occurs in the child's natural environment; therefore, the problem of transferring skills from school to home is eliminated.
2. Parents have direct and natural access to behaviors as they occur; therefore, functional objectives can be set and cultural considerations taken into account.
3. Learned behaviors are more likely to generalize and be maintained if taught in the home by the parent.
4. There is more opportunity for all family members to become involved and participate in the child's program.
5. Parents have access to the child's full range of behaviors, not just what is evident to the classroom teacher; therefore, they can work on skills for which there would be no opportunity in the classroom.

6. Training parents, who are the child's natural reinforcing agents, allows them to develop skills to deal with new behaviors as they arise.
7. Individualization of the child's goals and objectives is operational, as it is a natural result of the setting.

Inherent in a home-based philosophy is the belief that parents can be and are the child's best teachers, that the home is a stimulating learning environment, and that staff can play an educational role for the entire family.

Home-based programs are often necessary for other than philosophical reasons. Geographic and demographic considerations sometimes make home-based programs the only viable option.

Center-based programs, on the other hand, have a different set of advantages and philosophical underpinnings:

1. All families have a common setting for their children, who are allowed access to the variety of toys and materials available at the center, many of which may not be found at home.
2. A wide range of services are available, including counseling and parent groups.
3. Parents have an opportunity to view tapes, books, and other materials to help them understand their child's handicap and aid in his or her development.
4. Children are exposed to other children and thus have an opportunity to develop social skills important to their development.
5. Children have an opportunity for individual therapy, and their programs may have input from many disciplines.
6. Children have a chance to learn to interact with adults other than their parents.
7. Parents have a chance to observe and perhaps work with children other than their own.
8. Parents have an opportunity to talk to other parents and share feelings and experiences, thereby gaining emotional support.
9. Children may receive more actual program time.
10. Parents may need time away from their handicapped child; the center time allows them some respite.

Combined home-and-center-based programs profess to offer the advantages of both settings. Depending on how much time is spent in either setting and what activities occur, this may or may not be the case. Combined programs may also be somewhat more expensive because of dual transportation expenses. The ideal arrangement may be an individualized program that can offer either or both settings as deemed appropriate to the child and the family.

Continuum of Services The environmental options available exceed home-based, center-based, or combination programs. Public Law 94-142 specifies that programs for handicapped children must be provided in the "least restrictive" or most "normal" environment. A continuum of most restrictive to least restrictive environments might include the following:

----Institution
-----Home-bound (school-age)
------Segregated school
-------Regular school self-contained class
--------Self-contained class & integrated activities
---------Integrated class & resource room activities
----------Integrated class & support services activities
-----------Integrated class & integrated activities

In the case of handicapped infants, home is considered a natural environment. If a more "therapeutic" environment is deemed appropriate, the infant may attend a program either in a segregated school or a segregated classroom within a normal school. Occasionally, handicapped infant and preschool children are integrated with normal children.

Each "step" on the continuum has advantages and disadvantages, and there is research to support or reject each as a successful approach to serving children. The problem facing infant and preschool programs for handicapped children, particularly in public schools, is that frequently there are no "regular" infant or preschool classes of "normal" children with whom to integrate. Creative alternatives, however, can be found. For instance, integrating siblings or staff children can provide important normal models. Cooperative efforts with local nursery or day-care establishments can also offer more "normal" environments—for example, through exchanges or half-day arrangements between special preschool and day-care centers (for parents who work). Whenever possible, handicapped children should be provided opportunities to interact meaningfully with normal children. This may require some training of both the nursery school or day-care staff *and* the normal children. Whenever mainstreaming efforts are undertaken, they should be planned carefully to maximize successful interaction.

Table 1. Role of early childhood educator

Educator as facilitator:	Educator facilitates the child's interaction with the environment by modeling, demonstrating, questioning. The child plays a major role in decision making concerning activities. Discovery learning is vital.
Educator as teacher:	Educator "teaches" or transfers knowledge and skills. The child accepts information. Repetition and practice are important.
Educator as "engineer":	Educator manipulates the environment to ensure success. Modeling, shaping, and reinforcement are utilized. Measurement is precise and ongoing.
Educator as therapist or educational synthesizer:	A clinical or remediation approach is utilized based on developmental and behavioral principles. Knowledge and skills of various disciplines are integrated. A combination of approaches may be used.

Determination of the Nature of Program Interaction

The third component of the process model for determining the service delivery system focuses on the interaction between the child, staff, parents, and environment. The manner in which these elements interrelate (see Figure 1), flows directly from the nature of the program philosophy, and specifically from the staffing pattern selected, the theoretical model, the curricula utilized, and the program setting. How the educator and other staff perceive their roles directly affects how the environment is ordered and thus also the child's role in that environment. The role of the parents is often determined by these perceptions as well.

Role of the Early Childhood Special Educator
The role of the teacher is critical to program design, and will vary regardless of the team approach utilized. The teacher is responsible for planning and implementing the child's educational program and measuring its success. Depending on the educational model on

Role of Early Childhood
Special Educator
—facilitation
—direction, training
—remediation, therapy
—observation
—measurement

which the program is based, this role differs greatly. The early childhood special educator may be viewed as a facilitator, teacher, "engineer," or therapist (see Table 1).

Role of the Child and the Environment The role of the child within the environment can be seen to emanate from the definition of staff roles. Table 2 shows the relationships among the various elements. When the child assumes a more active role, the teacher tends to have fewer directive responsibilities. The materials and structure within the environment also vary, depending on whether the environment is meant

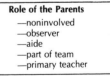

Role of the Child
—inactive/initiator
—passive/receptor
—self-directed

Role of the Environment
—natural
—facilitative
—controlled
—therapeutic

to stimulate exploration, provide information, or ensure success. The interrelationships among these three elements reflect a program's fundamental philosophy.

Role of the Parents The role of the parents may vary regardless of the preceding interrelationships. Parent involvement is explored extensively in Chapter 7, and thus is only briefly discussed here as it relates to the development of a service delivery system. The

Role of the Parents
—noninvolved
—observer
—aide
—part of team
—primary teacher

philosophy of the staff is reflected in their perceptions of what the parents' role in the program should be. Parental participation is also highly dependent on how the parents themselves view their role. The parents and/or staff may find one or more of the following to be appropriate parent roles:

1. *Noninvolvement* Occasionally, staff or parents do not feel it is in the best interest of the child (or the parents) for the parents to be involved in the program. Parents may not feel comfortable observing or working with their handicapped child, or their work schedules may not allow involvement. If highly specific therapy is needed that is unpleasant for the child, a staff person

Table 2. Role of the child and environment

Role of educator	Role of child	Role of environment
Educator as facilitator	Child is active—initiates own activity. Play is vital to development and learning. Manipulation, comparison, discovery are encouraged. Child interaction is important for cognitive and social-emotional development.	Self-initiated interaction with environment is key. Objects, people, events are foundations for cognitive restructuring. Arrangement of the environment to maximize discovery of concepts is important.
Educator as teacher	Child is a receptor of information. The relationship between the teacher and the child is the most important vehicle for learning. Imitation after demonstration is important.	Environment is structured to provide the needed information in the appropriate sequences. Repetition of presentation of information, objects, etc.
Educator as "engineer"	Child is a receptor of information and is shaped to perform desired behaviors. Child may be involved in measuring his or her own progress.	Environment is the source of reinforcement and can be structured to ensure learning and success. Objects, persons, and events are structured to reinforce desired behaviors.
Educator as therapist or educational synthesizer	Child may be both active and a receptor. Physical manipulation of child may take place. Reinforcement of desired behaviors is important. Self-initiation of activities is essential to maximize generalization. Play is also crucial.	Environment needs to be structured at times and unstructured at others. Environment is reinforcing and stimulates exploration.

may recommend that the parent not observe the sessions. It should be noted that at times noninvolvement may be the best "therapy" for a parent. As a general rule, however, noninvolvement should not be encouraged. If enough options are available, parents will be more likely to find a meaningful mode of participation. Bronfenbrenner (1975) has noted that those programs that teach parents how to work directly with their children are the most successful.

2. *Parent as observer*   Parents can learn a great deal about their child and how to deal with the child at home by observing staff working with their child. Staff can model and demonstrate positioning, feeding, the teaching of specific

skills, and managing behavior. Parents may then try these techniques at home. Such an informal method of working with parents is nonthreatening, and often encourages increased involvement by a hesitant or fearful parent. Parents also indicate that they have benefited greatly by observing children other then their own, as they are provided a better understanding of the strengths and weaknesses of their own child. A handicap that seemed devastating to the family may be viewed as "not so bad" when compared to more severely involved children in the program.

3. *Parent as aide*   The next step toward a higher level of parent involvement is aiding in the home or classroom. As the teacher or therapist works with the children, the parents assist with specific program tasks. This level allows for greater learning by the parent, as staff can provide continual feedback and encourage good teaching techniques. Often parents rotate the job of aiding in a classroom, thus allowing all parents to participate. The parent-as-aide can provide a welcome extra set of skilled, helping hands.

4. *Parent as partner*   As parents become more involved, particularly in home-based programs, they can become partners to the staff. Intervention techniques are taught to the parent, who practices the techniques in front of the staff. Staff provide ongoing feedback and support. Parents' suggestions are sought, and program planning becomes a joint effort, with the parent a key team member.

5. *Parent as teacher*   Many parents ultimately become proficient at intervention. They are able to plan a program with assistance from staff and can follow through on all intervention. The staff serve primarily as consultants and as a base for emotional support. Staff provide ongoing evaluation, therapy, and necessasry materials and equipment. Parents at this level of involvement are often tremendously valuable resources to assist other parents who are struggling with adapting to living and working with a handicapped child.

It is important for staff to discuss their philosophy regarding the role of parents in the program. A variety of alternatives need to be available in order to ensure that the program is individualized to meet the needs of families as well as children.

INTEGRATING PHILOSOPHICAL COMPONENTS

The development of a service delivery system based on a consistent philosophy is a complex task. The nature of the population, of staff's beliefs concerning learning and development, and of staff's perception of roles all determine a philosophy of early intervention. A step-by-step analysis of each of the previously discussed elements is essential to the program planning.

To summarize, each of the following elements needs to be assessed:

1. Funding sources, which may affect who may be served
2. The types, degrees, ages, and number of handicapped children needing service
3. The background of families to be served
4. The geographic distribution of families to be served
5. The services provided by other agencies that have an impact on young handicapped children
6. The services to be provided to young handicapped children
7. The staff needed to provide services
8. The staffing patterns desired
9. The theoretical model of learning espoused
10. The assessment instruments and curricula selected
11. The setting, including facilities and equipment
12. The interactive nature of child/staff/environment/parents

The details of job responsibilities, scheduling, specific instruments, materials and equipment will evolve from these philosophical foundations. Numerous problems in communication among staff may be avoided if a consistent philosophy is adhered to from the start of program planning.

REFERENCES

Ackerman, P.R., Jr., & Moore, M.G. Delivery of educational services to preschool handicapped children. In: T. Tjossem (ed.), *Intervention strategies for high risk infants and young children*. Baltimore: University Park Press, 1976.

Anastasiow, N.J. Strategies and models for early childhood intervention programs in integrated settings. In: M.J. Guralnick (ed.), *Early intervention and the integration of handicapped and non-handicapped children*. Baltimore: University Park Press, 1978.

Behavioral characteristics progression. The Office of the Santa Cruz County Superintendent of Schools. Palo Alto, CA: VORT Corporation, 1973.

Biber, B., Wickens D., & Shapiro, E. *Promoting cognitive growth from a developmental-interactionist point of view*. Washington, DC: National Association for the Education of Young Children, 1971.

Bluma, S., Shearer, M., Frohman, A., & Hilliard, J. *Portage guide to early education*. Portage, WI: Cooperative Educational Service Agency 12, 1976.

Boegehold, B.D., Cuffaro, H., Hooks, W.H., & Klopp, G.J. *Education before five*. New York: Bank Street College of Education, 1977.

Bronfenbrenner, U. Is early intervention effective? In: J. Hellmuth (ed.), *Exceptional infants*, Vol. 3. New York: Brunner/Mazel, 1975.

Fallen, N. *Young children with special needs*. Columbus, OH: Charles E. Merrill Publishing Co., 1978.

Furth, T.D., & Wachs, H. *Thinking goes to school*. New York: Oxford University Press, 1975.

Heber, R., Garber, H., Harrington, C., Hoffman, C., & Falendar, C., *Rehabilitation of families at risk for mental retardation*. Madison, WI: University of Wisconsin, 1975.

Hohman, M., Banet, B., & Weikart, D.P. *Young children in action*. Ypsilanti, MI: High/Scope Educational Research Foundation, 1979.

Holm, V.A., & McCartin, R.E. Interdisciplinary child development team: Issues and training and interdisciplinariness. In: K.E. Allen, V.A. Holm, & R.L. Schiefelbusch (eds.), *Early intervention: A team approach*. Baltimore: University Park Press, 1978.

Iacino, R., & Bricker, B.B. A model for preparing personnel to work with the severely-profoundly handicapped. In: N. Haring & D. Bricker (eds.), *Teaching the severely handicapped*, Vol. 3. Columbus, OH: Special Press, 1978.

Kamii, C., & DeVries, P. Piaget for early childhood education. In: M.C. Day & R. Parker (eds.), *Preschool in action*. Boston: Allyn and Bacon, 1977.

Lewis, C. The Montessori method. In: B. Boegehold, H. Cuffaro, H. Hooks, & G.J. Klopps (eds.), *Education before five*. New York: Bank Street College of Education, 1977.

Lillie, D.L., & Trohanis, P.L. *Teaching parents to teach*. New York: Walker & Co., 1976.

Mikulas, W. *Behavior modification*. New York: Harper & Row, 1978.

Montessori, M. *The Montessori method*. New York: Schocken Books, 1964.

Phillips, J.L., Jr. *The origins of intellect: Piaget's theory*. San Francisco: W.H. Freeman & Co., 1975.

Shearer, M.S., & Shearer, D.E. The Portage project: A model for early childhood education. *Exceptional Children*, 1972, *36*, 210–217.

Sternat, J., Messina, Nietupski, J., Lyon, S., & Brown, L. Occupational and physical therapy services for severely handicapped students: Toward a naturalized public school service delivery mode. In: E. Sontag, J. Smith, & N. Certo (eds.), *Educational programming for the severely and profoundly handicapped*. Reston, VA: The Council for Exceptional Children, Mental Retardation Division, 1977.

Webster's seventh new collegiate dictionary. Chicago: G. & C. Merriam Co., 1967.

chapter

3

Leadership and Administration

Leadership entails the capacity to assume responsibility and to manage. Effective leadership implies the ability to forsee necessary changes, to solve problems creatively, and to guide and influence the thinking of others. Strong, competent leaders are needed to confirm and strengthen the role of early childhood special education in the human service delivery system. Early intervention programs are unique in that they are by necessity cross-agency and transdisciplinary. They require highly knowledgeable and skilled individuals to plan, coordinate, implement, and evaluate program efforts.

Leaders in early childhood special education need more than administrative skill. A belief in the effectiveness of early intervention and a commitment to young handicapped children and their families are essential. As in any new field, there are many battles to be waged and obstacles to surmount in order to achieve desired goals. Considerable dedication and energy are required to ensure that these goals are not obscured.

Early childhood special education programs are often nontraditional in nature. Administrators therefore need to be open-minded and flexible in their approach to service delivery alternatives, staff patterns, and scheduling. In addition, early childhood programs, more than programs for school-age children, must be sensitive to parents' needs. Effective programs directly involve parents in their child's education (Bronfenbrenner, 1975). Sensitivity to parents' individual differences is crucial if effective program alternatives are to be developed and implemented.

Another major leadership characteristic in early childhood special education should be a willingness to work cooperatively with other agencies. To provide a full-service program requires coordinating multiple community resources. An administrator whose vision is limited only to those services and funding sources available in the sponsoring agency is unlikely to produce a maximum service delivery system. A creative problem-solving approach that looks at unique alternatives is often required in order to provide the full range of services needed by handicapped children and their families.

The above characteristics—knowledgeable, committed, flexible, sensitive, and creative—are important for any leader, but particularly so for administrators in early childhood special education.

PLANNING FUNCTIONS

The functions of the early childhood special education (ECSE) coordinator vary depending on the "developmental stage" of the program, that is, whether the program is in the initial planning phase, the implementation phase, or is ongoing. Decker and Decker (1976) discuss the functions of the administrator planning a program. These include: 1) identifying goals, 2) communicating the goals to others, 3) determining policies and procedures to accomplish the goals, 4) implementing policies, procedures, and activities, and 5) providing for feedback and evaluation.

One of the first things a program coordinator must do is develop goals for the program. These goals may derive from: 1) professional and personal belief, 2) funding sources, 3) the advisory board, and/or 4) implied or stated needs of families of children to be served (Hewes, 1979). Second, goals need to be communicated to those who will help in planning and administering the program. Goals should be discussed with upper level administrators, parents, staff, and community agency representatives. Communication of goals is essential, as it is paramount that all persons involved understand the purposes of the program. The third step is determining the processes by which the goals will be met. Objectives to be accomplished must be outlined, together with corresponding policies, procedures, and activities. The delineation of program roles and responsibilities in relation to these activities, along with time-lines for accomplishment, comprises the fourth step, implementation. The final step is to provide for feedback and evaluation, and includes: 1) establishing mechanisms for ongoing accountability regarding program objectives and processes, 2) providing for communication channels between administrators, staff, parents, and children, and 3) delineating formative (ongoing) and summative (annual) evaluation procedures.

Planning Goals, Objectives, and Activities

An examination of the processes involved in the above responsibilities can provide direction for program planning. Chapter 2 discussed the components of a program philosophy, from which program goals and objectives are derived. With the program philosophy as a foundation, goals may be articulated for several broad areas: services to children, services to families, staff development, coordination of community resources, and dissemination and demonstration (if the project is funded by a federal grant). Goal statements should indicate the direction and intent of accomplishments for each of these areas. For example: A goal for services to children is "to identify and serve handicapped children from birth to 6 years old." Objectives under each goal should be specific and measurable, and should be formulated with evaluation procedures in mind. For instance, an objective under the above goal might be, "To implement semi-annual screenings in three locations, screening at least 60% of the estimated population from birth to 6, within one year." Program coordinators will need to define objectives for each goal in each program area.

Once objectives are defined, the next step is to develop activities to attain the objectives. Table 1 provides an excerpt from a sample program plan outlining activities to meet the above-stated objective. Activities should be determined for each program objective. Of course, every program is unique, and goals, objectives, and activities will vary depending on local needs.

Table 1. Example of goal, objectives, and activities from a sample program plan[a]

I. **Services to Children**
    A. **Child Find**
        Goal: To identify and serve handicapped children from birth to 6 years old.

Objectives	Activities
1. To implement semi-annual screening in three locations, screening at least 60% of the estimated population from birth to 6 within 1 year.	1.1. Contact a minimum of 15 agencies in the school district and coordinate a meeting to discuss screening. 1.2. Coordinate screening efforts with other agencies, including social services, health, institutions. 1.3. Conduct a community awareness campaign to include: —presentations to 10 service clubs and organizations —5 articles in local newspapers —10 air spots on local radio stations —distribution of 1,000 fliers through grocery stores, food stamp stations, doctors' offices, schools 1.4. Conduct developmental screenings at three different locations in the school district twice a year in cooperation with other community services and agencies. 1.5. Refer children with significant delays in one or more developmental areas for further evaluation.

[a]This example is taken from the sample program plan for early childhood special education included in full in the Appendix at the end of the book.

Whenever possible, staff who will be involved in the program should be included in developing the program plan. This allows them the chance to gain a greater understanding of the rationale and processes underlying their responsibilities, and they may also develop an increased respect for their role in program evaluation (see Chapter 9). The reader is referred to the Appendix, where a sample program plan is presented.

Establishing Communication Links

The ECSE administrator is a key individual in promoting external (outside of the program) communication. Externally, the ECSE administrator must relate to building teachers and staff, building administrators, agency administrators, the school board or advisory board members, human service agency representatives, and the community.

It is desirable for public school ECSE programs to be housed in regular elementary school buildings. Establishing a level of understanding with all building staff from the beginning is extremely important. The presence of very young handicapped children, with the concurrent noise and constant influx of parents, may prove to be a discordant note in a traditional school setting. Prior to program implementation, it is therefore essential to arrange a meeting with staff to explain the rationale for early intervention and to justify the program design. Once the program is underway, cooperation from regular classroom teachers will enable mainstreaming efforts to proceed. The ECSE coordinator may need to provide inservice training to teachers concerning the children to be served, their handicaps, and special problems. The level of understanding and support that is established at the beginning of the program may set the tone for the whole year. Otherwise, the early childhood program may remain "that room" down the hall, enveloped in mystery and misconception.

Building principals are key figures for early intervention programs. The programs are, after all, housed in "their" buildings and come under their responsibility. Depending on the lines of authority, the principal may be the direct supervisor of the ECSE coordinator or may have parallel responsibilities. In either case, it is important to obtain the principal's commitment to the early childhood special education program. Advocacy and support by the building principal will facilitate: 1) more flexible staff usage, 2) non-early childhood staff cooperation, 3) materials and equipment exchange, and 4) program continuation. Especially with programs in early childhood, it is important to develop advocates in education and elsewhere who are not directly involved in the program. These "unbiased" individuals can often be persuasive in gaining continued program support from school boards and other school administrators.

There is also a need for direct communication with upper level district administrators and the school board in the case of public school programs, and with upper level agency heads in the case of nonpublic school programs. Creating channels for input will again allow positive feelings toward the early childhood program to develop over time. Providing evaluation data on progress and growth will enable the gradual building of support as a basis for later continuation requests. If communication lines are established early, a last-minute rush of emotional appeals may be avoided.

The ECSE coordinator must also relate to human service agencies. The number of agencies serving handicapped children and their families is impressive. If comprehensive services are to be provided, coordination of resources is essential. Chapter 4 provides detailed guidelines to assist in the development of interagency communication and cooperation. The ECSE coordinator should work to secure these communication channels during the program planning phase, thus assuring that as children enter the program, alternatives will be available to meet their needs in the most effective and efficient way.

The importance of interacting, as well, with the community at large must not be overlooked. If early intervention programs are to become permanent components of our education and human services system, it is imperative that the taxpayers understand *why* we need to serve handicapped infants and preschoolers. Without the public's support, a long-term commitment to early childhood special education cannot be established. Therefore, the ECSE coordinator must become a media specialist. Local newspapers can be notified of special events, and encouraged to write feature stories on the program. Television spots or other television coverage (for example, talk shows) are also effective. Talking to community organizations and parent groups helps recruit others to publicize the program concept. Pamphlets, newsletters, participation in community events—all contribute to community visibility and to ongoing support of early intervention programs.

Concurrent with establishing external communication links is the need for internal communication channels. The ECSE coordinator can facilitate ongoing staff discussion by ensuring the presence of feedback mechanisms among the staff, the administration, parents, and the community.

One way to guarantee communication is to build it into the schedule. Often administrators expect staff to meet before or after school hours to discuss children, special topics, or for parent conferences. This in effect, tells staff that such communication is an adjunct to, and not a crucial part of, their job. Perhaps one reason for educator "burn out" is that educators lack administrative support to perform many of their job roles. Administrators need to recognize the importance of these tasks. Team meetings, staff meetings, parent conferences, home visits, meetings with the coordinator, and other communication processes are *critical* to effective program operation, and should, therefore, be formally included in program planning and scheduling. The ECSE coordinator needs to include these responsibilities in job descriptions, as well as provide time and support for staff to adequately perform these functions. Staff should not be expected to do them on their "own time."

Establishing Policies and Procedures

Policies are statements of written assurance of a course of action, while procedures provide specific guidelines for meeting the intent of the policy. Policies are typically made by boards of education or other upper level administrators, while procedures are developed by local administrators in order to implement policy. Policies are developed for the following reasons: 1) to meet requirements of state or federal agencies, 2) to provide guidelines for achieving program goals, 3) to help avoid inconsistency, 4) as a basis for decision making, and 5) to ensure fairness and protection of program, staff, children and parents.

All public schools and most nonpublic schools have extensive policies and procedures that guide administrative governance. Early childhood special education programs must adhere to these policies and procedures, but may also want to establish additional policies that reflect their distinct population, range of services, and mode of operation.

There are many areas in which policy development is necessary or helpful. Decker and Decker (1976) cite the following policy areas:

1. *Administrative policy* including a) meeting legal requirements; b) the appointment and functions of the director and supervisory personnel; c) administrative operations.
2. *Child-related policy* including a) referral and assessment and placement; b) attendance; c) continuum of program services; d) termination of program services; e) assessing and reporting children's progress; f) provisions for child welfare (accidents and insurance) and medication; g) special activities (e.g., field trips and class celebrations); h) services to parents; i) confidentiality; j) parent involvement.
3. *Staff-personnel policy* including a) recruitment, selection and appointment; b) qualifications; c) job assignment; d) staff evaluation; e) tenure; f) separation; g) salary schedules and fringe benefits; h) absences and leaves; and i) personal and professional activities, including inservice requirements.
4. *Fiscal policy* including a) sources of funding; b) nature of budget (e.g., preparation, adoption and publication); c) categories of expenditures; d) guidelines and procedures for purchasing goods and services; e) system of accounts and auditing procedures; and f) accounting for per child expeditures.
5. *Public relations policy* including a) types of participation by the public (e.g., citizen's advisory committees and volunteers); b) use of program facilities; c) relations with various agencies and associations; and d) media used for communication with public (p. 17).

The ECSE coordinator must be familiar with school policies and procedures in each of these areas and be alert to the need for additional policies. A policy and procedures handbook should be developed that delineates the program's operating principles. This handbook "exerts a stabilizing effect upon the organization, serves as a guide to performance and provides a standard against which to measure accomplishment" (Marks, Stoops, & King-Stoops, 1971, p. 92). The time involved in developing such a manual and providing inservice training to the staff on its content and use will be rewarded by reduced conflict and misunderstandings. The manual will also serve as a reference for consideration of problems relating to specific policy areas.

Following is a discussion of the above-mentioned policy areas, specifically as they relate to early childhood special education.

Administrative Policy Policies relating to administration will vary depending on whether the program is in a public school, a not-for-profit, or a private agency. Within the public schools, policies relating to legal mandates and state regulations are required.

Compliance with Legal Mandates The coordinator/director of early childhood special education programs should be fully informed on all legal mandates and federal and state rules and regulations relevant to programs for young handicapped children. At present, early intervention programs in the public schools are subject to the same mandates as are programs for school-age children. Public Law 94-142 required that public schools were to provide handicapped children 3 to 21 years of age a free, appropriate public education by September, 1980. The requirements for the 3 to 5 age range, however, do not apply if the application of such requirements would be "inconsistent with State law or practice, or the order of any court" [(PL 94-142, 1975, Section 612(2)(B)]. (See Chapter 1.) With the demonstrated need for services and documented benefits of early intervention, however, many public schools are taking advantage of special incentive grant monies provided under PL 94-142 for services for preschool age children.

In order to be eligible for federal funds, the local education agency (LEA) must provide written guarantees of each of the following:

1. Assurance of active, ongoing child identification procedures for children birth to 21 years of age
2. Assurance of a "full service" goal and detailed timetable for implementation
3. A guarantee of complete due process procedures
4. Assurance of an effective policy guaranteeing the right of all handicapped children to a free, appropriate public education, at no cost to parents or guardian
5. Assurance of nondiscriminatory testing and evaluation
6. Assurance of the maintenance of an individualized education program (IEP) for each handicapped child
7. Assurance of special education being provided to all handicapped children in the "least restrictive environment"
8. A guarantee of policies and procedures to protect the confidentiality of data and information

9. Assurance of regular parent or guardian consultation
10. Assurance of a surrogate to act for any child when parents or guardians are either unknown or unavailable, or when the child is a legal ward of the state
11. Assurance of the maintenance of programs and procedures for comprehensive personnel development, including inservice training

These assurances should be supported by written policies. Even for nonpublic schools, most of these requirements apply.

If the public school does not have an appropriate placement for a child, nonpublic day-school programs or private settings may provide services. For states mandating services to handicapped children less than 5 years old, these nonpublic school services must be purchased. In states where preschool and infant programs are not mandated, public schools may serve as the vehicle for identification and referral to appropriate placements. Federally funded public agencies to which public schools refer young handicapped children should 1) meet the state standards that apply to local education agencies (LEAs), 2) maintain the child's IEP, and 3) accord children and families equal rights as in public schools. If referrals are made to nonpublic schools, the school district has an ethical responsibility to provide follow-up and periodic reevaluation. In agencies where these mandates do not apply, the practices are still valid and should be incorporated into administrative policies.

Identification The agency, whether public or private, needs to provide a clear, written description of each type of handicap for which services will be provided. There is currently a controversy regarding the advisability of "labeling" a child with a particular category of handicap. The trend toward noncategorical services aims at defining handicapped children by their special *needs* rather than by a specific handicapping condition. Many programs are currently providing services to handicapped children under the age of 5 on a noncategorical basis. PL 94-142, however, requires that data be reported by the disability of the child. The following have been designated as exceptionalities:

Blind
Communication disorder
Deaf
Deaf/blind
Developmentally disabled
Emotionally disturbed
Hard of hearing
Health impaired

Learning disabled
Mentally gifted (services not mandated through PL 94-142)
Mentally retarded
Multiply handicapped
Talented (services not mandated through PL 94-142)
Visually impaired

Attempts at noncategorical services have grouped the handicapping conditions as: physical, health, or sensory handicaps; emotional or behavioral problems; or exceptionality in mental ability. Designation of need for service by degree of severity of the handicap is another means by which states have tried to avoid the stigmatizing effect of labels. The terms mildly handicapped, moderately handicapped, severely handicapped, and profoundly handicapped have thus been used to identify children. Another method of grouping that is becoming more popular is by child needs, which are then grouped by service. The identification of needs such as curricular needs, training needs, physical environmental needs, classroom management needs, social-emotional needs, vocational/avocational needs, and home-school interaction needs can allow the child to receive services without having to attach a handicapping condition.

The handicap or "label" given to a child is still a means by which the federal government and others justify provision of services to the child and family. If trends continue, the future will, it is hoped, see development of a system that justifies the provision of services based on children's needs, without the necessity of child labeling.

Policies relating to identification procedures should be clearly delineated and should designate the means by which children will be assessed and their IEPs developed (see Chapter 5). Nondiscriminatory testing, team evaluation, staffing guidelines, assurances of placement in the least restrictive environment, and reevaluation, all require policy statements.

Due Process As outlined in PL 94-142, each school district must meet minimum due process requirements in identification, evaluation, and placement of handicapped children. The purpose of due process standards is to assure parents' involvement in all decisions concerning their child's educational program and to protect the child's right to a free, appropriate public education.

Procedures should be developed to address the following requirements of due process:

1. Parents must be informed (in their native language) of all the rights that are provided them under the law.
2. Parents have the right to be notified whenever the school wishes to evaluate their child, wants to change an educational placement, or refuses their request for an evaluation or a change in placement.
3. The school must obtain written permission from parents before evaluating their child.
4. Parents have a right to request an independent evaluation if they disagree with the results of the school's evaluation. Parents also have a right to request a reevaluation by the school if they question the appropriateness of the child's placement.
5. The child has a right to valid, comprehensive, unbiased testing by a multi-disciplinary team.
6. Parents have a right to review all the child's educational records, to request removal of false or misleading information, and/or to place a statement in the child's records indicating the portions with which they disagree.
7. Parents have the right to participate in developing their child's IEP. They should be given every opportunity to be involved in the child's staffing. Written permission from parents must be obtained before the placement of the child.
8. Parents have the right to an impartial due process hearing if they disagree with

decisions the school makes about their child's evaluation, placement, or services. They should be informed of their rights regarding such a hearing. Whenever possible, informal rather than formal processes should be employed to resolve conflicts. Due process hearings tend to create an adversary atmosphere that can result in negative feelings on the part of one side or the other after final decisions are made. Although rights are preserved, the resultant negative relations may not be constructive. Consequently, the school should develop procedures for informal discussion and mediation of differences that can be utilized prior to, and preferably eliminate the need for, the due process hearing. These informal negotiations may not in any way impinge upon parents' right to a written decision within 45 days of their request of a due process hearing.

9. A child has a right to a surrogate parent (*guardian ad litem*) when the child's parent or guardian is unknown, when the child's parents are unavailable, or when the child is a ward of the state.

All agencies, public or private, need policies guaranteeing due process. Specific procedures need to be clarified in writing for both formal and informal practices.

Full Service It is the aim of PL 94-142 that educational agencies provide a continuum of educational services that will enable children to be placed in the "least restrictive" educational setting that will meet their needs. A variety of program alternatives should thus be available. Deno and Mirkin (1977) have described a "cascade" of services, from the least restrictive to the most restrictive, progressing from regular education with program modifications, consultative services, resource room, integrated programs, self-contained classes, and special school, to homebound, hospitalized, or institutionalized.

In addition to placement in the appropriate educational setting, children are entitled to an IEP and "related services" that will meet their special needs. These related services include occupational therapy, nursing services, physical therapy, speech language services, social services, medical consultation, counseling services, psychological services, and transportation services. Many questions are now being raised as to which related services are required and which are open to the discretion of the local education agency (LEA). Policies regarding the school's position on related services should be developed. Litigation and legislation may soon dictate the direction of future policies.

Child-Related Policies The previously discussed policies concerning identification and placement are also child-related. However, there are additional ongoing concerns specifically relevant to young handicapped children that need to be addressed once children are receiving services, in particular, policies regarding confidentiality, the distribution of medication, and the involvement of parents. If the school district does not have policy statements and procedures for these areas, the ECSE coordinator may need to work with other agency staff to develop them.

Confidentiality A written policy regarding confidentiality is needed to guarantee the child's right to privacy. Procedures for retrieval and use of all information collected should be delineated as required by PL 93-380, the Education of the Handicapped Amendments of 1974, (Title V, Sections 513–514). The Council for Exceptional Children (1977) has outlined four levels of information that may be accumulated pertinent to a child's participation in special education services.

Level I, Basic Identifying Data—includes specific information regarding the child's name, address, academic achievement, attendance and health data.
Level II, Verified Data—includes test results, medical history, classroom testing.
Level III, Tentative Data—includes reports of professionals, reports from external agencies, anecdotal records.
Level IV, Professional Files—includes notes taken during interviews (may become Level III data if shared at staffings).

Each of these levels becomes increasingly more sensitive with regard to confidentiality. Levels I, II, and III are usually stored in one place, while Level IV data remain the professional's personal property. Level I data may be kept indefinitely, while Level II and III information must be destroyed or provided to parents within 5 years, or after the information is no longer needed; this is to prevent stigmatizing information from following the child long after special services have ended. In early childhood special education prevention of stigmatization is vital, as early intervention may correct or alleviate problems to such a degree that regular class placement is possible sooner in the child's academic school years. It is important that when data are no longer needed, parents be notified and that unnecessary and irrelevant information be deleted from the child's record. Procedures for periodic (annual) review of records should be established to ensure protection of the child's rights.

Policies and procedures should also be written with regard to the access of records—including parental access to records, the conditions of access, student access to records (for later years), and notation of who had access to the records and when.

Medication   Many young handicapped children need medications during the day. The program needs to establish a written policy and procedures for administering medication. Medical personnel are preferred for this responsibility; however, many programs do not have access to nursing or other medical personnel. Policies should designate the personnel responsible for administering medication, the conditions under which other persons may administer medication, and the methods by which medications will be locked and safely stored.

Parent Involvement   Public schools cannot require parental involvement in school programs. However, parent-child interaction and follow-through in ECSE programs is so crucial to maximum program effectiveness that a policy statement in this area is recommended. A statement of parent involvement alternatives should be included, along with another statement regarding why these options are felt to be significant to the child's growth. Procedures for initiating, conducting, modifying, and terminating such involvement should be outlined. The parent involvement component is discussed further in Chapter 7.

Staff-Personnel Policies   School districts and other public agencies may have existing policies regarding many staff-personnel issues. These do not need to be duplicated here, as such policies automatically apply to ECSE staff. However, the interdisciplinary or transdisciplinary nature of early intervention programs may necessitate policies that address the variations in staff roles and responsibilities. A statement of the philosophical intent of staff patterns may clarify for other administrators, staff, and parents the reason for overlapping and cooperative duties. Procedures need to be outlined describing the team processes that will be utilized, including team planning, programming, and evaluation.

Staff Development   Policies regarding staff development may also need to be written. Many professionals, though trained to work with handicapped children, may not have been trained to work with very *young* handicapped children. They also may not have had training in working with and understanding other disciplines. The ECSE administrator may want to design a continuum for ongoing professional development, from professional readings to inservice training, external classes, and degrees. (This is discussed further in Chapter 8.) Policies should be outlined delineating administrative expectations and how a staff member may become involved in staff development alternatives. Procedures for disseminating information derived from current education research, as well as methods for adopting new educational practices and materials, are also important.

Staff Evaluation   Staff members need written guidelines concerning their evaluation. Specific procedures on who will supervise, how supervision will take place, and how often it will take place are needed. Methods for establishing mutually agreed upon goals between staff and supervisor, and review and appeal procedures are also important staff safeguards to include in policy statements.

Fiscal Management Policy   Policies need to be developed with regard to how decisions concerning expenditures are made. The "bottom line" in fiscal decision making is that financial resources should be allocated on the basis of individual child need rather than on traditional estimates of service usage. Recording systems need to:

1. Track the costs of early childhood special education programs:
   a. The number of children receiving service
   b. Expenditures for identification and placement
   c. Cost of the early childhood programs
2. Account for all federal, state, and local monies expended for young handicapped children
3. Identify and record the total cost of educating the child in order to determine excess costs

A policy statement should be written to indicate that fiscal decisions are made based on the written IEP.

The sources of funding in ECSE programs may be more diverse than in school-age programs, and may coordinate, for example, with funds from Early, Periodic Screening, Diagnosis, and Treatment (EPSDT) and Child Find activities. Policies regarding cooperative fiscal arrangements should be stated, particularly with regard to those services for which the agency has "first-dollar" (or primary) responsibilities.

Existing school policies and procedures must be utilized for accounting and auditing procedures, but specific care should be taken in determining per-child expenditures. These figures may become very significant in program continuation discussions.

Public Relations Policies A representative for early childhood special education should be included in the public school district's special education advisory panel. It is also recommended that a separate, but cooperative, advisory board be formed for the ECSE program, whether public or private. Policies regarding this advisory board and procedures for selection and rotation of members need to be written. Suggested membership might include parents, staff, a regular education preschool or kindergarten teacher, an ECSE administrator, a consumer representative of a local advocacy organization, a professional from higher education or someone involved in training who prepares persons for employment in ECSE, and an administrator from the local school district.

Such an advisory board can provide a firm advocacy base and also serve as a link to the community. The policies regarding the advisory board need to take into account the duties of the members. As delineated by The Council for Exceptional Children (1977) the following might comprise a few of the responsibilities:

1) Assist in developing plans for identifying children who need special services.
2) Assist in the formulation and development of long-range plans for ECSE.
3) Assist in the development of priorities and strategies for meeting the identified and special education and related service needs.
4) Submit reports on committee's findings and recommendations for action.
5) Assist in dissemination and interpretation to the school board and community of committee's recommendations and plans for implementation (Policy Number 1005).

Policies with respect to interagency agreements and procedures for developing formal and informal agreement may also be considered part of public relations. (This is discussed in Chapter 4). Also in this area would be policies regarding the use of media and the need for parental permission for child involvement in such media coverage. Specific policies and procedures for assuring a positive community and school district image need to be outlined.

If the ECSE program will involve nonhandicapped children and/or work with nonhandicapped preschool programs outside the agency, guidelines for establishing and evaluating such efforts are needed. School policies relating to visiting groups (for example, staffing patterns, insurance) should be determined and coordinated with policies regarding mainstreaming. Identifying inconsistencies between policies may alleviate difficulties at later stages in the program.

Policies and procedures that need to be developed can be specified in relation to program goals, objectives, and activities. The reader is referred to the sample program plan in the Appendix for an example of how needed policies can be outlined at the same time that goals, objectives, and activities are developed.

MANAGEMENT AND SUPERVISION

In addition to program planning and establishment of policies and procedures, the ECSE coordinator has management and supervisory responsibilities that are critical to both planning and ongoing program operation. The determination of individual staff responsibilities, the establishment of a fiscal process, the supervision of staff, and the maintenance of a quality program are important administrative functions.

Staff Responsibilities

The initial careful planning of activities to be accomplished must be complemented by the hiring of persons qualified to perform those tasks. The ECSE coordinator must develop job descriptions that carefully delineate the individual duties to be performed, and that list the qualifications or competencies required to do them. Figure 1 is an example of a job description developed for a speech therapist in an early childhood special education program. Job descriptions should reflect the program philosophy, and will need to be modified as the program evolves.

In addition to describing the roles of the staff, the coordinator needs to encourage the development of communication ties among staff. This can be done by creating a program structure that fosters transdisciplinary interchange. Job descriptions, inservice plans, and flexibility in scheduling can all contribute to maximum communication.

Establishing a Fiscal Process

The ECSE administrator must identify funding sources (addressed in Chapter 10) and establish mechanisms for fiscal accountability—that is, plan, control, and monitor the budget. Planning the budget entails designating necessary expenditures for personnel, fringe benefits, instructional materials and equipment, facilities, administrative costs, contracted services, transportation, and other expenses. These expenses must be matched against the total projected revenue from basic revenue, special education formulas, entitlement funds, competitive grants, tuition charges, donations, and other sources. It is advisable to include parents, staff, and board members in the development of the budget. If funds are short, these persons can contribute to making the tough decisions regarding program priorities and budget cuts. Once the budget is balanced (overall income and expenditures are equal), business personnel can monitor the daily fiscal processes. The coordinator will need to approve material and equipment ex-

---

JOB DESCRIPTION

Position:

Speech/Language Therapist for an early intervention project for handicapped infants and toddlers and their families.

Requirements:

Master's degree in Speech Pathology
Certificate of Clinical Competence in Speech Pathology, the American Speech-Language-Hearing Association
3 years' experience in speech/language field and 1 year's experience with young children

Responsibilities:

1. Provides comprehensive speech and language evaluations for all children referred to the project.
2. Contributes to the development of child's objectives in the language areas.
3. Plays active role in case reviews, parent conferences, and IEP conferences. Plays role as case manager on a rotating basis with other team members.
4. Implements treatment services, conducts weekly individual therapy sessions, and aids parents in home program facilitation.
5. Plans and implements weekly classroom plan on a rotating basis with other team members.
6. Participates in group parent sessions.
7. Conducts evaluations of children every 6 months in appropriate areas.
8. Participates in self-evaluation process every 6 months.
9. Participates in staff development program and conducts some sessions.
10. Participates in dissemination activities, public awareness campaigns, and the screening components as needed.
11. Provides general consultative service to the project in all areas of speech, language, hearing, and general development of communication.

Figure 1. Sample job description for a speech therapist in an early childhood education program.

penditures and be wary of deficit spending. Cost overruns can cause financial difficulties and problems in public relations. Careful, ongoing budgetary monitoring is especially important in early childhood special education, where cost effectiveness is demanded by agency heads and legislators who may doubt the efficacy of early intervention programs.

Supervision of Staff

Supervision usually has a threatening and negative connotation, but if the goals of supervision are developed, understood, and shared with staff, the results can be positive. The primary purpose of supervision is to facilitate the professional growth of staff and to assist them in more effectively meeting the goals of the program and the needs of children and families.

It is important that staff have one person to whom they can turn for help in accomplishing their duties. Supervisory responsibilities should be supportive in nature. The supervisor:

1. Works to arrange a flow of information among the team, the parents, and the teachers

2. Provides needed information to parents or staff
3. Implements program activities on a realistic and manageable time-line
4. Develops standards for effectiveness
5. Organizes weekly review sessions
6. Studies the teaching-learning situation to ascertain how it can be improved
7. Provides constructive feedback to staff
8. Provides opportunities for continuous learning
9. Arranges for outside resources

The duties outlined above are not only the responsibility of the coordinator/ supervisor. Each staff member shares a number of these mutual tasks. Marks (1971) has identified these tasks as informational, managerial, supervisory, operational, or technical assistance.

The development of a staff organization and responsibility chart helps staff and parents to perceive the intricate interrelationships among the staff and their responsibilities. Figure 2 is an example of such a chart. Examination of the chart shows that there is an overlap in the nature of staff duties. An expanded chart might show the type of information, technical assistance, and so on, that each staff member shares.

Lines and methods of communication are essential if the children, who on the chart are connected to all team members, are to be served effectively and efficiently. The supervisor should clarify the specific nature of staff responsibilities and facilitate an interchange among staff. A good supervisor takes advantage of the expertise on the staff and thus reduces the need for "dictatorial" supervision.

Maintenance of a Quality Program

The accomplishment of the previously discussed facets of administration and supervision will contribute greatly to developing a quality program. In addition, the program coordinator must continually evaluate the program's progress toward its goals. In the chapters that follow, information is presented in more depth to assist further in coordinating community resources (Chapter 4), establishing assessment procedures (Chapter 5), selecting and using curricula (Chapter 6), involvement of parents (Chapter 7), staff development (Chapter 8), program evaluation (Chapter 9), funding (Chapter 10), and proposal writing (Chapter 11). The information presented in these chapters should provide a foundation for administration and leadership in early childhood special education.

SUMMARY

The coordinator of an early childhood special education program plays a critical role in the program's success. The individual is not only a planner and inter-disciplinary coordinator. He or she is also an advocate for children, families and

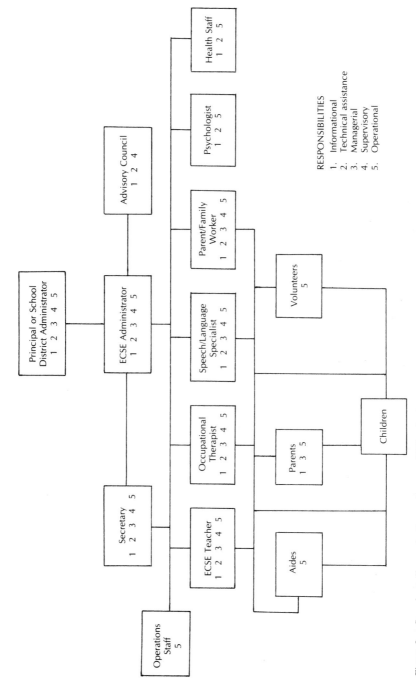

Figure 2. Sample staff organization and responsibility chart.

RESPONSIBILITIES
1. Informational
2. Technical assistance
3. Managerial
4. Supervisory
5. Operational

staff; a program and fiscal manager; a stimulator; an advisor; a mediator; an interpreter; an evaluator; and an educational prophet. The person to fill this role must be chosen wisely.

REFERENCES

Bronfenbrenner, J. Is early intervention effective? In: J. Hellmuth (eds.), *Exceptional infants*, Vol. 3. New York: Brunner/Mazel, 1975.

Decker, C.A., & Decker, V.R. *Planning and administering early childhood programs.* Columbus, OH: Charles E. Merrill Publishing Co., 1976.

Deno, S.L., & Mirkin, P.K. *Data-based program modification: A manual.* Reston, VA: The Council for Exceptional Children, 1977.

Hewes, D.W. *Administration: Making programs work for children and families.* Washington, DC: National Association for the Education of Young Children, 1979.

Marks, J.R., Stoops, E., & King-Stoops, J. *Handbook of educational supervision: A guide for the practitioner.* Boston: Allyn and Bacon, 1971.

Sciarra, J., & Dorsey, A.G. *Developing and administering a child care center.* Boston: Houghton Mifflin Co., 1979.

Special education administrative policies manual. Reston, VA: The Council for Exceptional Children, September 1977.

chapter 4

Coordinating Community Resources

Staff serving young handicapped children encounter daily a range of problems related to obtaining needed services for children and their families. The following are examples of typical service delivery gaps:

> Jimmy has cerebral palsy and a need for reflex integration and activities to develop fine and gross motor skills. However, there is not a physical therapist in this rural school district.
>
> Sally's mother is a single parent, with an eighth-grade education and no job. Sally is being neglected at home, both physically and mentally. Sally's mother needs a variety of services before she can be an effective mother to her developmentally delayed daughter. Program personnel realize that although their responsibility is to provide services to the child, in order for these services to be effective, Sally's mother needs education, job training, and homemaking assistance.
>
> Freddie has chronic health problems, would benefit from corrective surgery on his spine, and needs a prosthetic device. The family does not have the resources to adequately meet Freddie's needs.
>
> Barbara's family is having a difficult time handling the multiple responsibilities associated with their daughter's severe handicaps. Barbara's mother has had a nervous breakdown and her father, working two jobs, is physically and emotionally unavailable to help. The family would like to place Barbara in a residential setting temporarily while they deal with family crises. The program staff is unaware of any options other than the state institution, which is in another city.

The above cases illustrate some of the innumerable problems that service providers face in coping with a delivery system that is, on the whole, extremely fragmented. The inadequacies revealed by the above cases include:

1. The need for more specialized personnel to supplement and enhance a program's services

2. The need for more services for a child's family
3. The need for support services not ordinarily provided by education
4. The need for knowledge of existing community resources
5. The need for knowledge of local, state, and federal agencies that can provide assistance

One way these needs may be addressed is through a coordinated, community effort that is child-oriented rather than agency-oriented.

A CONTINUUM OF SERVICES

A major goal of most agencies serving young handicapped children and their families is to provide a broad spectrum of high quality care and treatment in a supportive environment. The needs of both child and family may be numerous, as a result of the lack of traditional support systems in our society. As Pollard, Hall, and Keeran (1979) point out: ''In today's mobile culture, many families have not established adequate resources and social networks (relatives and friends) to provide necessary support to meet vital life problems; therefore, a formal community-based intervention system is necessary'' (p. 7).

Clearly, no one agency has the resources to provide a total continuum of services to deal with all the problems—mental, physical, social, educational, and financial—that may impinge upon a handicapped child's family. Most families, however, do not know how to maneuver through the maze of existing community services and also may be unaware of many services that exist. Moreover, many families may not even appreciate the extent of their own and/or their child's needs. There is a demand, therefore, for a *system* with well defined and highly integrated resources.

> Effective access to services requires each agency in the service delivery system to serve as a resource to the individual and the family, and to provide linkage to all other services within the system. A high degree of communication, cooperation, and coordination is therefore required among all the elements of the service delivery system (Pollard, Hall, & Keeran, 1979, p. 7).

RATIONALE FOR INTERAGENCY COORDINATION

There are numerous advantages to interagency coordination, one of the most important being the *elimination of duplication* of services. In early childhood special education, many agencies may provide similar services from different funding sources. Screening, for example, may be done by a variety of agencies. Coordination of the screening and other services would eliminate much duplication and *release dollars for other needed services*.

Interagency coordination also provides a clearer picture of existing gaps in services. For example, a review of resources may reveal a paucity of mental health services for the emotionally disturbed preschool-age child. Cooperative efforts can then be developed, using existing resources in the Head Start programs, public schools, mental health centers, and other community agencies. *Identification of gaps in services can thus lead to the initiation of efforts to provide needed services.*

The reduction of duplicated services and the elimination of gaps in services can, in turn, result in a *more effective use of personnel and resources* and facilitate the development of a total continuum of services for handicapped children and their families.

Interagency cooperation can also enable *horizontal as well as vertical extension of the service delivery system.* Horizontal extension adds depth to existing services, while vertical expansion allows for an increased number of services. In other words, an agency would have more alternatives to rely on in meeting a child's and family's needs. Elder (1979) has described how interagency agreements could assist the schools in meeting the mandates of PL 94-142.

> In their implementing regulations, PL 94-142 and Section 504 of the Rehabilitation Act of 1973 require that each handicapped child must be provided all services necessary to meet his or her special education and related needs. If this statement were read as mandating that schools must assume all costs, it would place an impossible financial burden on school districts to pay for services they have never before provided and can ill afford. However, there is no requirement in any of the legislation that schools can plan only services in the IEP which the schools pay for. That is, nothing in law or regulations prohibits schools from meeting IEP requirements by utilizing other nonschool community services and funding where they are available. Arrangements with other sources of funds at any level, cost-sharing across agencies, and even tapping the too-often-overlooked insurance benefits which pay for needed services should be worked toward in developing interagency agreements. By developing joint funding in interagency agreements, resources can be maximized and the question of which agency provides the first dollar for services can be resolved (pp. 203–204).

By utilizing other available monies, or cost-sharing, the school districts can coordinate a wide range of services for a child.

The coordination of resources not only meets individual and family needs, it also *meets community needs.* Taxpayers are demanding wiser expenditure of tax money. California's Proposition 13, for example, is a clear directive to state and local agencies to develop unified service delivery systems, to simplify the bureaucracy, and to stop "wasting" the taxpayers' money. There is unlikely to be a large increase in dollars available for human services. Consequently, coordination is imperative to ensure maximum use of services.

Coordination of existing resources facilitates as well *comprehensive planning for effective utilization of future resources.* It allows, too, for agencies to make joint application for grants, with increased probability of funding if interagency coordination is demonstrated.

The coordination of resources through a specific local and state human service agency *allows parents and service providers a central facilitation agency.* The coordination of intake, referral, service delivery, and follow-up by education agencies will encourage consistent program management. If interagency agreements exist with a broad range of agencies, the child and family could have access to all needed services through one organization in the service delivery system.

Expanding cooperation and communication among agencies has the further advantage of *helping to build a support base for various programs*. As representatives of other agencies become familiar with the services provided, as they invest time and resources in establishing a high quality continuum of services, they will want to help ensure that these services continue. Interagency coordination can thus be a basis for good public relations and continuing support for early intervention programs for young handicapped children.

The "time" for interagency agreements may have arrived. As a result of increased recognition of the above-mentioned benefits (at no extra cost), many state and federal legislators and policymakers are beginning to mandate interagency coordination. Particularly at the federal level, joint policy statements are being developed. The office of Special Education Programs, the Bureau of Community Health Services, the Rehabilitation Services Administration, and an increasing number of other agencies are encouraging interagency coordination and, in many cases, requiring grant recipients to incorporate interagency agreements in their proposals. While the pressures to coordinate services would appear to come from the federal and state levels, the burden of developing workable agreements, however, must begin at the local level.

BARRIERS TO COORDINATION OF RESOURCES

The benefits previously described would lead one to believe that all administrators would be racing to develop interagency agreements. In fact, however, there has been great reluctance on the part of state and local level agency heads to become involved in interagency efforts. Why the hesitation?

Pollard, Hall, and Keeran (1979), in describing the basis for this reluctance, cite the following barriers to coordination:

1. The competitiveness of long established institutions
2. The lack of an organizational structure that brings agencies together around areas of mutual interest
3. The parochial interests of agencies and organizations that make them myopic to the needs of the broader community
4. The lack of experience in the techniques of coordinated planning
5. Awkwardness in interdisciplinary communication and lack of respect among many professional groups whose skills are needed by the handicapped
6. Failure to recognize that programs for handicapped persons are coequally a major responsibility of several government agencies at federal, state, and local levels
7. The temptation of system delivery designers to become so preoccupied and fixated on the "system design" that they lose sight of the functional whole of the system and of the individual agencies working to meet the needs of handicapped persons (pp. 7–8).

Elder (1979) has discussed additional factors that hinder interagency coordination. He states that resistance to more work on the part of agency personnel is an important factor. (The development of interagency agreements is time consuming and often difficult. Unless all parties perceive the benefits to be accrued, they will not see the value of expending more effort.) The attempt to protect "turf" is also seen as significant. Problems with variations in client eligibility criteria and ethical issues relating to confidentiality of information are other realistic concerns. Differences in terminology or "professional jargon" furthermore make interagency communication difficult—program plans, for instance, are variously called individualized education programs (IEPs) by education, individualized program plans (IPPs) by institutions, and individualized rehabilitation plans (IRPs) by vocational rehabilitation. Each of these terms has a slightly different meaning to the professionals from these agencies.

Elder also indicates that the segregated and fragmented delivery system in general thwarts coordination. Inadequate communication and coordination among and across federal and state agencies serves as a poor example for local agencies. Without effective exemplars, local agencies do not perceive the rewards to be gained, nor do they have a model to follow in initiating the complex interagency planning process. Finally, states Elder, all of us resist change when we are uncertain of the benefits or have to drastically alter long-standing processes and procedures.

OVERCOMING BARRIERS

The difficulties of overcoming the above problems should not be minimized. A successful coordination effort can, nevertheless, be accomplished by careful planning and consideration of possible barriers. It may be necessary to start "small," with the needs of individual children as the initial impetus for coordination.

People at the program level need to be involved in planning for coordination. A facilitator from each agency should oversee the process as it evolves, working with both program and administrative staff. A coordination facilitator should work on the project full-time, or else have the development and implementation of interagency agreements a major function of his or her job. The political nature of the process demands a sensitive, astute person who can work successfully with many different personalities. The role of each party needs to be clearly delineated at the beginning of collaborative efforts; this demands that facilitators have knowledge of existing resources, services provided, funding mechanisms, and regulations. Facilitators must also secure a definite commitment from agency heads. If full support is not obtained, agreements can break down at any time—and too often at the most critical stage of implementation.

THE INTERAGENCY PLAN

The development of interagency agreements can be compared to the process of developing an IEP for a handicapped child (NASDSE, 1980). In the school, the interdisciplinary team developing an IEP evaluates the child's strengths and weaknesses, determines his or her needs, establishes goals and objectives, and plans activities to correct problems and facilitate growth. The IEP is reviewed annually and continually modified as the objectives need to be updated or when the plan is not working effectively. In the community, the multiple agencies within the service delivery system are analogous to the interdisciplinary team. The inter-agency team looks at the whole system (like the whole child), analyzes strengths and weaknesses, and plans a course of action, stating who will be responsible for each part of the plan to meet the stated goals and objectives. The interagency plan (like the IEP) needs to be monitored and evaluated throughout the year and changes made to ensure maximum effectiveness.

Getting Started

One of the first steps is to determine which agencies are most likely to have interrelated services. (This exercise can be especially meaningful if keyed to the needs of specific children.) Representatives from each of these agencies need to meet to discuss the service areas that are most demanding for them. The benefits of possible interagency cooperation and coordination are more likely to be visible after a discussion of mutual concerns and problems. Once needs have been identified relating to individual children and groups of children, it is possible to form an interagency coalition to gather and examine data to aid in more general problem solving.

The initial coalition may include, but not be limited to, representatives from the following community groups and agencies:

Public and private schools
Private or public agencies serving normal and handicapped children
State and local agencies representing institutions for the handicapped
State and local agencies representing mental health
State and local health agencies
Local medical personnel
State and local social services agencies
Head Start agencies
Parent groups
Public service organizations

The flowchart shown in Figure 1 outlines the process by which the coalition can operate. After the initial formulation of roles and responsibilities, the core coalition can develop a list of important state and local agencies. Coalition members can then begin to gather data from their own and other relevant community service agencies and organizations.

Coordinating the Components

Aiken (1975) has identified four key elements requiring coordination in a fully integrated service delivery system: 1) clients, 2) programs and services,

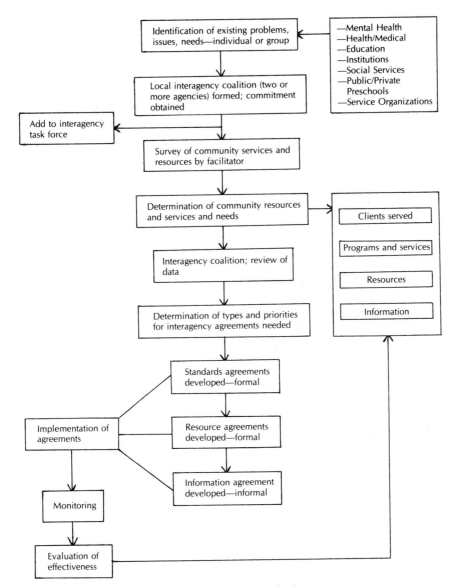

Figure 1. Process model for developing interagency coordination.

3) resources, and 4) information (see Figure 1). In order to make decisions about where cooperative efforts need to be undertaken in these areas, the coalition needs to examine data on: Who are the children being served? not being served? What programs and services are being offered to young handicapped children? What resources are available to young handicapped children and their families? Where are there gaps in services and deficient resources? How are programs, services,

and resources funded? What interagency efforts already exist? What are the variations in eligibility requirements? cost? staff limitations?

Clients   First, who are the young handicapped children receiving services? An analysis of the numbers of children being served in each age group, birth to 3 years and 3 to 6 years is needed. It is also important to determine what handicaps are being served. Perhaps there are many programs for young mentally retarded children but very few for hearing impaired children. Also, the degree of severity of the handicapped children being served has to be ascertained. Severely involved children may be receiving the majority of services to the exclusion of the mildly involved children. By examining these data, areas of overlap in services to particular target groups can be found. Gaps in services to an age level, type of handicap, or severity level can also be readily seen (see Form 1, Target Population, page 85).

Programs and Services   Analysis of the programs and services offered by various agencies and organizations will reveal further duplication and gaps. Requesting information about whether an agency provides a specific service directly, purchases the service, or does not provide the service but has a need for it, is important. Such data can not only facilitate development of interagency agreements, but can also contribute to the planning for a future service delivery system. Kazuk, Greene, and Magrab (1979) discuss a system for analyzing community resources. The following list of services is based on their listing of possible services that should be explored within each agency:

Screening	Nursing service
Diagnosis	Pediatric service
Specific discipline evaluation (e.g., speech and language)	Vision specialist
	Mobility training
Multidisciplinary evaluation	Nutrition consultation
IEP in PL 94-142	Case management
Comprehensive individualized planning	Parent education
	Legal (protective/advocate)
Counseling parents	Recreation services
Special education (classroom or home-based)	Residential services
	Respite care
Regular education	Foster care
Mainstreaming	Day-care
Consultation	Transportation
Follow-up	Homemakers service
Referral	Home nursing
Speech therapy	Preventive services
Language therapy	Public education
Physical therapy	Staff training
Occupational therapy	Financial assistance
Psychiatric therapy	Equipment
Psychological service	Instructional materials

Resources and Information The accumulation of information about each of the above service and resource areas can provide an eye-opener to overlaps, duplication, and gaps. Again, this information can not only be helpful for the immediate development of interagency agreements, but also is crucial for sagacious future planning (see Form 2, Service Provided/Needed, pages 86–88, for gathering data).

Information concerning how programs are funded is particularly relevant to interagency planning. By using funding sources in varied ways or financing services from several different federal programs, the number of services available to young handicapped children can be increased greatly. "It is clear that existing resources beyond those now utilized in special education can be coordinated with other federal programs to benefit children with handicaps" (Audette, 1978, p. 2).

Thus, in making decisions concerning first-dollar agreements, the source of funding and eligibility for services is critical (see Form 3, Program Funding Source, pages 89–93). Information relating to available personnel, facilities, equipment, and materials is all necessary.

Accumulating Data

In order to gather data relating to the above areas, a relatively simple procedure for data collection, as described below, can be instituted. First, however, a word about cooperation. Staff from the various agencies already spend much time filling out forms. They will not be eager to expend a great deal of energy to answer an outside agency's request for information. To promote cooperation, it is therefore essential that representatives from as many agencies as possible be involved on the interagency coalition. In the initial planning for the data collection process, each coalition representative will need to convince his or her staff of the benefits of collaboration.

A sample format for data collection is offered in the following section. The procedure can be modified to meet individual community needs. An effort has been made to keep the forms simple and the tabulation process quick.

THE DATA COLLECTION PROCESS

The following discussion focuses on a five-step process that uses five sequential recording forms to coordinate community resources for young handicapped children and their families. This Community Resources Packet is presented as a model to be adapted to meet local needs. A complete set of the packet's forms can be found at the end of this chapter (pages 85–94). These forms include:

Form 1—Target Population: This form is designed to determine the number, type, and degree of handicapping conditions currently being served (see page 85).

Form 2—Services Provided/Needed: This form assesses which of 40 services are provided by an agency either directly or through purchase of service. It also seeks information on services that are needed (see pages 86–88).

Form 3—Program Funding Source: This form allows agencies to indicate the *primary* source(s) of funding for various services that their agency offers (see pages 89–91).

Form 4—Service Delivery Barriers: This form allows agencies to indicate the problems they are encountering that may be hindering their ability to fully deliver effective and efficient services (see pages 92–93).

Form 5—Summary of Population and Services: This form is used by the coordinating agency to summarize data and determine overlaps in age, severity, handicap, or services. It also summarizes services that are needed by all agencies involved, services needed by other agencies that the school provides, and services provided by other agencies that the school district needs (see page 94).

One agency, serving as the coordinating agency, should initially complete a Community Resources Packet which contains Forms 1 through 4. Packets should then be taken to other participating agencies for completion. Comparison and analysis follows using Form 5. The following steps delineate the process in further depth.

Step 1 The Community Resources Packet is completed first by an early intervention program representative from the coordinating agency. The coordinating agency could be the public school or any community agency in a position to facilitate the development of interagency collaboration. (The coordinating agency may be selected by the coalition of agencies.) The coordinating agency's representative should fill in the shaded columns on each form.

Target Population (Form 1) Using the shaded boxes, the coordinating agency indicates the number of children currently being served by age (birth to 2 years; 2 to 3 years; 3 to 5 years), under the headings of mildly, moderately, or severely handicapped. Within each age range, the number of children served for each category of handicapping condition—indicating the primary diagnosis—is then recorded. Although data may be collected noncategorically, an effort should be made to provide a "nonduplicated" count by primary handicapping condition.

For instance, as shown in the example in Figure 2, the coordinating agency (in this case a public school) may be serving 10 moderately handicapped and 20 severely handicapped children in the birth to 2 years age range. Of those, 2 are blind or visually impaired, 5 are orthopedically handicapped, 13 are mentally retarded, 5 are severely disturbed, and 5 are language impaired. This is a nonduplicated count by primary handicap.

Services Provided/Needed (Form 2) Using the shaded boxes in each column, the coordinating agency indicates with a check for each of the 40 services listed if the service is purchased by the agency from another agency, is provided directly by the agency, or is not provided. If the service is not provided, but is needed, then the fourth column should be checked. An area for comments about the importance of particular services is also included on this form. An excerpt from a completed Form 2 is shown in Figure 3.

FORM 1: **TARGET POPULATION**

Please fill in each white box with the number of children served for each age range, including both the severity level and category of handicapping condition. Indicate only one handicap per child, the primary diagnosed handicap.

Age Range	Level of Handicap			Primary Diagnosis								
	Mildly Handicapped (Mi)	Moderately Handicapped (Mo)	Severely Handicapped (Se)	Blind or Visually Impaired (B/VI)	Deaf or Hearing Impaired (D/H)	Orthopedically Handicapped (OH)	Health Impaired (HI)	Mentally Retarded (MR)	Emotionally Disturbed (ED)	Learning Disabled (LD)	Language Impaired (LI)	Multiply Handicapped (MH)
Birth to Two Years (0–2)		10	20	2		5		13	5		5	
Two to Three Years (2–3)		8	5		1	3		9				
Three to Five Years (3–5)	15	10	7	2	1	4	2	10	3	4	6	

Figure 2. Excerpt from Form 1, Target Population.

FORM 2: **SERVICES PROVIDED/NEEDED**

Using Form 2 below, please check those services that your agency provides. Check the Purchase of Service column if your agency purchases service from another agency. Check the Direct Service column if your agency provides that service at your facility. Check Do Not Provide Service if the service is not available through your agency. Check Need for Service if that is a service that your agency could utilize.

Services	Purchase of Service	Direct Service	Do Not Provide Service	Need for Service	Comment: In the spaces below elaborate on specific factors of importance in relationship to that service.
(S) Screening	1				
(SDE) Specific Discipline Evaluation (e.g., speech and language)	2	✓		✓	need physical therapist
(MDE) Multidisciplinary Evaluation	3	✓			

Figure 3. Excerpt from Form 2, Services Provided

Program Funding Source (Form 3)   This form is designed to gather information concerning the funding sources utilized to pay for services. These data will be most helpful when interagency agreements are formed, as flexibility in this area will allow for restructuring of payment for services. The coordinating agency places a check in the shaded boxes to indicate which funding source is being used to pay for particular services. No check is placed where a service is not provided.

For example, if funds from PL 94-142 are being used to pay for screening, evaluation, and the development of the individualized education programs, then checks are placed in those respective boxes. Counseling is provided for parents of young handicapped children and is also paid for by funds through PL 94-142. (See Figure 4.)

Service Delivery Barriers (Form 4)   Information from this form serves many purposes. It allows agencies an opportunity to relate to one another their concerns about shortages of staff, money, and facilities, and other insufficiencies. It also provides a means by which to compare problem areas and to develop interagency agreements to solve some of the problems. (This form may also be used as an initial discussion base to aid program staff in identifying mutual problems and concerns.) The form is filled out by placing a check in the boxes that indicate problems that inhibit the most effective performance of a particular service. (See Figure 5.)

In the example in Figure 5, a school district has had difficulty organizing a Child Find effort because of lack of knowledge about utilizing community resources to provide comprehensive screening services. They have also had a time lag between referral for evaluation and the actual performance of the evaluation, primarily as a result of a shortage of support staff to do the needed evaluations.

Form 3:   **PROGRAM FUNDING SOURCE**

Funding Program	Screening (S)	Specific Discipline Evaluation (SDE)	Multidisciplinary Evaluation (MDE)	Individualized Education Program (IEP)	Individualized Program Plan (IPP)	Counseling Parents (CP)
PL 94-142	√	√	√	√	√	√
Title I, Disadvantaged						
Title I, 89-313						
Bilingual						
Title XIX, Medicaid, EPSDT						

Figure 4.   Excerpt from Form 3, Program Funding Source.

FORM 4: **SERVICE DELIVERY BARRIERS**

Services	Insufficient money to pay for service	Insufficient staff to provide comprehensive service	Insufficient materials and equipment	Lack of appropriate facilities	Lack of responsiveness from community resources	Hesitancy on part of staff to provide service	Time lag between when service is needed and when it is delivered	Lack knowledge about how to provide this service adequately
(S) Screening 1					√			√
(SDE) Specific Discipline Evaluation 2								
(MDE) Multidisciplinary Evaluation 3			√					√

Figure 5. Excerpt from Form 4, Service Delivery Barriers.

Step 2 A transparency is made of each form completed by the coordinating agency. These transparencies will be used to make response comparisons between the coordinating agency's early intervention services and the other community agencies' services.

Step 3 Community Resources Packets are taken to the other agencies or coalitions of community resources for young handicapped children. The procedures for filling out the forms are carefully explained to the person agreeing to serve as the agency representative in the interagency collaborative effort. How the information will be utilized in developing cooperative efforts to benefit the agencies in their delivery of services to children and their families is also discussed. Emphasis should be placed on the agencies filling in their response in the *unshaded* boxes.

Step 4 Each representative explains the interagency collaboration process to the staff at his or her agency and enlists their help and support in providing information to complete the forms. This is an important step; staff must understand their role in collaborative efforts if successful interagency agreements are to be implemented.

Step 5 Comparison and analysis of the data gathered take place as the cooperating agencies return their forms to the coordinating agency.

First, the transparencies of the forms from the coordinating agency are laid directly on top of the corresponding pages of the forms from the second agency. The responses from each agency then are compared. The coordinating agency's responses should appear in the shaded column and the second agency's responses should appear in the unshaded column, as shown in the example in Figure 6. As can be seen in this example, there is no duplication in population served in either the birth to 2 years or 2 to 3 years category. There is an overlap, however, in the 3 to 5 years age range, both in the severity level served (mildly handicapped) and in the handicapping conditions served (mentally retarded and language impaired).

FORM 1: **TARGET POPULATION**

Please fill in each white box with the number of children served for each age range, including both the severity level and category of handicapping condition. Indicate only one handicap per child, the primary diagnosed handicap.

Age Range	Level of Handicap			Primary Diagnosis								
	Mildly Handicapped (Mi)	Moderately Handicapped (Mo)	Severely Handicapped (SE)	Blind or Visually Impaired (B/Vi)	Deaf or Hearing Impaired (D/H)	Orthopedically Handicapped (OH)	Health Impaired (HI)	Mentally Retarded (MR)	Emotionally Disturbed (ED)	Learning Disabled (LD)	Language Impaired (LI)	Multiply Handicapped (MH)
Birth to Two Years (0–2)		10	20	2		5		13	5		5	
Two to Three Years (2–3)		8	10		1	3		9				
Three to Five Years (3–5)	10 15	10	7	2	1	4	2	10 3	3	4	6 7	

Figure 6. Excerpt from Form 1 to compare two agencies.

Form 5: **SUMMARY OF POPULATION AND SERVICES**

Agencies	Age served overlap	Severity level overlap	Handicap overlap	Service overlap	Write in initials of services that are duplicated
1. Maple Head Start	3-5	Mi	M.H.		
2.			L.I.		

Figure 7. Excerpt from Form 5, Summary of Population and Services.

Form 5, Summary of Population and Services, should be used to record these duplications. First, the agency's name is written in the left-hand column of the Summary of Population and Services form (see page 94). Then, any duplication of age, severity levels, or handicaps served should be transferred from Target Population (Form 1) to the appropriate column on Form 5. For each instance of overlap, enter the age range and the initials for the severity level and primary handicap (Mi, Mo, Se, ED, MH, etc.) in the appropriate boxes of Form 5's matrix (see Figure 7).

Form 2, Services Provided/Needed, would be compared for the two agencies in much the same way. A section of one agency's form compared with a school district transparency might look like the example in Figure 8. When transferred to the Summary of Population and Services, the information would appear on the form as shown in Figure 9. In this example, follow-up and referral are two duplicated services; consultation and speech therapy are two services Maple Head Start needs that the school can provide.

This process of comparison to the coordinating agency is repeated for each participating agency. No conclusions are drawn from these data at this time, however. Discussion of the implications will take place later with all of the agencies concerned.

It should also be noted that these forms can be utilized by any two agencies. Transparencies can be made of any one set of forms for comparison to any other set. In the example discussed above, the public school early intervention program was the agency acting as the service coordinator, but other agencies can also use this process to meet the needs of individual children or groups of children. Furthermore, although designed for coordination of early intervention programs, the forms and procedures could be used to examine services to older children.

At first glance, this data collection process may seem extremely complicated, time-consuming, and, in fact, one procedure that ''can surely be skipped.'' Accurate, detailed data collection, however, is *critically important* to successful interagency coordination and, in turn, to maximum service efficiency and effectiveness. A collection tool, such as the Community Resources Packet, once

FORM 2: **SERVICES PROVIDED/NEEDED**

Services		Purchase of Service	Direct Service	Do Not Provide Service	Need for Service	Comment *In the spaces below elaborate on specific factors of importance in relationship to that service.*
(C)	Consultation	10			√	need consultation on specific language problems
(F)	Follow-up	11	√			limited
(R)	Referral	12	√			
(ST)	Speech Therapy	13	√	√	√	

Figure 8. Excerpt from Form 2 to compare two agencies.

79

FORM 5: **SUMMARY OF POPULATION AND SERVICES**

Agencies	Age served overlap	Severity level overlap	Handicap overlap	Service overlap	Write in initials of services that are duplicated	Write in initials of services needed by all agencies involved	Write in initials of services the agency purchases that the school could provide	Write in initials of services the agency offers that the school needs
1. Maple Head Start					F, R	C, ST		
2.								

Figure 9. Excerpt from Form 5, Summary of Population and Services.

adopted, can facilitate this process of identifying duplication, overlaps, and gaps in service delivery.

INTERAGENCY AGREEMENTS AND EVALUATION

Once the information is available, planning groups can develop a variety of agreements to ensure a quality continuum of services. Formal written agreements can be developed to address standards for services and sharing of resources. Informal agreements may also be useful for dealing with specific situations. Attention also needs to be paid to the implementation of the agreements and ongoing program monitoring.

In order to demonstrate the effectiveness of interagency coordination, evaluation will also be necessary. The form for evaluation of interagency cooperation shown in Figure 10 is offered as an example of a questionnaire to assess qualitative aspects of the effort.

The coordination and evaluation process that has been delineated can be useful for: 1) determining community needs prior to requesting funding, support, or writing a grant proposal, 2) raising the community and legislative awareness level concerning duplication and gaps in services, 3) solving problems related to needed services for individual children, 4) evaluating the program's impact on the community service system, and 5) evaluating the effect of coordination on individual children and their families.

A CASE STUDY

Perhaps the best way to demonstrate the usefulness of the process just described is to examine the case of Paul. Paul is a 4-year-old, severely handicapped child with Down syndrome. He has been in an institution for 2 years, but has recently been assigned to a foster family in the local community. Paul was referred to Child Find for a complete evaluation. After gathering background information on Paul, representatives from the institution and social services were included on the evaluation team.

A complete assessment of Paul was done utilizing a multidisciplinary team. The results of that assessment revealed the following needs: 1) need for cognitive activities to stimulate imitation, problem-solving, discrimination, and basic classification concepts; 2) need for early language activities to stimulate imitation and production of sounds, recognition of objects and communicative intent; 3) need for motor activities to strengthen muscle tone, develop bilateral coordination, and encourage locomotion; 4) need for social interaction with developmental-age peers to develop onlooker behaviors and beginning social exchange; 5) need for development of attachment to foster parents and development of trusting relationship with adults; 6) need for glasses to correct vision; 7) need for follow-up of medical problems related to heart condition and respiratory problems; 8) need for

Evaluation of Interagency Cooperation

The following form will be used to help us assess the effectiveness of our cooperative efforts.

1.. Overall, I would say the cooperative effort among agencies in our district has been (circle one):

1	2	3	4	5
Virtually nonexistent	Not very good	Average	A substantial effort has been made	Good cooperation and coordination exists

2. Rank how you perceive the efficacy of various aspects of interagency efforts (1 = low, 5 = high):

	Low				High
Increased communication	1	2	3	4	5
Increased knowledge of available community resources	1	2	3	4	5
Increased flexibility in providing services	1	2	3	4	5
More services available	1	2	3	4	5
Elimination of gaps in services	1	2	3	4	5
Reduction of duplication of services	1	2	3	4	5
More effective use of personnel and resources	1	2	3	4	5
Better long-range planning	1	2	3	4	5
Other (specify):	1	2	3	4	5

3. Barriers that continue to exist include (indicate with a check):

_____ Insufficient money to pay for needed services
_____ Insufficient staff to provide comprehensive service
_____ Insufficient materials and equipment
_____ Lack of appropriate facilities
_____ Lack of responsiveness from community resources
_____ Hesitancy on the part of staff to coordinate services
_____ Lack of time to accomplish coordination
_____ Lack of knowledge about how to go about the coordination
_____ Lack of parent cooperation
_____ Lack of facilitative legislation
_____ Prohibition by regulations
_____ Unavailability of qualified staff

4. How could interagency cooperation be improved?

Figure 10. Sample questionnaire for evaluation of interagency cooperation.

hearing aid to correct hearing loss; 9) need for training of foster parents concerning care and education of Paul; and 10) need for appropriate day-care when not in program, as both foster parents work.

It was apparent that the school district would not be able to meet all of Paul's needs. Yet, all aspects were important to effectively serve Paul and his family. In fact, it became clear that support services were essential if the foster care arrangement was to succeed. Consequently, the analysis of community resources revealed the following:

1. Paul was eligible to have glasses and hearing aid paid for by Title XIX or Title V.
2. A special morning preschool program that focused on cognitive, language, motor, and social-emotional development was available in the school district and could be paid for by monies through PL 94-142.
3. Physical therapy services, not available through the school, could be purchased through Medicaid.
4. Training for foster parents was available through Title XX social services monies. The parents were also put in touch with a local parent's group through the state department of education and with the local Association for Retarded Citizens (ARC).
5. Therapeutic day-care services were identified for the afternoons. Funds available through state legislation to the state department of social services were used to help with funding.

SUMMARY

Interagency coordination is a dynamic process that demands agency commitment to work effectively. School districts, as the one agency with whom all children must relate until adulthood, are one logical coordinating agency. Any agency, however, may serve as the coordinating agency. Beginning the coordination effort with the first referral of a child is important. All agencies previously associated with the child and with his or her family should be involved in the evaluation and staffing of the child. Agreements developed may be informal or formal; child specific or program related; directed at standards, resources, or information. Regardless of the nature of the agreements, interagency cooperation and coordination must be viewed as vitally important.

REFERENCES

Aiken, M.T. *Coordinating human services: New strategies for building service delivery systems*. San Francisco: Jossey-Bass, 1975.
Audette, R. *Interagency agreements to support special education programs for children with handicaps: A manual for establishing program relationships in Colorado*. Unpublished paper prepared for Colorado Department of Education, Denver, 1978.
Elder, J.O. Coordination of service delivery systems. In: P.R. Magrab & J.D. Elder (eds.),

Planning for services to handicapped persons: Community, education, health. Baltimore: Paul H. Brookes Publishing Co., 1979.

Elder, J.O., & Magrab, P.R. (eds.), *Coordinating services to handicapped children: A handbook for interagency collaboration.* Baltimore: Paul H. Brookes Publishing Co., 1980.

Kazuk, E., Greene, L., & Magrab, P.R. Case study for planning coordinated services. In: P.R. Magrab & J.O. Elder (eds.), *Planning for services to handicapped persons: Community, education, health.* Baltimore: Paul H. Brookes Publishing Co., 1979.

National Association of State Directors of Special Education (NASDE). Proceedings from the State Implementation Grant Conference, Denver, CO, unpublished report, 1980.

Pollard, A., Hall, H., & Keeran, C. Community service planning. In: P.R. Magrab & J.O. Elder (eds.), *Planning for services to handicapped persons: Community, education, health.* Baltimore: Paul H. Brookes Publishing Co., 1979.

COMMUNITY RESOURCES PACKET
FOR
YOUNG HANDICAPPED CHILDREN AND THEIR FAMILIES

Note: Please fill out in pencil.

Agency_____
Address_____
Contact Person_____
Phone_____

FORM 1: TARGET POPULATION

Please fill in each white box with the number of children served for each age range, including both the severity level and category of handicapping condition. Indicate only one handicap per child, the primary diagnosed handicap.

Age Range	Level of Handicap			Primary Diagnosis								
	Mildly Handicapped (Mi)	Moderately Handicapped (Mo)	Severely Handicapped (Se)	Blind or Visually Impaired (B/Vi)	Deaf or Hearing Impaired (D/H)	Orthopedically Handicapped (OH)	Health Impaired (HI)	Mentally Retarded (MR)	Emotionally Disturbed (ED)	Learning Disabled (LD)	Language Impaired (LI)	Multiply Handicapped (MH)
Birth to Two Years (0–2)												
Two to Three Years (2–3)												
Three to Five Years (3–5)												

COMMUNITY RESOURCES PACKET

(continued)

MAJOR SERVICE AREAS in relation to birth to five population

FORM 2: SERVICES PROVIDED/NEEDED

Using Form 2 below, please check those services that your agency provides. Check the Purchase of Service column if your agency purchases service from another agency. Check the Direct Service column if your agency provides that service at your facility. Check Do Not Provide Service if the service is not available through your agency. Check Need for Service if that is a service that your agency could utilize.

Services		Purchase of Service	Direct Service	Do Not Provide Service	Need for Service	Comment — In the spaces below elaborate on specific factors of importance in relationship to that service.
(S) Screening	1					
(SDE) Specific Discipline Evaluation (e.g., speech and language)	2					
(MDE) Multidisciplinary Evaluation	3					
(IEP) Individualized Education Program	4					
(IPP) Individualized Program Plan	5					
(CP) Counseling Parents	6					
(RE) Regular Education	7					
(SE) Special Education	8					
(M) Mainstreaming	9					

	Service	No.				
(C)	Consultation	10				
(F)	Follow-up	11				
(R)	Referral	12				
(ST)	Speech Therapy	13				
(LT)	Language Therapy	14				
(PT)	Physical Therapy	15				
(OT)	Occupational Therapy	16				
(PTT)	Psychiatric Therapy	17				
(PGT)	Psychological Service	18				
(N)	Nursing Service	19				
(PED)	Pediatric Service	20				
(VS)	Vision Training	21				
(MT)	Mobility Training	22				
(NU)	Nutrition Consultation	23				
(CM)	Case Management	24				
(PAR)	Parent Education	25				
(RE)	Recreation	26				
(L)	Legal (protective/advocate)	27				
(RS)	Residential Services	28				
(RC)	Respite Care	30				
(FC)	Foster Care	31				
(DC)	Day Care	32				
(T)	Transportation	33				
(HS)	Homemakers Service	34				
(HN)	Home Nursing	34				
(PS)	Preventive Services	35				

(continued)

FORM 2 *(continued)*

Services	Purchase of Service	Direct Service	Do Not Provide Service	Need for Service	Comment *In the spaces below elaborate on specific factors of importance in relationship to that service.*
(PE) Public Education	36				
(SFT) Staff Training	37				
(FA) Financial Assistance	38				
(E) Equipment	39				
(IM) Instructional Materials	40				
Other: *(Please List)*					

FORM 3: **PROGRAM FUNDING SOURCE**

Place a check (√) in the appropriate box to indicate which state or federal source(s) supplies funding for the service. More than one source may be checked if appropriate.

Funding Program	(S) Screening	(SDE) Specific Discipline Evaluation	(MDE) Multidisciplinary Evaluation	(IEP) Individualized Education Program	(IPP) Individualized Program Plan	(CP) Counseling Parents	(RE) Regular Education	(SE) Special Education	(M) Mainstreaming	(C) Consultation	(F) Follow-up	(R) Referral	(ST) Speech Therapy	(LT) Language Therapy
PL 94-142														
Title I, Disadvantaged														
Title I, 89-313														
Bilingual														
Title XIX, Medicaid, EPSDT														
Title XX														
Title V, Maternal Child Health														
Crippled Children's Program														
SSI														
Title V of the Economic Opportunity Act (Head Start)														
State funding—Developmental Disabilities														
—Exceptional Children's Education Act														
—Mental Health														
Other: (Please list)														

(continued)

FORM 3 (continued)

Funding Program	(PT) Physical Therapy	(OT) Occupational Therapy	(PIT) Psychiatric Therapy	(PGT) Psychological Service	(N) Nursing Service	(PED) Pediatric Service	(VS) Vision Training	(MT) Mobility Training	(NU) Nutrition Consultation	(CM) Case Management	(PAR) Parent Education	(RE) Recreation	(L) Legal (protective/advocate)	(RS) Residential Services
PL 94-142														
Title I, Disadvantaged														
Title I, 89-313														
Bilingual														
Title XIX, Medicaid, EPSDT														
Title XX														
Title V, Maternal Child Health														
Crippled Children's Program														
SSI														
Title V of the Economic Opportunity Act (Head Start)														
State funding—Developmental Disabilities														
—Exceptional Children's Education Act														
—Mental Health														
Other: (Please list)														

FORM 3 *(continued)*

Funding Program	Respite Care (RC)	Foster Care (FC)	Day Care (DC)	Transportation (T)	Homemakers Service (HS)	Home Nursing (HN)	Preventive Services (PS)	Public Education (PE)	Staff Training (SFT)	Financial Assistance (FA)	Equipment (E)	Instructional Materials (IM)	Other:
PL 94-142													
Title I, Disadvantaged													
Title I, 89-313													
Bilingual													
Title XIX, Medicaid, EPSDT													
Title XX													
Title V, Maternal Child Health													
Crippled Children's Program													
SSI													
Title V of the Economic Opportunity Act (Head Start)													
State funding—Developmental Disabilities													
—Exceptional Children's Education Act													
—Mental Health													
Other: *(Please list)*													

FORM 4: **SERVICE DELIVERY BARRIERS**

This is an opportunity for you to get it all "off your chest." Put checks (✓) in the boxes that indicate why you have a problem with a particular service.

Services	Insufficient money to pay for service	Insufficient staff to provide comprehensive service	Insufficient materials and equipment	Lack of appropriate facilities	Lack of responsiveness from community resources	Hesitancy on part of staff to provide service	Time lag between when service is needed and when it is delivered	Lack of knowledge about how to provide this service adequately	Lack of parent cooperation	Lack of facilitative legislation	Prohibition by regulation	Unavailability of qualified staff	Other:
(S) 1 Screening													
(SDE) 2 Specific Discipline Evaluation													
(MDE) 3 Multidisciplinary Evaluation													
(IEP) 4 Individualized Education Program													
(IPP) 5 Individualized Program Plan													
(CP) 6 Counseling Parents													
(RE) 7 Regular Education													
(SE) 8 Special Education													
(M) 9 Mainstreaming													
(C) 10 Consultation													
(F) 11 Follow-up													
(R) 12 Referral													
(ST) 13 Speech Therapy													
(LT) 14 Language Therapy													
(PT) 15 Physical Therapy													

Code	Service	Number
(OT)	Occupational Therapy	16
(PTT)	Psychiatric Therapy	17
(PGT)	Psychological Service	18
(N)	Nursing Service	19
(PED)	Pediatric Service	20
(VS)	Vision Training	21
(MT)	Mobility Training	22
(NU)	Nutrition Consultation	23
(CM)	Case Management	24
(PAR)	Parent Education	25
(RE)	Recreation	26
(L)	Legal (protective/advocate)	27
(RS)	Residential Services	28
(RC)	Respite Care	30
(FC)	Foster Care	31
(DC)	Day Care	32
(T)	Transportation	33
(HS)	Homemakers Service	34
(HN)	Home Nursing	34
(PS)	Preventive Services	35
(PE)	Public Education	36
(SFT)	Staff Training	37
(FA)	Financial Assistance	40
(E)	Equipment	41
(IM)	Instructional Materials	42
	Other: (Please list)	

93

FORM 5: **SUMMARY OF POPULATION AND SERVICES**

Agencies	Age served overlap	Severity level overlap	Handicap overlap	Service overlap	Write in initials of services that are duplicated	Write in initials of services needed by all agencies involved	Write in initials of services the agency purchases that the school could provide	Write in initials of services the agency offers that the school needs
1.								
2.								
3.								
4.								
5.								
6.								
7.								
8.								
9.								

chapter

5

Screening and Assessment

Under the provisions of PL 94-142, local education agencies (LEAs) that are receiving federal funds are charged with locating, identifying, and evaluating handicapped children from birth through 21 years of age. The plans for Child Find, as this process is entitled in the law, must be submitted to state education agencies (SEAs) and included in their state plan. Typically, many other state and local agencies are also involved in identifying handicapped children (see Chapter 4).

In most states, Child Find is not yet fully operational, particularly for non-school-age populations. As a major vehicle for accomplishing the law's ultimate goal of ensuring a free, appropriate public education for all handicapped children, the success of Child Find is dependent upon vigorous enforcement efforts. Considering the small percentage of handicapped infants and preschoolers who are presently being served (see Chapter 1), it is hoped that Child Find efforts will not diminish but, rather, will escalate in the coming years. This chapter provides a process model to facilitate the screening and assessment of young children. It should be noted that each state, school district, or agency is free to develop its own process model. The model here is intended as a general guideline, and also suggests qualitative considerations in relation to particular aspects of the process.

SCREENING

Screening can be defined as the process of identifying from a total population those children who may have special needs and/or the need for further assessment. Screening should entail relatively quick, inexpensive procedures that will "raise a red flag" over areas of concern. It is *not*, however, diagnostic.

Screening to determine "special needs" could be interpreted to encompass innumerable medical, psychological, and educational problems. Lillie (1977) offers some guidelines for determining which deficiencies are appropriate for screening and deserve expenditure of time, money, and effort. First, the problem that screening seeks to identify should be relatively prevalent and treatable. Second, the screening should occur when the condition is *most* amenable to treatment. Third, methods should be available to improve or correct the problems identified.

Screening infants and preschoolers for developmental and other disabilities not only allows children to receive needed services at an earlier more remediable age, but it provides important data to assist schools in long-range planning for special services.

Community Screening

The screening process should be planned and coordinated in cooperation with other community agencies and organizations that provide services to young handicapped children and their families. Screening of the child under 5 years of age presents a unique set of problems and thus necessitates community involvement. First, the young child is usually not in a setting (i.e., school) where he or she is observed in relation to developmental and academic tasks, and therefore the problems may not be evident to a teacher as they often are in the case of teacher referrals of school-age children. Certain health related problems (for example, epilepsy, heart conditions) may be identified by the medical profession, but concomitant learning problems may not be associated with the condition. In like manner, high risk populations (such as abused and neglected children) may be identified by agencies, but the developmental implications may not be noted. The *developmental* rather than academic nature of screening young children therefore requires screening instruments and procedures different from those for school-age children. In addition, the screening of very young populations is a relatively new endeavor; thus, appropriate and discrete instruments are often not available.

As a result of the above difficulties, a coordinated community screening effort for the under-5 population is recommended. Coordination can help eliminate duplication of effort, and can provide more comprehensive screening.

One of the first items required is a survey of community resources to determine what agencies are serving handicapped children and their families, the type and degree of service each agency provides, whether the person, agency, or organization will participate in Child Find, and how. The next step involves developing an interagency steering committee to plan and coordinate screening efforts (see Chapter 4 for a further discussion of coordinating resources).

Chazdon, Harvey, and McNulty (1978) suggest a planning process that includes the following activities.

1. Outline goals of the screening program with the other community agencies involved in the Child Find or the interagency committee.
2. Confirm agency commitment through formal (signed, written) agreements or informal (verbal or written) agreements that designate persons responsible for specific responsibilities.

3. Utilize existing screening programs. Discuss and agree on joint methods and procedures.

4. Define the population to be screened. Decide what geographic location will be covered; the age range to be emphasized; whether there will be eligibility requirements; approximately how many children will be screened; whether transportation will be provided; and whether day-care for siblings will be provided.

5. Coordinate community screening and the public school screening program to prevent overlap of services and to set up an appropriate referral process.

6. Determine the screening areas to be tested—for example, developmental (motor, speech and language, social, self-help, adaptive, cognitive, perceptual), hearing, vision, health, and dental.

7. Determine screening instruments to be used. Criteria to consider include reliability, validity, standardization, brevity, ease of administration, and cost efficiency.

8. Establish screening sites, such as public schools, preschools and day-care centers, health care settings, community agencies or facilities, and/or the child's home.

9. Arrange dates and times for screening, taking into consideration logical times of the year (avoid major holidays or seasons with typically bad weather); family concerns (such as work); and child concerns (such as meals and naps).

10. Publicize all relevant information so that other agencies are aware of it.

11. Determine how the community will be notified of the screening. Start planning a public awareness campaign.

12. Determine what parental permission is required; permission is not needed for mass screening, but is needed for subsequent diagnostic assessment.

13. Plan for the training of screening staff.

Screening Process

Depending on procedures and instruments selected by the interagency steering committee, the actual screening process will vary. It is recommended that a multidisciplinary team be used. Professionals representing individual discipline, particularly in areas such as speech and language, can make valuable clinical observations of the child during screening. However, paraprofessionals can be trained to do most aspects of screening quite effectively.

The major components of the screening process are outlined in Figure 1. Basic elements that need to be included are discussed below.

Parent Interview The purpose of the interview is to obtain family, medical, and developmental information from parents. This includes information on difficulties that may have developed during pregnancy, delivery, postnatally, or in the early years. Any concerns the parents may have about the child's development are noted. Information on medical or health related problems within the family is also taken. It is also important at this time to explain to the parents the purpose of the

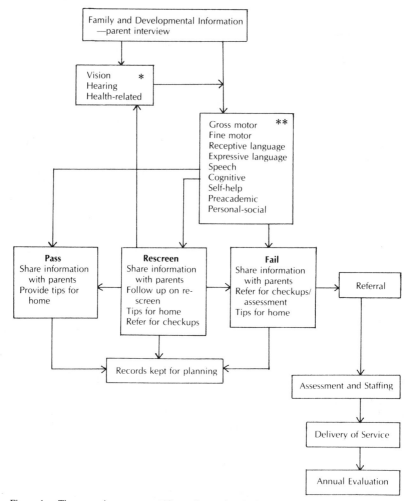

Figure 1. The screening process. (*Screening optional, depending on interagency screening plans. **Screening varies, depending on instruments chosen.)

screening process and how the results will be used.

Acuity and Health Screening Vision, hearing, or health related screening may be done by appropriate volunteers or agency staff, depending on the goals of screening. It is recommended that this aspect of screening not be omitted.

Developmental Screening Screening instruments vary in the developmental areas they address. Usually the major components include fine and gross motor (and/or self-help), expressive and receptive language (often including a speech section), and cognitive or adaptive reasoning. Frequently a section is included that examines behavior relating to social-emotional development. Some instruments geared for kindergartners look at preacademic skills as well.

In determining the processes and procedures for screening, care should be taken to avoid "over-identifying" or "under-identifying," that is, identifying children who really are *not* handicapped or missing those who *are* handicapped and in need of service. Careful selection of instruments, and development of local criteria for pass-fail cutoff is thus extremely important.

Determination of Status Another means of avoiding the problem of over- or under-identification is to develop a review system. Children who obviously pass do not need to be discussed. Children who have failed several sections of the screening, however, should be referred automatically for further evaluation. Data from the screening of this "questionable" group of children should be discussed by the team and determination made as to whether the child should be rescreened in one or more areas or referred for an in-depth evaluation in specific areas. Rescreening is advised rather than "passing" a child who has performed "questionably."

Sharing Results Parents of all children should have the screening results interpreted for them, along with a review of the purpose of screening. Regardless whether the child "passed" or "failed," the parents should be informed that a screening examines only a few selected behaviors. A "fail" does *not* constitute a confirmation of a problem or a diagnosis, just as a "pass" does not ensure a problem-free future. Parents should also be advised if further checkups are needed. Also, activities or suggestions for home are often welcomed at this time by parents. If the child is being referred for further evaluation, a personal interview with the parents is important to explain the procedures that will take place and to provide support to parents who may be fearful of the assessment process.

Record Keeping Careful records should be kept on all children undergoing screening, as this will equip service providers with valuable information for long-term planning. Issues of confidentiality need to be addressed as part of the interagency planning process. Permission can be obtained from parents for cross-agency sharing of information in accordance with due process procedures.

ASSESSMENT

Children who have been referred by other agencies (such as social services), by professionals (such as doctors or therapists), or by parents, *and* who have failed the screening must be evaluated further. As stated in the *Federal Register*, December 30, 1976:

> Evaluation (assessment) means procedures used to determine whether a child is handicapped and the nature and extent of the special education and related services that the child needs. The term means procedures used selectively with an individual child and does not include basic tests administered to or procedures used with all children in school, grade, or class. (p. 56989)

Thus, evaluation implies an *individual* assessment that usually results in a determination or "diagnosis" of a handicapping condition. Chazdon et al. (1978) provide some insight into the educational diagnosis.

Literally, diagnosis means "knowing thoroughly." Use of the term diagnosis [in education] is taken from the medical model which involves giving examinations and interpreting symptoms in order to find the cause of the disorder and to prescribe treatment. In the field of education, it may refer to the labeling of specific disorders or categories (1978, p. 137).

Whereas medical diagnosis refers principally to identifying symptoms and prescribing a treatment, diagnosis in early childhood special education seeks to examine in-depth a full range of learning-related problems (physical, emotional, and mental) that have been identified in screening, and then makes recommendations on how best to answer a child's needs, taking into account multiple perspectives. Educational diagnosis thus may entail a somewhat broader approach than medical diagnosis.

Screening may be done by trained paraprofessionals, but diagnosis must involve professionals from a variety of fields, including medicine. The specific purposes of educational diagnosis or assessment are first to determine whether a handicap or handicaps exist and, if possible, to clarify the etiology of the problems (Cross & Goin, 1977). Another intent is to provide information regarding a child's *needs*. Harbin (1977) emphasizes the importance of collecting information on a child's level of functioning in specific areas of development, on determining his or her learning characteristics, and on carefully interpreting the information collected. The resulting assessment is used to determine the placement of the child in the least restrictive and "most productive" environment possible (J. Melcher, personal communication, 1978). The information is also used to develop a comprehensive and specific plan for the child's day-to-day educational program. Assessment data should, moreover, assist in "outlining the evaluation procedures that are to be used in determining the effectiveness of the child's individual educational program in meeting identified goals and objectives" (Ingram, 1980).

In summary, assessments should provide some "global" information about the child (How does the child compare to other children his or her age?); it should provide educators with specific information for the classroom (What skills is the child ready to learn?); and it should, finally, give direction to the staff who will be working with the child (In what ways does this child learn most effectively?). Table 1 summarizes the global and specific questions that the assessment process should address.

Composition of Assessment Team

Ingram (1980) has outlined seven points, originally noted by Higgins (1977), that should be considered in organizing a team to conduct evaluations under the provisions of PL 94-142:

1. The public agency responsible for determining that the child has a specific handicap will use a *team* to evaluate that child.
2. The official from the education agency responsible for the administration of special education programs will be responsible for appointing team members.

Table 1. Purposes of assessment

Global information for placement	Specific information for the classroom
1. Does a handicap exist? (diagnosis)	1. What are the child's strengths and weaknesses? (profile)
2. What is the etiology of the handicap?	2. What is the treatment for the problems or condition?
3. What is the child's developmental level?	3. What skills does the child need to acquire?
4. What placement is most appropriate and least restrictive?	4. What environment is most appropriate for learning?
5. What services does the child need?	5. a. How does the child learn most effectively? b. What skills is the child ready to learn?
6. What services does the family need?	6. What suggestions are there for the family to do at home?
7. How far has the child progressed?	7. How will we know whether our intervention is successful?
8. What follow-up will be provided?	8. What information will follow the child?

3. The composition of the team must include the child's regular teacher or a teacher licensed or certified by the state agency and appointed by the official representing the educational agency completing the assessment.

4. One additional person certified or licensed by the state education agency to conduct individual diagnostic examinations (school psychologist, speech clinician, or resource teacher) must be included on the assessment team.

5. Members constituting the team shall be chosen on the basis of their knowledge of procedures used in the evaluation of children.

6. Each individual team member must be qualified to perform the specific assessment tasks he or she has been assigned.

7. After the evaluation, the team should meet at least once to discuss the evaluation and to reach a decision as to the child's performance (Ingram, 1980, pp. 6–7).

EDUCATIONAL ASSESSMENT PROCESS

The assessment process can be divided into five phases:

Phase I: Assessment planning
Phase II: Assessment (analysis)
Phase III: Interpretation (synthesis)
Phase IV: Program planning (staffing)
Phase V: Classroom assessment

The first four phases are completed by a multidisciplinary team assigned to evaluate the child. The final phase, classroom assessment, is conducted by those

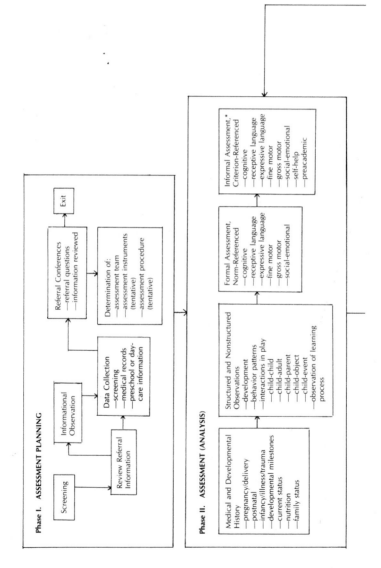

Phase I. ASSESSMENT PLANNING

Screening → Informational Observation → Referral Conferences
—referral questions
—information reviewed → Exit

Review Referral Information → Data Collection
—screening
—medical records
—preschool or day-care information → Determination of:
—assessment team
—assessment instruments (tentative)
—assessment procedure (tentative)

Phase II. ASSESSMENT (ANALYSIS)

Medical and Developmental History
—pregnancy/delivery
—postnatal
—infancy/illness/trauma
—developmental milestones
—current status
—nutrition
—family status

Structured and Nonstructured Observations
—development
—behavior patterns
—interactions in play
   —child-child
   —child-adult
   —child-parent
   —child-object
   —child-event
—observation of learning process

Formal Assessment, Norm-Referenced
—cognitive
—receptive language
—expressive language
—fine motor
—gross motor
—social-emotional

Informal Assessment,* Criterion-Referenced
—cognitive
—receptive language
—expressive language
—fine motor
—gross motor
—social-emotional
—self-help
—preacademic

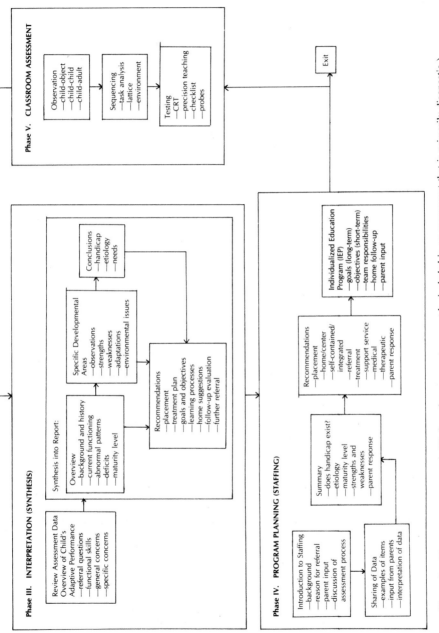

Figure 2. The assessment process. (*Informal assessment may not be included in an assessment that is primarily diagnostic.)

evaluation team members who work directly with the child after the child has been placed in the appropriate setting.

Each of these phases is examined in depth in the remainder of this chapter. The flowchart in Figure 2 illustrates the total process.

Phase I: Assessment Planning

After an agency receives a referral on a child, planning is necessary to determine the nature of the assessment to follow. The person responsible for handling the initial referrals, usually an intake social worker or the program coordinator, begins by reviewing the information accompanying the referral. Occasionally, additional information is needed, and the intake person may need to contact the parents, send for medical records, or talk to the child's preschool or day-care teacher. Informal observations of the child are advised whenever possible. After gathering the needed data, the intake worker then prepares "referral questions" to guide further evaluation. These questions may emanate from the professional screening, for example: What are the child's linguistic capabilities? At what level is the child functioning cognitively? Does the child have an identifiable motor handicap? Or, the teacher or parent might ask more informal questions such as: Why doesn't he talk well? Why doesn't he pay attention and "mind"?

The intake person calls a referral conference of the full evaluation team to review all referral questions and pertinent data and to ascertain whether any assessment, a full assessment, or a partial assessment is indicated. The team should consider the following four questions:

First, how could the child function better in his or her present environment? If the data do not justify further evaluation, the child may be able to return to his or her present placement, with recommendations for environmental modifications. This possibility is perhaps too often neglected, lending credence to the frequently voiced belief that children are often unjustifiably placed in special programs (Shepard, Smith, Davis, Glass, Riley, & Vojir, 1981).

Second, what additional information is needed? Multidisciplinary evaluation is important to obtain a complete picture of the child's performance (Cross & Goin, 1977). However, unnecessary evaluation should be avoided. Information from other sources should be used whenever possible.

Third, who would be the most appropriate individuals to obtain the needed information? Traditionally, professionals are trained to perform specific roles and functions, or to administer certain types of instruments. Social workers, for example, are trained to gather relevant data through interview techniques. Speech and language pathologists, in addition to being trained in assessing speech and language skills, are often trained to do feeding assessments, behavioral observations, and family interviewing. Administrators need to know the skills of the various team members in order to use their abilities to best advantage. Staff should be qualified to do the testing needed, particularly when using standardized tests (see Phase I in Figure 2).

Fourth, what instruments or procedures are most appropriate to obtain the needed information? This question is particularly important, as there are numerous instruments on the market with varying capabilities. It is important for staff to be familiar with new instruments, as well as with current research regarding all instruments. Each instrument should be analyzed to determine:

Validity—Has the test been proven to measure what it purports to measure?

Reliability—Does the test provide a consistent estimate of behavioral performance?

Standardization—Was the test standardized on a sample population with demographic characteristics similar to those of individuals to be tested? Administration and scoring procedures should also be standardized in order that interpretation of test results be as accurate as possible.

Bias—Is the test biased or discriminatory against any cultural minority? Is it biased so that children with a particular handicap (for example, blindness or deafness) will be penalized by standardized administration?

These considerations are particularly important for the global purposes of assessment as outlined in Table 1. In addition to studying test manuals for the above information, staff should be familiar with O.K. Buros's *The Seventh Mental Measurements Yearbook*, and F. Davis's *Test Analysis: Screening and Verification Instruments for Preschool Children* (see references). Diagnosis, developmental level, and placement decisions have tremendous implications for the child and should not be treated lightly. Psychoeducational testing done in Phase II should utilize appropriate instruments for these purposes. For classroom assessment in Phase V, a wider variety of instruments is legitimate. Discussion of the informal, criterion-referenced assessment that takes place in Phase II should also be a part of the assessment planning phase.

Phase II: Assessment (Analysis)

A few guidelines for organization and implementation of the assessment process should be noted.

1. Assessment should be systematic, thorough, and accurate.
2. Assessment needs to take place with full due process rights accorded the child and the family.
3. Assessment should take place in the child's native language.
4. When the child has a known handicap (such as cerebral palsy or visual impairment) the nature of the handicap should be considered during the collection and interpretation of assessment data.
5. A combination of norm-referenced, criterion-referenced, observation, and Piagetian devices should be used in assessment.
6. The importance and effect of the assessment environment on the child should be kept in mind. Everything possible should be done to ensure the child's best performance.

7. Rapport with the child is very important. The child needs to feel comfortable with the environment and the tester before assessment begins.
8. Confidentiality needs to be guaranteed and procedures established for cross-agency information sharing.

Organization of the Process   With various teams carrying out different assessment responsibilities, several assessment procedures may be occurring simultaneously. However, there should be an overall pattern to assessment and a process model should be followed. A recommended process is delineated in Phase II of Figure 2.

Medical and Developmental History   The medical history is typically obtained directly from the child's physician (after parents have granted permission for the release of information). However, most agencies have their own intake forms that request medical information from the parents, usually through an interview. Many parents have had to compile their child's medical and developmental history several time in the past so the doctor's records may be fairly complete. Only information not available in the records should be sought from the parents. It is wise to first determine what experiences the parents have had with other agencies and what their level of understanding is concerning their child's medical history. Some parents have been shocked and dismayed, for example, to learn that a label of cerebral palsy or of autism has been placed in their child's medical records without their knowledge. Negative feelings may be avoided if the staff do not *assume* the knowledge level of parents concerning the problems of their child and the information contained in records.

Information relating to the child's medical and developmental history may provide clues to the etiology of the child's problems. This "piece of the puzzle" may have implications for treatment (as in the case of epilepsy or endocrinological disorders), or it may provide some help to parents who almost universally want to know "why?" Most medical and developmental history data forms include questions concerning:

Pregnancy   Difficulties the mother may have had, including illness, trauma, infection, blood disorders, nervous condition, or other abnormal conditions.

Delivery   Data on the gestational age, birth weight, duration of and difficulties in labor are all significant.

Postnatal   The child's Apgar score, difficulties with breathing, blood, jaundice, or physical abnormalities.

Infancy   Illnesses, trauma, seizures, and high fevers are examples of information sought.

Developmental milestones   Extreme delays or unexpected cessation of expected normal behaviors such as babbling and use of words, sitting, crawling, and walking are often indicators to both parents and professionals that there may be reason for concern.

Nutrition   Difficulty with feeding, unusual eating habits, or poor nutrition may cause problems not only in development but also in parent-child interactions, and is thus an important area for exploration.

Family situation   Although sometimes sensitive to discuss, the nature of the family situation is important. Patterns of interaction, marital status, stresses, support systems, sibling relationships, extended family relationships, all may relate to the problem either diagnostically or therapeutically, and may have implications for the most appropriate means of intervention.

Observation   The formal testing process is often highly structured and takes place in an environment that is unnatural for the child. Consequently, the behaviors that are observed under the testing situation might *not* be indicative of the child's typical behavior patterns. It is, therefore, extremely important to observe the child in a variety of other more familiar settings, including home and day-care or preschool. Varying the time of observation may also make a difference in the types of and quality of behaviors observed; for example, the child's "best" time might be right after eating or a nap. Observation may be done by any or all of the team members involved in the assessment. The social worker often makes a home visit to obtain the medical and developmental history—this is a good opportunity to observe the child in his or her natural environment. The teacher or developmental specialist might also want to observe the child in his or her nursery or preschool program.

Structured Observation   Several types of structured observations may be used in assessment. One of the most frequently employed is a checklist that analyzes developmental areas. The following types of questions may be listed with alternative responses to be checked: How does the child move? How does the child communicate? How does the child solve problems? How does the child react to modeling? What types of prompts are most effective? What signals are needed to arouse attention? How does the child react to failure? In observing the child eating, playing, or dealing with frustration, inferences can be made about how the child adapts within various environments. Any deviations in performance under differing circumstances should be noted, as they may be relevant to program planning.

A second type of structural observation is commonly done with children who exhibit maladaptive or bizarre behaviors. The observation consists of observing the child and obtaining baseline data on the frequency, duration, and intensity of the behaviors exhibited. In addition, the observer watches what happens in the child's environment—such as actions on the part of the child or by any other person in the room that precede the behavior. These are known as "antecedents" to the behavior. The observer also notes "consequences"—what happens to the child and others in the room after the behavior occurs. In addition, the observer records what is reinforcing or motivating to the child within the environment.

These quantitative data on frequency counts, reinforcers, antecedents, and consequences are then used to assess what may be causing the behavior and how the behavior might be modified to become more acceptable.

Nonstructured Observation   Some professionals find it useful to observe the child without a checklist or baseline chart. They prefer to take "raw data," writing down everything they observe the child doing—movement, language patterns, and so on—and including a qualitative description. This allows the whole team to analyze the data later. Raw data or nonstructured observations are actually synthesized in the analysis rather than in the data taking. Data should be examined systematically, studying patterns of interaction between: the child and other children; the child and his or her parents; the child and other adults; the child and objects; the child and events within the environment.

Guidelines Regardless of whether structured or nonstructured observations are used, the following general suggestions are offered:

1. Observe the child in a variety of times and settings.
2. Observe the child at play. Behavior patterns and skills that have become functional will be observed in play, as will problem-solving abilities and motivating factors.
3. Look for patterns of behavior and situations that affect behavior.
4. Look for the child's individual way of learning or processing information.
5. Develop a structure to analyze observational data.
6. Note how and where the child was observed and the length of the observation.

Information about the child and the family that is gained through observation is a critical, yet often overlooked, aspect of assessment. Observations can be particularly useful in Phase IV, Program Planning. Structured and nonstructured observations should be built into the assessment process from the beginning and not added as an afterthought or haphazardly.

Formal Assessment Assessment is conducted to measure human capacity, ability, behavior, or performance (Ingram, 1980). Formal assessment is the use of norm-referenced or standardized tests. In norm-referenced testing, an individual's performance is measured against others of the same age. Salvia and Ysseldyke (1978) point out that in norm-referenced assessment, content learning is important only to the extent that it allows rank-ordering of individuals, from those who have acquired a few skills to those who have acquired many. Norm-referenced testing, then, by affording an overall perspective on how the child compares with his or her peers, is relevant in screening, to compare a child against regional or national norms, to make placement decisions, or to evaluate progress from year to year. Ingram (1980) characterizes norm-referenced tests as using specific administration procedures, definite scoring criteria, and distinct methods—which should be thoroughly discussed by the team—for interpreting scores. The child's *actual* performance is obtained from a combination of norm-referenced and criterion-referenced testing.

With the under-5 population, a variety of norm-referenced tests are available to assess each of the areas usually measured: sensorimotor, gross and fine motor, receptive language and expressive language, cognition or adaptive reasoning, and social-emotional development.

If a full battery of tests is being administered to a child, a comprehensive test is typically completed first. The Bayley Scales of Infant Development are frequently used with children under 2½ to obtain information on the child's language, cognition, motor development, and behavior. With preschool-age children the McCarthy Scales of Children's Abilities are popular, providing information on subareas in verbal, perceptual, qualitative, memory, and gross motor development. Whether one of these or other tests are used, the purposes of inclusive tests are the same: 1) to gain an overall understanding of how the child is functioning compared to other children of the same age, 2) to pinpoint strengths and weaknesses within the child's ability range, and 3) to provide direction for further assessment.

It is important to note that the use of an inclusive test is only the beginning and should never be viewed as a complete assessment. Rather, the comprehensive overview allows team members to garner clues as to further in-depth testing that needs to be done. For example, areas of weakness on the Bayley may indicate a need for further cognitive evaluation using the Uzgiris and Hunt Scales (ordinal scales that are not standardized); or, after completing the McCarthy, more Piagetian (not standardized) testing might be desired to judge how the child processes cognitive information. Additional testing using other normative tests in subareas of speech or linguistic patterns may also be advisable. The original testing plans of the team should always be regarded as tentative. For example, a team may determine initially that only a psychological test and a speech and language evaluation are needed. However, the motor subtasks of the psychological test may indicate some difficulty with motor planning. An occupational therapist or physical therapist can then be added to the assessment team to provide the needed in-depth motor evaluation.

Data gathered from normative testing should be combined with that collected through observation and through informal assessment processes to provide a "total" picture of the child. The developmental specialist or teacher plays a significant role in all of these areas, but particularly in relation to criterion-referenced testing.

Informal Assessment   The purpose of an informal criterion-referenced device is to compare the child not to other children but to a set of standards (usually derived from norm-referenced tests). The criterion-referenced test (CRT) allows the teacher to determine the level at which the child is functioning and to measure the child's progress over time, not in terms of an overall score but in terms of specific developmental skills.

The advantage of a CRT is that it allows the teacher to construct tests to measure specific skills that may not be evaluated on norm-referenced tests. Howell, Kaplan, and O'Connell (1979), provide directions for developing CRTs.

1. The person developing the CRT determines what specific skills or behaviors need to be assessed.
2. A performance objective is then written that describes how the child will be

tested. The objective includes: a) what *behavior* the child must perform, b) under what *conditions* the child will attempt the activity, and c) the *criteria* for how well the child must perform in order to pass the test. As with formal assessment instruments, CRTs need to be valid, reliable, and relevant to the particular child being tested.

3. The performance objective (that can also be used in the child's program plan) can be used to construct a CRT. If reliability is to be ensured, the CRT must specify: a) the directions for administering and scoring, b) the criteria for successful accomplishment, and c) the necessary materials and/or test items.

4. The criteria for successful completion of the test are determined by the developer of the CRT. Howell et al. (1979) recommend that individuals who are "considered to possess the skill measured by the CRT be identified and administered the CRT." Their minimum level of performance is then adopted as the standard for "passing" the test. In actuality, the setting of criteria is usually done rather subjectively, with the standard whatever the CRT developer believes to be reasonable. A high standard (for example 70%–80%) is frequently used. It is important to note that this numerical criterion is useful only for indicating that this skill does *not* need further work. However, if the child does not perform the skill to criterion, he or she does not "fail" the item. An item analysis should be done to determine the starting point for remediation. The test tells only the present performance level and where remediation should begin. If the child has *no* success with the CRT, it is probably an inappropriate CRT.

A sample criterion-referenced test and scoring sheet is shown in Figure 3.

The CRT can be of great value to the assessment team, both in determining where and how the child is functioning and also in planning the child's educational program. Developing a CRT takes time, however. Fortunately, a great many criterion-referenced devices already exist, and the teacher can utilize those most relevant to the child being assessed. In addition to the traditional developmental areas assessed by norm-referenced tests, criterion-referenced assessment devices may also contain subareas addressing preacademic and self-help skills. Additional CRTs can be developed as needed. (The reader is referred to Cross & Goin, 1977, for sources of CRT-based assessment instruments.)

Guidelines for Formal and Informal Assessment   The following guidelines are offered on the utilization of formal and informal assessment.

1. Utilize normative data to provide inter-individual comparisons (skill levels of child compared with age peers).
2. Utilize a comprehensive normative test to provide an overview of the child's strengths and weaknesses.
3. Utilize normative assessment to provide direction for further testing.
4. Keep the assessment plan flexible, so that assessments can be added or deleted as necessary.
5. Utilize criterion-referenced data to supplement normative data and to provide

Task:	The child will name each of four common objects when shown.
Materials:	A set of color pictures including a doll, a cup, a dog, and a book. One scoring sheet.
Directions:	Say to the child, "Tell me what this picture is." Hold up the picture for 5 seconds. Say, "What is this?" Repeat procedure for each of the pictures. Do not tell the child whether he or she is correct or incorrect. Do not let the child see what you are marking. Use a stopwatch or a watch with a second hand, held out of the child's field of vision. Timing should begin as you present the picture to the child.
Scoring:	Wait 5 seconds for a response. Put the picture face down on the table. If the response is incorrect, mark "incorrect" on the scoring sheet. If the response is correct, mark "correct" on the scoring sheet. If the child hesitates, wait the full 5 seconds before putting the picture down and mark "incorrect."

Scoring Sheet

Skill: Picture recognition and naming

Task: Names each of four common objects

Subject: _____   Age: _____

Examiner: _____   Date: _____

Stimulus: Response (check one):
                                   Correct: Incorrect:

1. doll   1. _____   1. _____
2. cup   2. _____   2. _____
3. dog   3. _____   3. _____
4. book   4. _____   4. _____

Criterion for acceptable performance: 100%

Figure 3.   A sample criterion-referenced test and scoring sheet.

intra-individual comparison (specific skill levels of an individual child compared).

6. Develop new CRTs as needed for individual children.

7. Consider any biases the test may have when given under standardized conditions, and supplement the assessment with instruments designed to show maximum performance levels.

Phase III: Interpretation (Synthesis)

Whereas Phase II emphasized analysis of the child's capabilities and performance, Phase III focuses on the interpretation and synthesis of data that have been collected (see Phase III in Figure 2). Team members are responsible for their own sections of the evaluation, but it is crucial that discussion and exchange of information take place prior to writing the final report. If possible, the team should come to consensus concerning the major referral questions. It is helpful to raise some transdisciplinary questions that are relevant to all members of the team and to the parents. This may prevent fragmenting the child into "pieces," in which each team member talks about his or her "piece."

For example, a question such as "In what ways does the child communicate his or her needs?'' will provide an opportunity for the speech and language specialist to share information obtained about the child's expressive language capabilities. The question will also serve as a base for comments from the occupational therapist concerning how the child uses movement to communicate needs. The psychologist may have input regarding the interpersonal or social communication patterns with the parents. And the developmental specialist or teacher may be able to add conclusions gained from observation and testing on how the child communicates needs in a group and how he or she communicates needs when frustrated.

Interactive discussion around referral questions such as the above leads to more fruitful interchange than merely sharing normative test scores and developmental levels. One purpose of assessment is to provide information for daily programming for the child. A discussion focused on *functional* questions will facilitate the emergence of functional data. After an informal discussion of the assessment data, team members need to incorporate their assessment data, observations, conclusions, and recommendations into a final report.

Organization and Synthesis of Data   The organization and synthesis of data should respond to the questions asked in Table 1. Information relevant to both global and specific concerns should contribute to the final recommendations presented in the evaluation report. The following suggested format for the written report is an adaptation of one presented in Knobloch and Pasamanick (1974). The modifications presented here facilitate use of the format in educational assessment. Note that in a written team report such as this, it is necessary to address various areas of evaluation by discipline; thus the report is usually analyzed by developmental area. However, for the purposes of generating functional recommendations during oral staffing sessions, information can best be discussed in relation to the referral questions.

Format for the Written Report on Assessment Data

I. Identifying Information
    A. Name.
    B. Birth date.
    C. Age (or corrected chronological age).
II. Reason for Referral
III. History (use past tense)
    A. Birth weight and duration of gestation.
    B. Pregnancy, labor and delivery, and neonatal period. Mention abnormalities specifically associated with high-risk pregnancies.
    C. Significant illnesses.
    D. Convulsions: type of episodes, age of onset, frequency, duration, association with fever, and treatment.
    E. Developmental history: Indicate if normal or in what areas significant deviation occurred, and age at which deviation first was noted. Note specifically if deterioration has occurred.

IV. Informal Observations
    A. Indicate the location and duration of observations.
    B. Discuss interactions observed.
        1. Parent-child.
        2. Child-child.
        3. Child-adult.
        4. Child-objects.
        5. Child-events.
V. Tests Administered
    A. List normative tests or sub-tests administered.
    B. List criterion-referenced tests administered.
    C. List other descriptive procedures used (e.g., Piagetian interview).
VI. Qualitative Description of Test Behavior
Mention specific patterns that characterize the behavior of the child. Comments on general description, adjustment to the examination, interest and attention, and quality of exploration of materials are included.
VII. Neuromotor Abnormalities
    A. Abnormal patterns.
    B. Description of any seizures observed during the examination.
    C. Mention visual or auditory deficits.
VIII. Interpretation of Test Results
Discuss each behavior in each developmental area separately—adaptive behavior or cognitive, gross motor, fine motor, receptive and expressive language, and personal—social behavior. The assigned maturity level or range is included after each sub-heading. Strengths and weaknesses for each area are discussed. Give examples of behaviors that were observed that indicate patterns of growth or deviation.
IX. Summary of Results
    A. Indicate the general maturity levels and the quality of the behavior.
    B. Indicate an etiology if data are present to warrant.
    C. Summarize major areas of need.
X. Recommendations
Make specific recommendations for the following areas:
    A. Placement.
    B. Treatment.
    C. Educational programming.
    D. Referral.
    E. Home stimulation.
    F. Family support. (Adapted from Appendix A, pp. 447–479.)

The recommendations sections should derive from the staffing discussion, with the family contributing to the final recommendations. The interpretation of data should be based on objective, empirical data. Emphasis should be placed on the child's and family's *needs* rather than on a diagnostic label.

Phase IV: Program Planning (Staffing)

The fourth phase is concerned with the formal presentation of assessment data and the joint determination of the child's educational placement and program plan (see Phase IV in Figure 2). The rules and regulations for implementation of Part B of the Education for All Handicapped Children Act (*Federal Register*, August 23, 1977, Section 121a. 344) indicate that meetings, usually termed "staffings," will be held for the purpose of determining a child's handicap and developing an individualized education program (IEP). A variety of professionals and the parents participate to ensure that children are not misclassified or unnecessarily labeled as being handicapped and that due process procedures under PL 94-142 are safeguarded.

The act's regulations stipulate that participants in staffings should include a supervisory representative of the public agency providing special education services, the child's teacher, one or both of the parents, a member or members of the evaluating team, the child, where appropriate, and other individuals at the discretion of the parent or agency.

The staffing committee provides a professional interpretation of test results, determines whether or not the child is eligible for special education services, and identifies the child's specific educational needs. The committee also recommends services to meet identified needs in the most appropriate and the least restrictive environment possible.

Role of the Parents The staffing process can seem threatening to parents who walk into a room to find a group of professionals seated around a table talking about their child. Staffings usually tend to be rather formal, with staff using professional jargon. All of this can stifle the parents' desire to offer information, voice an opinion, or even ask a question. Parents should be viewed as equal members of the staffing team, with valuable information to contribute—after all, who is likely to know the child better? Attempts need to be made to make the parents feel comfortable and to let them know that their input is important. For example, it is a good idea for a staff person who knows the parents well to sit next to them to make them feel more at ease. Every effort should also be made to keep jargon to a minimum and to explain unfamiliar terms to parents throughout the staffing. Public Law 94-142 also stipulates that parents should be fully advised of their due process rights prior to the staffing.

Staffing Process As the staffing process begins, the case coordinator presents background information relating to the reason for the child's referral for evaluation. The parents' perceptions and/or concerns about their child should be included at this time. Asking parents to express their concerns at the outset helps to make staff aware of parents' attitudes and may, as well, make parents more receptive to the assessment information. Parents, however, who do not perceive their child as having a problem, and who are upset that the child was referred for evaluation, may become defensive about information that is presented. In either case, the assessment team needs to present data very carefully to parents, giving multiple examples of how deficits or delays may be observed at home.

The staffing coordinator then describes the assessment process used, and explains the questions the team sought to answer, how the information was obtained, and why specific instruments or procedures were chosen. The medical and developmental history is traditionally shared first, with additional input from the parents if desired or needed. Team members then discuss the observational and test data gathered. Information is provided on the child's general level of functioning, specific strengths and weaknesses, and learning processes observed. It is often a good idea to give examples of the test items given, and relate them to behaviors that the parents may observe. For example, the speech and language pathologist might say that the child had difficulty remembering a sequence of three commands. The test item can be stated, "I asked Tommy to pick up the pencil, go put it on the table, and then put it under the chair. He was only able to remember the first two requests." The therapist might then ask the parents, "What usually happens at home when you ask Tommy to do several things in a row? For example, 'Pick up your toys, hang up your coat, and wash your hands for dinner'." If the parents note that Tommy usually leaves out one or more of the requests, they then may begin to appreciate the relationship between everyday behaviors and test items. They may also begin to understand their child's present level of functioning. The parent may add, "I just thought he was being naughty when he didn't mind me." This type of discussion around test data helps parents later to comprehend the reasons for specific goals and objectives and also makes recommendations for home follow-through more meaningful.

After a thorough discussion of all aspects of the assessment, the parents' response is again requested so that any misconceptions may be clarified. For instance, after discussions of visual perceptual problems, it is not uncommon for parents to conclude that there is something wrong with their child's eyes; clearly, in this case, a further explanation of "visual perceptual" is needed. A summary of the general conclusions of the assessment is then provided, answering these major questions:

1. Does a handicap(s) exist?
2. Is there a known etiology?
3. What is the range of the child's levels of functioning?
4. What are the child's strengths and weaknesses?
5. What are the child's needs?

Recommendations regarding the child's placement and treatment plans are made based on the answers to these questions. The staffing committee discusses placement alternatives that would best meet the child's and family's needs. Considerations of home-versus center-based, self-contained versus integrated, or variations of these may be determined. The possibility of providing additional services through another community agency, such as a cerebral palsy center, might also be discussed. Often it is helpful to list the child's needs and match them with required services. Transportaion, medical needs, and therapy are examples of possible essential services. The family's needs must also be considered, particularly when infants are being served. A need should *not* be excluded from identification because the agency has limited staff or services. Means can be sought to provide *all* needed services through joint agency planning (see Chapter 4).

Parent Needs in Staffing Before discussing the last aspect of the staffing, the IEP, it is important to digress briefly to emphasize that the needs of parents are often unconsciously overlooked at staffings.

Listening to and absorbing a discussion of diagnosis and placement is often very difficult for parents. The full impact of the diagnostic information and the implications for the child's future may take weeks or months (in some cases even years) to be understood (Turnbull & Turnbull, 1978). One suggestion might be to make a tape recording of the staffing available to parents, so that they can listen again later to further clarify points in their own mind. Professionals can provide a great service to parents by 1) listening to their concerns; 2) providing time for information to be assimilated; 3) making themselves available for further discussion at another time; 4) not expecting parents to be emotionally and physically equipped to perform all the follow-through desired by the team; and 5) providing support services when needed to help parents cope with the difficulties encountered in having a handicapped child.

The IEP The final task of the staffing committee is to develop the child's individualized education program. The IEP is a written statement developed by the multidisciplinary staffing committee (including the parents) that outlines the *annual goals* to be met, the specific *instructional objectives* to be accomplished, and the *educational services* that will assist the child in reaching the specified goals and objectives.

As directed by PL 94-142, the IEP is to include:

1. The present educational level of the child
2. Annual goals
3. Specification of short-term instructional objectives
4. Statements concerning the specific education or related services that are to be provided for the child
5. The extent to which the child will be participating in the regular education program (unfortunately, regular infant and preschool programs may not exist in the agency)
6. Projected dates for initiation of services and the anticipated duration of services
7. An evaluation plan outlining the procedures to be used in determining if annual goals and objectives have been met, and a statement reflecting how effective the service patterns have been in meeting goals and objectives (*Federal Register*, August 23, 1977, Section 212a. 348)

Present Performance Level Utilizing the assessment data, statements regarding the child's present performance in each developmental area should be given. Physical, medical, and sensory functioning should also be noted.

Goal Statements   The areas that are *priorities* for intervention need to be decided. A *general* goal statement is first written to indicate long-range directions. An example of a goal statement would be "to increase communication skills." Next, annual goals are delineated. In the (then) Office of Special Education's Policy Paper on IEPs (The Individualized Education Programs, 1980), an annual goal is defined as "a statement which describes what a handicapped child can reasonably be expected to accomplish within one calendar year" (p. 21). This is technically equivalent to a long-term objective.

Long-Term Objectives   The long-term objective or annual goal statement, as redefined by the U.S. Office of Education in 1980, should be written to state what specific skills will be acquired within one year. Objectives are written in the same manner in which CRTs are developed (see pages 109–111). Van Etten, Arkell, and Van Etten (1980) state that the components of an instructional objective include: the learner for whom the objective is intended; a statement of the precise, *observable behavior* that the learner is expected to display; the *conditions* under which the learner is expected to display the behavior; and the criteria for successful performance of the behavior. An example of a long-term objective would be, "By June 1, Tommy will identify 20 common household items when requested with 80% accuracy."

Short Term Objectives   Short-term objectives are written in the same manner, only they indicate steps or skills that will be accomplished on the way to achieving the long-term objective. In relation to the above stated long-term objective, an example of a short-term objective might be: Given the verbal cue "Show me the cup," Tommy will point to the cup four out of five consecutive trials.

Short-term objectives are usually derived from long-term objectives, and indicate where instruction is to begin. Van Etten et al. (1980) suggest the following guidelines for selecting objectives:

1. Incorporate major parental concerns with regard to skills for the child.
2. Consider physical or medical concerns in selecting skills needed.
3. Select skills that will contribute to the child's *functional* independence.
4. Select skills that are functionally related from various developmental areas.
5. Consider how valuable it is to the child to learn a particular skill at a particular time.
6. If a child is in the program for a brief time period, select critical skills to be achieved.
7. Consider objectives that can be accomplished in small groups.
8. Objectives should fit into a developmental sequence.
9. Select skills that are appropriate for the child's rate of learning.
10. Select skills that can be used in the home so that maintenance and generalization of skills is facilitated.
11. Classroom objectives should complement those of other team members.

Educational and Related Services   The special education services to be received, as well as services beyond the classroom that will be provided, are designed on the IEP. Federal rules and regulations (*Federal Register*, August 23, 1977) specify the following as "related services":

> Transportation
> Speech pathology and audiology
> Psychological services
> Physical and occupational therapy
> Recreation
> Counseling services
> Medical services for diagnostic and evaluation purposes
> School health services
> Social work services
> Parent counseling and training (pp. 42479–42480)

Art, music, dance, and physical education are also considered related services when appropriate.

Participation in Regular Education Many public schools do not currently provide education to normal infants and preschoolers, which limits the type of environment available for "least restrictive" placement. However, whenever possible, joint efforts between early childhood special education programs and local preschools should be planned to provide opportunities for mainstreaming. Any formal arrangement for mainstreaming should be noted on the IEP.

Projected Dates for Initiation and Duration of Services Most personnel interpret the initiation and duration of services to refer to the amount of time projected for each objective. Thus, the team notes the anticipated length of time needed to accomplish the objectives.

Appropriate Evaluation Procedures The procedure to be used to evaluate performance needs to be stated. Continuous measurement, checklists, and probes are examples of methods of evaluating progress.

The development of the IEP is the culmination of the assessment process. Although all team members and parents have input, the developmental specialist or early childhood special educator and other team members who will work directly with the child have the major responsibility for writing the IEP.

Guidelines for Staffings

1. Parents must be notified of the staffing and given every opportunity to attend.
2. Parents must be informed of their right to be responsible by counsel and of their right to appeal.
3. The staffing process should be discussed with parents beforehand so that they will not be overwhelmed by the process.
4. The social worker, case manager, or teacher (a person with whom parents have established a rapport) should sit by the parents to offer support and to encourage their involvement.
5. Remarks to be presented should be prepared using lay language; terms that parents and other staff might not understand should be defined.

6. Practical examples of the child's behaviors, such as the parents might observe at home, should be given to help illustrate deficits found in testing.
7. Major referral questions should be addressed in the summary of test data.
8. Recommendations should derive from data gathered.
9. Family needs as well as the child's needs should be considered.
10. Services needed by the child and family should not be disregarded because of shortage of staff or funds; instead, interagency agreements should be pursued.
11. IEPs should be developed consistent with federal and state guidelines.

Phase V: Classroom Assessment

Classroom assessment is the continuous evaluation of the child's progress. It usually occurs after the child has been placed in the program, and is performed by the teacher and other team members. Classroom assessment begins with the IEP and proceeds throughout the year. Depending on the level of severity of the child's handicaps, the program philosophy, and the curricula utilized, this assessment will take different forms, though the overall process is similar (see Phase V in Figure 2).

Each day in the classroom (or in the home) the staff observe the child and note the child's interactions with objects, events, and people within the environment. Specific attention is paid to:

The times when the child is most attentive and receptive
The length of time of maximum concentration
The materials, toys, people, and events that are most stimulating to the child
The methods (demonstration, modeling, imitating, physical or verbal prompting, questioning, and so on) that are most effective in promoting learning
The mode of response preferred by the child
The sensory modalities stressed by the child
The physical setting that is most conducive to exploration and involvement
The types of peer involvement that encourage social growth
The adult-child interactions that are most effective in promoting positive growth (types of reinforcement, directive, and/or playful interactions)

As the staff assess the child within the environment, patterns begin to emerge that are useful for program planning. This type of observation over time usually cannot be done during diagnostic assessment (except in diagnostic placements), but, as a program tool, it holds the key to successful teaching. (The child's patterns may also change, so observations need to be ongoing.)

Observational data play an important role in the second aspect of classroom assessment, the sequencing of skills to be assessed. The most common method of sequencing involves task analysis. Howell et al. (1979) define task analysis as "the process of isolating, sequencing and describing all of the essential components of a task" (p. 81). Van Etten et al. (1980) describe the following five steps of task analysis:

1. Identify the terminal behavior (task) to be learned, as stated in the instructional objective.
2. Derive the components of the task and then sequence them.
3. Determine any prerequisite skills needed for the subtasks.
4. Eliminate nonessential and/or redundant component and prerequisite skills.
5. Consider the need for task-slicing of component skills (p. 164).

Task analysis allows the staff to assess exactly where a child is in relation to learning a particular skill. It is especially helpful when working with severely and profoundly handicapped children.

Another method of assessing a child's progress in relation to a learning sequence is the use of a developmental lattice in which tasks are listed in vertical steps, with the earliest developmental prerequisites at the bottom. Interrelationships are also depicted among skills as they relate horizontally. An excerpt from a language/cognitive lattice is shown in Figure 4.

The advantage of a lattice is that the interrelated nature of various skills and areas of development can be seen clearly. Determining which skills on a lattice the child is able to perform may reveal that one reason the child is not learning a skill is that he or she does not possess a related, concurrently developing skill. For example, a blind child may not be crawling much, even though the physical ability is present; one explanation may be that the child is not actively pursuing objects for play, a cognitive skill emphasizing the use of vision. The teacher may then alter the child's program to encourage locomotion toward a desired auditorially stimulating toy.

In programs for mildly handicapped children, sequencing of specific events within the environment may allow the teacher to observe a child's developmental level within a series of structured events. The teacher, for example, may request that the child decide on an activity, carry it out, and describe what he or she has done. Depending on how the child proceeds, the teacher obtains information on the child's cognitive abilities (knowledge of time, sequencing, memory) as well as the child's language and motor abilities. From such an observational assessment, the child's program can be modified to provide activities that will help to develop multiple skills at appropriate levels.

Finally, the staff do ongoing testing in a variety of ways. Precision teaching models that utilize charting of skills, CRTs, checklists, probes, and anecdotal records are all ways of assessing progress. Again, the methods chosen will depend on the population and the philosophy.

SUMMARY

The assessment model presented in this chapter emphasizes the dual nature of child evaluation. Assessment should present inter-individual information on the nature of the child's performance in relation to other children of the same age. Such data are useful for placement and service decisions. Assessment should also present intra-individual information on the specific skills that the child possesses and those

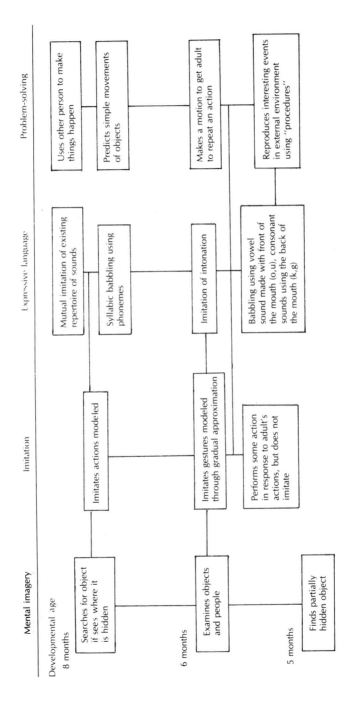

Figure 4. Excerpt from a language/cognitive lattice. (From Linder, T., *The Colorado Guidelines for Preschool Special Education Programs*. Denver: Colorado Department of Education, 1981.)

121

skills that are ready to be learned. These data are necessary for decisions concerning the child's classroom program as well as to provide a means for measuring the child's progress within that program.

A five-stage assessment design is recommended that includes assessment planning, assessment (analysis), interpretation (synthesis), program planning (staffing), and classroom assessment. The inclusion of classroom assessment in the design demonstrates the ongoing nature of evaluation assessment. It is a dynamic process that should be an integral part of the child's program—from before he or she enters the special education service delivery system until "graduation" from the system.

REFERENCES

Buros, O.K. (ed.). *The seventh mental measurements yearbook.* Highland Park, NJ: Gryphon Press, 1972.

Chazdon, C., Harvey, D., & McNulty, B.A. (eds.). *Child Find. A handbook for implementation, procedure and recommended guidelines.* Denver: Colorado Department of Education, 1978.

Cross, L., & Goin, K. (eds.). *Identifying handicapped children. A guide to casefinding, screening, diagnosis, assessment and evaluation.* New York: Walker and Co., 1977.

Davis, F. *Test analysis: Screening and verification instruments for preschool children.* Harrisburg: Commonwealth of Pennsylvania, Department of Education, 1977.

Harbin, G. Educational assessment. In: L. Cross & K. Goin (eds.), *Identifying handicapped children. A guide to casefinding, screening, diagnosis, assessment and evaluation.* New York: Walker and Co. 1977.

Higgins, J.P. Present levels for performance and assessment: Some basic considerations. In: S. Torres (ed.), *A primer on educational programs for handicapped children.* Reston, VA: The Council for Exceptional Children, 1977.

Howell, K.W., Kaplan, J.S., & O'Connell, C.Y. *Evaluating exceptional children. A task analysis approach.* Columbus, OH: Charles E. Merrill Publishing Co., 1979.

The Individualized Education Programs, Part B, Education of the Handicapped Act as amended by PL 94-142. BEH Policy Paper, U.S. Department of Education, Office of Special Education, May, 1980.

Ingram, C.F. *Fundamentals of assessment.* New York: D. Van Nostrand Co., 1980.

Knobloch, H., & Pasamanick, B. (eds.). Appendix A: Examination techniques. In: *Gesell and Amatruda's developmental diagnosis. The evaluation and management of normal neuropsychologic development in infancy and early childhood.* New York: Harper & Row, 1974.

Lillie, D.L. Screening. In: L. Cross & K. Goin (eds.), *Identifying handicapped children. A guide to casefinding, screening, diagnosis, assessment and evaluation.* New York: Walker and Co., 1977.

Salvia, J., & Ysseldyke, J. *Assessment and remedial education.* Boston: Houghton-Mifflin Co., 1978.

Shepard, L., Smith, M.L., Davis, A., Glass, G.V., Riley, A., & Vojir, C. Evaluation of the identification of perceptual-communictive disorders in Colorado. Laboratory of Educational Research, University of Colorado, Boulder, February 20, 1981.

Turnbull, A.P., & Turnbull, H.R. *Parents speak out: Views from the other side of a two way mirror.* Columbus, OH: Charles E. Merrill Publishing Co., 1978.

Van Etten, G., Arkell, C., & Van Etten, C. *The severely and profoundly handicapped. Programs, methods, and materials.* St. Louis: The C.V. Mosby Co., 1980.

chapter

6

Selecting and Using Curricula

Curriculum generally refers to "systematic procedures for organizing educational activities; the procedures include both content (what to teach) and method (how to teach)" (Lillie, 1975, p. 2).

Content areas in elementary school typically revolve around the "three Rs," reading, writing, and arithmetic. However, programs at the preschool level have taken various approaches to curriculum, as outlined in Chapter 2. Programs for handicapped preschool children have evolved from and expanded upon these different themes, styles, and techniques.

What are the "essentials" to be taught to handicapped children? In response to that question, a variety of assessment instruments and curricula have been developed in early childhood special education. These curricula differ in a number of significant ways. It is therefore important that the team or persons responsible for selecting or designing a curriculum for their program be cognizant of the various program areas or components that may be included in these curricula as well as the different instructional sequences that may be proposed.

MAJOR PROGRAM AREAS

Major program areas are the general domains targeted for instruction—the basic units, or components, of the curriculum. These components may focus on 1) *developmental areas*, 2) *specific skills areas*, or 3) *enrichment areas*. Many early childhood curricula are divided into components according to general *developmental areas* such as gross and fine motor skills, expressive and receptive language, cognitive or adaptive reasoning, and social-emotional behavior. Other curricula may designate major program areas by *specific skill areas*, such as self-help skills, pre-reading, and pre-math skills, and communication skills. Sensory skill areas, as visual or auditory perception, may also be represented. Still other curricula will designate major program components that integrate developmental or skill components into *enrichment activities*, such as art, music, and dance.

Generally, five categories are recognized as appropriate areas of instruction for young handicapped children: 1) motor development, 2) self-help skills (activities for daily living), 3) sensorimotor and cognitive development (pre-academic), 4) communication (language), and 5) social/interpersonal development (socialization, personal-social, social-emotional) (Van Etten, Arkell, & Van Etten, 1980).

Regardless of the component's title in the curriculum—whether it is designated as a developmental area, skill area, or enrichment area—it is important that each of the above domains be represented in some way in program planning. Particularly for handicapped children, difficulties with one area may have a profound influence on other areas of development. Emphasis on one curriculum component may result in an unbalanced program, one that does not totally meet each child's individual needs. The necessity for a transdisciplinary or interdisciplinary team approach is evident to maximize information exchange and ensure optimal programming for each child in all developmental areas.

SEQUENCE WITHIN CURRICULUM COMPONENTS

Cohen and Gross (1979) have identified four variations of curriculum sequences. A curriculum may utilize all four types of sequences or may emphasize one or two. The important consideration for the team is to use a curriculum that pinpoints the instructional needs of their population and is consistent with their program philosophy.

The variations of sequences of abilities include:

1. *Arrangement according to targets in a specific area.* In this type of sequence, targets, or terminal objectives, for skill development within very specific areas are identified. In the area of self-help, for example, feeding, toileting, and dressing might be identified as instructional subareas; skills would then be listed in each subarea and broken down into step-by-step sequences, or task analyses, for instruction. Such sequences are typically used in behaviorally oriented programs.

2. *Arrangement according to developmental milestones.* In some cases, a curriculum will list all the milestones a child generally accomplishes in a given year. For example, a curriculum might list the following skills under the cognitive area for a 3-to 3½-year-old:

    Copies a circle
    Copies a four-block train with chimney
    Initates straight cross
    Puts together a two-piece puzzle

It is important to note that the items are not listed as prerequisites to the next item in the sequence. This sequence listing is probably most appropriate for mildly handicapped children who acquire skills without intensive training.

In other instances, the curriculum may list objectives in developmental sequences leading to major milestones. For example, in the development of object permanence, the curriculum may list:

Finds object hidden under one screen
Finds object hidden under one of two screens
Finds object hidden under one of two screens alternately
Finds object after successive visible displacements

With the former listing of milestones by age, if the child were unable to perform one of the skills, the teacher might not know what prerequisite skills were necessary. The latter listing of developmental sequences therefore allows the teacher to determine a teaching sequence based on developmental prerequisites. It is particularly appropriate for severely involved children, since the sequences can be finely differentiated.

3. *Arrangement according to constructs.* Some curricula designate conceptual constructs to be attained as the basis for activities. Piagetian constructs, such as ordination, cardination, and conservation, provide areas that are then broken down into developmental tasks. Part of a sequence under the construct of seriation might include:

Understanding of *big* and *little*
Understanding of *tall* and *short*
Understanding of *largest*
Understanding of *tallest*
Understanding of *middle*

Curricula designed to develop specific constructs are, in general, experientially rather than behaviorally oriented.

4. *Arrangement according to stimulus characteristics.* Developmental progressions in areas such as vision and audition may relate to characteristics of the stimulus. For example:

Prefers circular to linear arrangements
Shows preference for checkerboard over regular lattice or arrangement of circles, squares, diamonds
Fixates somewhat longer on male and female patterns than on other patterns
Discriminates between differing facial orientations

Such stimulus character arrangements would be useful in designing programs for visually impaired, hearing impaired, or learning disabled children.

Since most early childhood programs are noncategorical in nature, the ideal curriculum would probably incorporate elements of each of the above-mentioned sequence formats. The ideal curriculum to meet all handicapped children's needs is yet to be developed, however, and the intervention team is advised to select a variety of curricula as resources. There are many good curriculum ''packages'' on the market. These are convenient for teacher use, but need significant modification in order to address adequately the individual needs of children. Often staff will need to find, develop, or modify subcomponents, objectives, task analyses, or activities. Assembling a variety of available resources is important to facilitate ongoing program development. All handicapped children are different, and their programs and strategies should reflect individual needs and learning styles.

This text does not recommend one specific curriculum or set of curricula; indeed, to do so would be inappropriate. An effort is made, however, to delineate recommended program areas and subareas of importance in early childhood special education programs. A rationale for inclusion of each area is suggested to emphasize the interrelated nature of the various components. A team of professionals should collaborate closely to further expand and delineate needed subcomponents for the children they will be serving.

GROSS AND FINE MOTOR DEVELOPMENT

Rationale

The development of volitional movement can be said to be the foundation for development in all other areas. Yet it is, perhaps, the most overlooked curricular area in many programs, with the exception of programs for physically handicapped children.

The development of gross and fine motor skills is usually sequential and fairly predictable, with skills emerging with experiences and as the nervous system matures. With the handicapped child, however, there may be delays and/or deviations in motor development that will interfere with the normal sequence of skill acquisition. These delays or deviations will undoubtedly impinge on other areas of development. Problems in gross and fine motor development will affect perceptual-motor, self-help skills, cognition, language, and social-emotional development.

In order to function well in the environment a child needs balance, stability, coordination of both sides of the body, rotational abilities, a fairly broad range of motion, adequate muscle tone and muscle strength, and volitional control of movements. Without these abilities, the child cannot achieve maximum interaction with his or her environment. For example, inadequate head and trunk control will limit visually directed reaching, and consequently reduce fine motor manipulation of objects. Difficulty with balance in sitting may limit bilateral manipulation of objects. The child who must concentrate his or her efforts on resisting the pull of gravity will need to use his or her extremities as props rather than exploratory tools. The child with inadequate motor control may not be able to explore his or her own body or move around in order to explore the environment as a normal child does. The child may consequently have reduced or limited visual, tactile, auditory, gustatory, and olfactory experiences. This reduction of sensorimotor experiences may result in limited body awareness and delayed or inaccurate development of form and space perception (Fantz & Yeh, 1979).

Limited motoric exploration may affect a child's cognitive development as well. For example, major cognitive skills, such as object permanence, tool use as a means to attain desired ends, classification of objects according to shape, and sequencing of objects in order of size, are all achieved after much manipulation and experimentation with the objects in the child's environment. The child learns through acting upon the environment. Motor problems result in a limited ability to move and to manipulate objects, to cause events to occur, and to interact with people. The result is reduced learning opportunities.

The development of language skills may also be adversely affected by motor problems. Inadequate head and trunk control may interfere with breathing patterns and thus affect phonation required for speech. Inability to control oral musculature will affect speech production. Limited exploration of the environment may result in formation of fewer concepts and thus a reduced ability to label objects and environmental events. Both receptive comprehension and expressive language may be delayed, especially as related to spatial concepts and actions.

Inadequate head and trunk control, lack of stability, and disequilibrium may hinder development of feeding, dressing, toileting, and other self-help skills. In addition, difficulties with music tone, muscle strength, and motor planning may affect academic skills such as writing, cutting, and drawing. Numerous academic skills for young children require gross and fine motor coordination.

Emotional development and the growth of social skills are greatly influenced by the child's physical abilities. When attachment between mother and infant is first taking place, the child communicates primarily through physical cueing. Looking, touching, cuddling, smiling, and crying are all behaviors with motor components to which the mother reacts (Brazelton, Koslowski, & Main, 1974; Klaus & Kennel, 1976). The physically handicapped child may not have adequate cueing mechanisms to encourage reciprocal positive interaction. Predominant extensor patterns, for example, may inhibit cuddling. Reduced smiling behaviors (Cicchetti & Sroufe, 1975; Emde, Gaensbauer, & Harmon, 1976) may diminish playful interaction. Increased and intense crying may result in less handling and inattention or possibly more holding but less mutual needs gratification. The child with motor problems is at greater risk for "attachment failure" (Foley, 1980). Later in the child's development, this cycle of insufficient needs fulfillment may expand to include teachers and peers.

The child who does not perform competently in skill areas may recognize his or her limitations. This awareness of physical inadequacy may, in turn, inhibit the development of self-concept and social interaction. Play opportunities and social interaction may be limited or reduced, with possible consequences of inadequate or delayed social skills. The child may experience a delay in developing independence as a result of continued assistance from caregivers.

Often, cognitive delays coincide with motoric delays, but in many instances the motorically involved child is simply unable to demonstrate the cognitive skills of which he or she is capable. The result is frustration for the child and often misdiagnosis by staff who perceive the child as cognitively delayed as well.

As can be seen by these few examples, the motor area is a critical component of the curriculum. Although the type of curriculum chosen for the gross and fine motor areas will depend largely on the needs of the identified population of children, important elements that any motor curriculum should include can be identified. These are discussed below. Staff should examine the various curricula under consideration to determine whether or not assessment, sequences, and program strategies for these motoric elements adequately address the needs of the children they will be serving. No effort is made in the discussion below to list all skills that should be included in a motor curriculum component, but staff are encouraged to look for curricula in which related skill areas are developmentally sequenced, rather than being grouped by all motor skills that are normally attained at a given age.

Reflexes and Reactions

The importance of reflexes and automatic reactions should be recognized. Reflexes facilitate the development of motor and cognitive skills. Integration of certain reflexes is essential to the appropriate development of gross and fine motor skills. However, reflexes are not targets that can be "trained." Instead, volitional movements that are incompatible with the reflex are appropriate for program objectives. It is not possible, for instance, to train a "grasp" reflex; however, "holding" as a skill can be a curriculum objective. The importance of having a physical or occupational therapist on the team (or available for consultation) to work on developing program plans in the motor area can be seen readily.

Assessment

Prior to the development of program objectives, the therapist will want to evaluate the child's reflexes and reactions. Bobath (1974) looks for delayed or abnormal development with:

> 1) an insufficiently developed postural reflex mechanism, showing itself, for instance, in poor head control, lack of rotation within the body axis, and lack of balance and other adaptive reactions, and 2) a lack of inhibition showing itself in unduly prolonged retention of the primitive patterns of earliest childhood (p. 2).

Connor, Williamson, and Siepp (1978) recommend that analysis of motor skills the child has acquired should take into account the following practical considerations.

1. What components of movement are necessary in order for the child to have mastered a particular skill? Does the skill involve integration of primitive reflexes, righting reactions, equilibrium reactions, and/or protective reactions? How have the child's movement patterns affected normal sensorimotor development?

2. For what future skills can a particular skill be considered an important component? For many handicapped children it is important to rank skills to be learned in order of priority, as progress is slow. It is therefore necessary to select skills that are crucial to present and future development.
3. What areas of cognitive, language, and social development are likely to be facilitated by a motor act? If a particular motor skill will facilitate more rapid growth in other developmental areas, it may become a priority.

Motor Sequences

After evaluating the child's motor development in relation to the above questions, the child's motor program can be planned. The curriculum should include activities to facilitate the integration of primitive reflexes and the development of righting, equilibrium, and protective reactions as well as activities for development of sequences of motor skills. The following are subareas of gross motor development. Each area listed should be broken down into developmental sequences in the curriculum.

Head-righting—prone	Progression on hands and knees
—supine	Progression to sitting
—upright	Progression to crawling
Joint stability—upper arms	Progression to standing
—trunk	Progression to walking
—hips	Progression to jumping
—legs	Progression to skipping
Rotation—prone to supine	
—prone to sitting	
—rotation in standing	

The fine motor component of the curriculum should illustrate and define progressions in the differentiation and progressive development of prehension and fine muscle control. Included should be sequences related to:

Progressions in visually tracking objects or visual pursuit	Progressions in coordination of use of two hands simultaneously
Progressions in focusing	Progressions in throwing of objects
Progressions in head and trunk control	Progressions in catching
Progressions in reaching	Progressions in thumb and finger opposition
Progressions in voluntary grasp	
Progressions in voluntary release	Progressions in drawing
	Progressions in writing

Each of the above-mentioned progressions may be sequenced in varying degrees of detail. For severely involved preschool children, it may be necessary to develop subtle, more finely differentiated steps in the developmental progression. It may also be necessary to task analyze individual steps within a progression into chains of behaviors to attain mastery of one of the steps in the progression. A task analysis can be thought of as the breakdown of a skill into its component parts, which are then taught in a step-by-step instructional sequence. The developmental prerequisites for the functional acquisition of the skill and its generalization to related tasks must be taken into consideration in writing a task analysis.

In the developmental task analysis that follows, the goal or behavioral objective is for the child to write the letter A. The prerequisites to this task in other developmental areas need to be identified before beginning instruction on this specific fine motor skill. For example, the child must have good postural stability, be able to adaptively hold a pencil, be able to plan motor movements, have representational understanding of sounds, have communicative intent, and have a desire to write. Obviously, there is more to the goal of writing the letter A than the rote replication of the three lines that form an A. The prerequisites in the areas of language, cognition, and social-emotional development must be addressed prior to, or (when appropriate) concurrently with, the desired skill in order to ensure successful skill acquisition. The task analysis in the developmental progression below lists three skills prerequisite to writing the letter A. The teacher needs to determine which developmental prerequisites are relevant for a particular child.

I. *Progression*—Writes the letter A
    A. Makes horizontal strokes in imitation
    B. Makes Λ strokes in imitation
    C. Recognizes that a letter represents a sound
    D. Traces letter A (*task analysis*)
        1. Traces heavily marked letter A on top of the letter
        2. Traces lightly marked letter A on top of the letter
        3. Traces letter A on a piece of translucent paper placed over the letter A
        4. Connects many dots which form the letter A
        5. Connects a few dots which form the letter A
    E. Writes letter A

In the above example, the child had acquired the prerequisite skills in the developmental progression up to the point of tracing letter A. At this point the task was analyzed and taught through backward chaining (or teaching the last step in the task analysis first). After successful acquisition, the child can then proceed to the next step in the developmental sequence.

SENSORY INTEGRATION

Rationale

Sensory development in the child has been studied extensively over the past 10 to 15 years. Research on visual perception (Campos, Langer, & Krowitz, 1970; Fantz & Yeh, 1979; Haith, 1980; Kessen, 1976), auditory perception (Brackbill, 1970; Bridger, 1961), tactile perception (Brackbill, 1970), vestibular/proprioception (Korner & Thoman, 1972; Pick & Pick, 1970), gustation (Nowlis & Keesen, 1976), and olfaction (Engen & Lipsitt, 1965) has shown the importance of these sensory systems to the developing child. The integration of information sent to the central nervous system (CNS) from each of these systems provides the foundation of the child's *perceptions* of the world and consequently the basis for his or her *conceptual* understanding. If inadequate or inaccurate sensory messages are being delivered to the child's CNS, or if there are problems with processing the information once it reaches the CNS, the child's other developmental areas may be adversely affected.

For example, inadequate perception of gravity and the body in space may interfere with the child's efforts to coordinate movements. The development of motor skills is affected by the child's awareness of his or her body's movements in space. Without accurate information from tactile and kinesthetic and/or proprioceptive systems, the child will not have optimal volitional control of body movements. Refinement of fine motor skills may be also impeded, as inadequate perception of spatial relationships may interfere with basic skills such as reaching for objects, accurately placing objects, or manipulating objects in goal-oriented actions.

Cognitive growth may also be delayed or hampered by the inadequacy of sensory systems. If the information processed by the brain is inaccurate or inconsistent, the child may develop a distorted understanding of his or her environment. A child who has difficulty making sensory discriminations may be hesitant to interact with the environment. For example, a child who is tactilely defensive may withdraw from contact with persons or objects. The child consequently does not absorb as much information about the environment as a normal child would, does not optimally interact and experiment in order to ascertain the relationships between objects and events, and may therefore be delayed in problem-solving abilities.

Behavioral problems may also be seen in children with inadequate sensory systems. The child may be overly sensitive to stimuli, or easily frustrated by the inability to process and "classify" environmental perceptions. A child with difficulty discriminating among, for instance, visual or auditory patterns may react by withdrawing from such stimulation or may exhibit behavioral problems as a result of being "overwhelmed" by sensory stimuli. Continued failure in interpersonal and object interaction may also result in an impoverished self-concept.

The area of sensorimotor, perceptual-motor, or sensory integration, as it is variously titled, is becoming an increasingly important curriculum area. Its pivotal nature is reflected in its close relationship to gross motor, fine motor, and cognitive development, as well as progressions of skills—such as tracking and object manipulation—that are common to more than one developmental area.

Developmental Sequences in Sensory Integration

Identification of areas of instruction in sensory development involves providing activities that maximize the use of strongly developed sensory systems and enhance those that are impaired. Van Etten, Arkell, and Van Etten (1980) divide primary sensory curriculum component tasks into three major areas:

Tactile
Accepts touch
Allows directed body movement
Explores with mouth
Localization of touch
Responds to and begins to dis-
    criminate between various tactile
    stimuli
Uses tactile sense to explore en-
    vironment
Thermal awareness

Visual
Sensation
Visual fixation
Visual tracking
Convergence
Eye contact
Reaching and grasping
Eye-ear coordination
Eye-hand and eye-foot coordination
    activities

Auditory
Cries or startles in response to sound
Responds by quieting, stopping
    movement
Localization
Discrimination (p. 210)

These tasks can be subdivided and extended as necessary to include more discriminating and/or higher level targets. The other areas of sensation, including proprioception, should also be included in the curriculum. Again, the importance of an occupational or physical therapist is emphasized, as this team member can have valuable input both in terms or assessment of sensory deficits and in planning remedial strategies.

COGNITIVE DEVELOPMENT

Rationale

The cognitive, or adaptive reasoning, curriculum area is heavily emphasized in most programs. The relationship between cognitive ability and academic or school success is well established, and thus, justification for its inclusion hardly seems necessary. Yet it is important to appreciate the impact of cognitive delays on the other areas of development.

Problems in cognitive development may affect the rate at which motor skills are acquired. The child may take longer to understand the various properties of objects and the functional use of these objects, so complementary motor "schemata" or patterns may also be delayed. The child may have a reduced comprehension of environmental events and a resultant decrease in desire for object or interpersonal interaction that allows the practicing of motor skills to take place. In addition, the lowered capacity for applying motor skills in new situations may act to hinder the generalization of motor actions. For example, the child who learns to poke his or her fingers in the holes of a pegboard may not generalize that skill to holes in other toys, and the motor skill of finger differentiation is then not practiced as often. Therefore, "classification" of motor schemata into complex motor planning actions may take longer to accomplish.

The child with delayed cognitive development may rely heavily on a trial-and-error or a perserverative approach to learning and thus may not develop a sufficient number of problem-solving strategies involving movement and manipulation. The child may, for instance, persist in one approach to putting a puzzle together. By not experimenting with moving the puzzle pieces into different positions, the child is not exercising precise finger movement, eye-hand coordination, or perceptual discrimination.

The overall delay in learning skills will also influence the rate, quality, and quantity of language acquisition. Diminished conceptual understanding will affect both receptive and expressive abilities. Higher level symbol representations will be understood primarily through concrete experiences. Abstract concepts will take longer to comprehend or may never be functional aspects of the child's language system. Learning irregular language forms of plurals, past tense, and other syntactic structures may be difficult. Generalization of grammatical rules may also take much longer in the cognitively delayed child.

In relation to social skills, the child may not comprehend subtle social cues that are necessary for appropriate behavioral adjustment. The understanding of cause-and-effect relationships in social situations involves cognitively higher level skills than understanding cause-and-effect relationships in concrete situations involving objects. The cognitively delayed child may therefore take longer to understand why an action or event makes someone "angry," "sad," "happy," and so on.

As previously mentioned, the cognitively delayed child may have at his or her disposal fewer problem-solving skills, and thus may be unable to see alternative means for accomplishing a goal. This can lead to frustration not only in dealing with concrete problems involving object use for obtaining a desired end but in interpersonal interactions when dealing with social problems. The implications for the development of the self-concept are evident.

Self-directed play may remain longer at the lower level of "isolated" or "parallel" play (Parten, 1932). The child's level of representational thinking may be inadequate to process symbolic information necessary for cooperative and dramatic play. For example, whereas a normal preschool child may use blocks to represent buildings, roads, towers, and bridges, the cognitively delayed child may still be constructing "patterns" with blocks. He or she cannot visualize the block as anything other than a piece of wood. Socialization skills that develop through cooperative dramatic play will consequently be affected.

The discrimination and generalization of social skills may be problematic. The child may, for example, learn that "hugging and kissing" is positively reinforcing and may then, indiscriminately and inappropriately, hug and kiss everyone. On the other hand, the child may learn not to perform an inappropriate action—such as screaming—at school, but this learning may not generalize to the home. Such situation-specific learning can cause increased problems particularly in the area of social skills.

Developmental Sequences in Cognition

Given the significance of the cognitive area and its impact on other areas of development, the skills outline in this area of the curriculum is necessarily comprehensive. The following are suggested skill areas in cognitive development. These need to be further defined according to the needs of the population being served.

Attending to stimuli
Tracking stimuli
Hand regard
Visually directed grasping and reaching
—bilateral
—unilateral
Object permanence progression
Means-end progression
Differentiated object usage progression
Social object usage progression
Representational object usage (beginning classification) progression
Object's relation in space progression (utilization of space relations)
—places objects in, out, on top of
—builds vertical structures
—builds horizontal structures
—builds vertical-horizontal structures
Operational causality progression
Gestural imitation progression
Vocal imitation progression
Classification by characteristic of objects progression
—color
—shape: circle, square, triangle, rectangle
—understands same and different
—size
—function
—multiple characteristics
Drawing progression
—marks
—scribbles
—controlled strokes: vertical, horizontal, angle, circle, cross
—reproduction of forms
—draws people
—copies letters
—writes letters spontaneously
—writes name
—writes numbers
Class inclusion progression
—within one set
—within a hierarchy

Concept of ordering progression
—big, little, largest
—tall, short, tallest
Concept of seriation progression
—size
—color
—number, cardinal correspondence
—correspondence of sets
—ordinal correspondence
Rote counting
One-to-one correspondence progression/ rational counting
Numeral identification
Comparison of sets progression
—all, empty
—each
—more/less
—same
Conservation progression
—length
—number
—continuous quantity
—discontinuous quantity
—volume
Addition progression (in relation to above)
Subtraction progression (in relation to above)
Time concepts
—now, today
—past present, and future words
—duration of time
—part of day (morning, afternoon, night)
—before/after
—time on the clock
Money concepts
—identify coins
—identify uses of money
—understand value of coins and bills
—reading numerical amounts
Calendar concepts
Measurement
Fractions

LANGUAGE DEVELOPMENT

Rationale

Examination of the impact of the area of language development on the total development of the child reveals the necessity of including both receptive and expressive domains in any curriculum for handicapped children.

Inadequate language comprehension may indirectly affect gross and fine motor performance. If the child does not accurately hear or interpret verbal directions, the child will not be able to respond correctly—which usually entails a motor component. This may be misinterpreted by the teacher as an inability to perform the skill requested.

A deaf, hearing impaired, or severely language impaired child may need to substitute or supplement oral language with sign language. Thus, the development of parallel language systems, oral and gestural, may be indicated.

The relationship between language and cognition is a controversial issue (Bruner, 1972; Bruner, Olver, & Greenfield, 1966; Piaget, 1962, 1963, 1973), but regardless of which serves as the foundation for the other, the interdependence of the two areas is undeniable. Language is a primary means by which one demonstrates understanding of concepts, processes, and events, particularly comprehension of abstract concepts and relationships. A child's inability to demonstrate cognitive understanding through verbal expression may lead to lowered appraisal of cognitive skills and consequent lowered expectations on the part of the teacher. Concurrently, reduced motivation and/or frustration on the part of the child may result. Conversely, some children learn to parrot extensive phrases without true comprehension of the content. These children may be viewed as having cognitive skills at a higher level than are actually present. Thus, the teacher's level of expectations for such children may be too high, with resultant frustration for both.

In the area of social skills, the child who cannot effectively make his or her needs known and cannot verbally express feelings may resort to alternative means of self-expression. For example, acting-out behaviors, or engaging in actions that are abusive to self or others, may be manifested. On the other hand, withdrawal from interpersonal interaction may also occur. Children with lower language skills may not be sought out by peers for social interaction (Guralnick, 1978). In either case, socialization skills are adversely affected. Other children may also become frustrated and reduce interactions with the child who does not comprehend or cannot communicate well.

There appear to be some cognitive prerequisites that underlie language development. Bates (1976) has identified some of these precursors: 1) awareness of object permanence, 2) awareness of spatial relations, 3) awareness of the understanding of means-end, 4) development of deferred imitation, 5) development of rational and pretend play, and 6) development of communicative intentions. These target areas should be included in or referenced in the language area of the curriculum.

Developmental Sequences in Language Acquisition

The relationship of skills to one another within a developmental sequence is important. For example, a 5-month-old is observed to use arm movements to try to get an interesting event to recur. The child also responds with body movements and babbling to someone speaking to him. These responses are important to social, cognitive, and language development. As another example, the development of object permanence, a cognitive skill, is related to the development of inner language and the association of words with objects not present in the child's view. As staff develop or utilize existing sequences of language skills they need to relate each substep to prerequisite or co-requisite skills in other developmental areas (see, for example, the excerpt from a language/cognitive lattice in Chapter 5, Figure 4). The number of skills and degree of specificity may vary depending on the population being served. Sequences for preschool children, suggested by Cohen and Gross (1979), would take into consideration:

Lexical production progression
Lexical comprehension progression
Production of semantic relations
   progressions
  —single-word usage
  —two-word productions
  —three-word productions
  —complex productions

Comprehension of relational meaning
Production and comprehension of
  grammatical form
  —sentence elaboration
  —inflectional development
  —interrogative usage

SOCIAL-EMOTIONAL DEVELOPMENT

Rationale

The development of social relationships is probably most closely tied to the parallel development of cognitive constructs. But it is also intertwined with increased differentiation of motor skills, enabling more complex and volitional interpersonal interaction. Increased language comprehension and expression enhances higher level social interchange as well.

The impact of delays or deviations in emotional development may have compounding effects on skills acquisition in other areas. A child who is passive and withdrawn or fearful of interaction may not interact as frequently or intensely with objects and people in the environment. Both practice and generalization of motor skills and cognitive problem-solving efforts may be affected. The child who behaves impulsively and has a short attention span may have difficulty in planning sequences of movement. He or she may display unsystematic, ineffective problem-solving approaches that may later affect academic performance. Inability to see others' points of view may cause social difficulties, but probably will also be reflected in an inflexible approach to accomplishing or attaining desired goals. Emotional problems may also result in overdependence on adult assistance, with a consequent delay in independence and a lack of self-confidence, risk taking, and exploration.

Language acquisition may also be affected. The child who is socially delayed may not verbalize as frequently in interactive situations. Play with language— manipulation and experimentation with vocabulary, grammar, syntax—may not be fully experienced. Modeling behaviors may not be exhibited. Language may appear delayed when, in fact, the child is merely not using language to the fullest extent possible. This will not only affect teacher interaction, but may also interfere with peer interaction, as children tend to seek out other children at their same language level (Bloom, 1974; Guralnick, 1978). The child who does not respond appropriately to directions or does not seem to comprehend language may be demonstrating lack of compliance or withdrawal rather than language delays.

Observation of children's social patterns is extremely important. Unfortunately, the social-emotional area has been concerned primarily with elimination of maladaptive behavior rather than fostering the development of social sequences. Many curricula include a list of skills in the social-emotional area that are designed to "prepare" the child for academic settings; for example, the child needs to: attend for 20 to 30 minutes; follow three directions; wait for his or her turn. These are important skills, but they need to be addressed within a developmental framework. Children with emotional problems or delayed social development may not be able to perform at a social level that is as advanced as their demonstrated cognitive level. For instance, cooperative efforts and games with rules may be too difficult for a child still at the level of parallel play. The significance of attachment (Ainsworth, 1973; Bowlby, 1969; Klaus & Kennel, 1976), separation (Ainsworth, 1973; Bowlby, 1973; Mahler, 1975), and individuation (Mahler, 1975) are becoming increasingly apparent to professionals working with young handicapped children (Foley, 1980). The relationship of play behaviors to the development of social and emotional, cognitive, language, and motor skills (Garvey, 1977) is recognized and is particularly important for handicapped children (Linder, 1980).

Social-Emotional Sequences

The following suggested subareas of social-emotional development focus on progressions that take into consideration the above-mentioned precursors to healthy emotional development and appropriate and responsible social interactions. The lack of certain subskills (for example, cuddling) may indicate a concern that has implications for another area of development (for example, motor). The intervention may not be to "train" the skill, but to raise the level of awareness in the family and team as to the social impact of the lack of these behaviors. Also, interventions (such as, positioning) that will optimize opportunities for pleasurable interaction would be indicated.

Indiscriminate social responsiveness
   (signaling behaviors)
   —crying progression
   —smiling progression
   —vocalizing progression

Differential social response
   —to face
   —to patterns
   —to parent

Contact seeking/formation of dependence relationship
—indication of preference for mother/ differentiation of strangers
—indication needs progression
—fear of strangers progression
—response to separation
Differentiation of self
—reaction to mirror image progression
—exploration of others
—reference to self
—identifies self in picture
—sees others' perspective
—knows sex

Establishment of independent activities
—locomotion progression
—manipulation of objects progression
—plays near adults
—explores expanding environment progression
Goal directed interaction
—plays by self
—object use progression (cognitive)
—parallel play progression
—on-looker behavior
—cooperative play progression
—sharing progression
—awareness of emotions progression
—dramatic play progression

The development of checklists or lattices of important progressions will allow staff to observe children and determine their level of interactive skill. It is important to emphasize, however, the interrelated nature of development. As previously discussed, each area of development affects every other area. The staff need to be aware of this in their observations in order to avoid misinterpreting observational information. The team approach should help circumvent this pitfall.

Once the specific needs of the children in each developmental area have been identified, the staff can begin the search for appropriate curricula. The greater the developmental delays, the greater will be the need for sequences with discrete breakdowns and progressions with smaller "steps" in between. The activities recommended can also be analyzed to determine whether they are the most appropriate. The greater the abilities of the child, the more need there is for integrated, experiential programs. Activities should provide for optimal challenge and a degree of novelty (Furth & Wachs, 1975).

CONSIDERATIONS FOR GIFTED HANDICAPPED CHILDREN

It should not be assumed that every handicapped child is delayed in all areas. Every child has strengths and weaknesses. Many normal and gifted children have handicaps, yet can function at above-average levels in cognitive and other developmental areas. Provisions need to be made to provide for advanced level activities for these children. For example, physically handicapped, emotionally disturbed, or language impaired children may also be very bright. Programs can be individualized so that areas of deficits are addressed, while advanced work is provided in appropriate areas. Enrichment activities in drama, art, and music are important for all children and should be included in the curriculum. For gifted handicapped children, opportunities to develop creative talents in the visual and performing arts can provide a needed boost to self-esteem as well as a means to capitalize on abilities.

Curricula for handicapped children need to be broad and encompass developmental, skill, and enrichment areas. They also need depth, so as to be able to meet the individual needs of a great variety of children with a wide range of abilities.

UTILIZATION OF CURRICULA

Curricula may be utilized in a variety of ways. They may be followed like a "bible," adopted as a guide for planning, used as a supplement to an existing program, or serve as a resource for new ideas. The manner in which any set of curricula is implemented should reflect the program philosophy.

The previous discussion has focused on curriculum content and variations in presentation of content. Two other considerations, structure and methodology, are germaine to curriculum implementation.

Structure

Included in the structure are:

1. The amount of time allocated to content areas
2. The amount of time spent in functional versus structured practice activities
3. The amount of time devoted to purposeful integration of developmental areas
4. The amount of "free time" versus facilitated play
5. The role of the environment
6. The role of the staff
7. The role of the child
8. The role of the parent

Examination of each of these elements will reveal why different programs that have adopted the same curriculum may function in extremely diverse ways.

Time Allocated to Content Areas The amount of time given to each content area of the curriculum is one indication of the relative priority of that area. Table 1 gives examples of daily schedules from three different programs. An examination of the three schedules may show that a high percentage of the day may be devoted to one area of development (see also Table 2, section A). Of course, in any one activity there are many developmental areas involved, but the area that is targeted from the curriculum is emphasized. In a program using primarily a cognitively oriented curriculum (Program I), for example, one would expect to find a high percentage of the day devoted to cognitive and language development. Program II has time allotted for group activities that will emphasize language development. Program III, which emphasizes individual work with children in each of the developmental areas, attempts to balance the program across all areas.

Practice Time versus Functional Time The analysis of time spent in practicing skills in drill-type activities versus practicing skills through application in functional activities is another measure of program difference (Table 2, section B). Program I's philosophy is that learning takes place best when children practice

Table 1. Daily schedules for three preschool programs

Time	Program I	Program II	Program III
8:30–8:45	Child planning time (cognitive, language) + + ∞	Circle time— Names (language) + ○	Free time (cognitive time, motor sequence) + + ∞ *
8:45–9:00	Block play (cognitive, fine motor, social-emotional) + + ∞ **	Puzzles, etc. (fine motor, cognition) + ∞	Individual cognitive targets + ○
9:00–9:20	House play (cognitive, language, social-emotional) + + ∞ **	Labeling pictures (language) + ○	Individual language targets + ○
9:20–9:50	Sharing time (language, social-emotional) + ∞	Drawing pictures (fine motor) + + ○	Individual fine motor targets + ○
9:50–10:15	Snack time/toilet (self-help, language, cognitive) + + ∞	Snack time/toilet (self-help) + + ○	Snack time/toilet; individual feeding, toileting targets (self-help) + + ○
10:15–10:35	Small group work (cognitive, fine motor) + ∞	Obstacle course (gross motor, language) + ∞	Group game (social-emotional, gross motor) + + ∞
10:35–10:55	Recess—outdoor play (gross motor, social emotional) + + ∞ **	Story time (language) + + ∞	Individual gross motor targets + ○
10:55–11:20	Story time (language cognition) + + ∞	Music (language) + + ∞	Free time (cognitive, fine motor, social-emotional) + + ∞ *
11:20–11:40	Art or building (cognitive, fine motor) + + ∞ **	Group games (gross motor, social-emotional) + + ∞ **	Directed finger painting (sensorimotor) + ○
11:40–12:00	Cleanup, home (self-help, motor) + + ∞	Cleanup, home (self-help) + + ○	Dress, home (self-help) + ○

Key: + + Functional activity; + Practice activity; ∞ Purposeful integration; ○ Single area or incidental integration; ** Facilitated play; * Free time.

skills in functional settings; therefore, 80% of the child's time is spent in informal play activities. Program II puts more emphasis on directed skill practice than does Program I. Staff feel that the children need some guided practice to bring them to a functional level, but 60% of the day is still spent in functional application of skills.

Table 2.   Comparison of three daily preschool schedules (see Table 1) according to four factors

A. Percentage of Activities Targeting Development Areas:

Program I	Program II	Program III
Cognition—60%	Cognition—10%	Cognition—30%
Language—50%	Language—50%	Language—10%
Fine motor—20%	Fine motor—20%	Fine motor—20%
Gross motor—10%	Gross motor—20%	Gross motor—20%
Self-help—20%	Self-help—20%	Self-help—20%
Social-emotional—40%	Social-emotional—10%	Social-emotional—30%
		Sensorimotor—10%

B. Percentage of Functional Activities vs. Practice Activities:

Program I	Program II	Program III
Functional	Functional	Functional
(+ +)—80%	(+ +)—60%	(+ +)—40%
Practice (+)—20%	Practice (+)—40%	Practice (+)—60%

C. Percentage of Activities Purposefully Integrating Development Areas:

Program I	Program II	Program III
Purposeful integration	Purposeful integration	Purposeful integration
(oo)—100%	(oo)—30%	(oo)—30%
Single area or inciden-	Single area or inciden-	Single area or inciden-
tal integration (o)—0%	tal integration	tal integration
	(o)—70%	(o)—70%

D. Percentage of Free Time vs. Facilitated Play:

Program I	Program II	Program III
Facilitated play	Facilitated play	Facilitated play
(**)—40%	(**)—10%	(**)—0%
Free time (*)—0%	Free time (*)—0%	Free time (*)—20%

Program III spends the greater portion of the day in directed skill practice, during which each child's individual targets are worked on. Functional application of skills take place in free time, snack time, and group games.

Integrated Time versus Segregated Time   Another indication of how a curriculum is being used is the amount of time spent in activities that focus on integrating areas of development (Table 2, section C). Many programs allot time to work on specific curriculum areas such as language or fine motor skills (as in Programs II and III, with 70% of nonintegrated activities). Such programs recognize that other areas of development may interact in accomplishing the activity, but the staff do not *purposefully* extend the activity to skills in other developmental areas. For example, in an activity designed to practice action verbs using objects that move, the teacher will focus simply on the child's producing the appropriate verb form and will move to the next child or next object when the correct answer is given. In a developmentally integrated program, the teacher might incorporate cognitive skills as well, by asking classification questions about what other object is the same shape, the same color, or has the same function. The teacher might also incorporate motor skills by having the child demonstrate use of the object in a variety of ways, or might provide the opportunity for social interaction by having two children use the object together.

Segregated activities have the advantage of being focused; consequently, it is easier to count correct responses to reach criteria on a specific skill. When working with a group of children, it is less taxing on the teacher to concentrate on objectives in one area of development only. Most activities that a child performs independently, however, incorporate a variety of skills. It is more functional for the child to also experience these interrelationships in school activities, as such interaction may facilitate transfer of learning to other situations.

The typical curriculum is divided into sections for each developmental area. This segregated approach has encouraged fragmented teaching of skills, and the viewing of children in parts rather than as a whole. As the team concept of working with handicapped children becomes more accepted, an increase in purposefully integrated program activities will likely result. Even for the severely or multiply impaired child who is practicing a specific skill, incorporation of other program areas can be accomplished. By working on a skill in a variety of ways, in multiple settings, and in combination with other skills, generalization is more likely to occur. Functional application of the skills also needs to be emphasized.

Integration of program areas, whether in skill practice activities or functional activities, requires familiarity with each child's total program plan, as well as sufficient preparation time to organize composite activities. Staff need time to plan as a *team* to determine time priorities for each content area, for skills practice, and for functional application and integration for each child. The amount of time each team member will allocate to individual and group time must be determined as well.

Free Time versus Facilitated Play   The importance of play to the normally developing child is now well accepted (Piaget, 1962, 1963, 1973). Social-emotional, language, motor, and cognitive development are all enhanced through play activities (Garvey, 1977; Weikart, Epstein, Schweinart, & Bond, 1978). The benefits of play to the handicapped child are also recognized (Devoney, Guralnick, & Rubin, 1974; Shores, Hester, & Struin, 1976). Play experiences for the handicapped child, however, may need a greater degree of guidance and facilitation, depending on the child's handicaps, degree of impairment, and developmental level. Programs vary in the amount of time they allow for play, as well as in the degree to which play is an actual part of the curriculum. Some programs will allow ''free time'' for children to do whatever they wish with the toys in the room (as in Program III). Others arrange specific areas with selected toys to encourage appropriate skill practice (Program I). In programs where play is an integral part of the curriculum, staff will facilitate appropriate interaction, exploration, manipulation, and language usage.

It is recommended that staff examine their use of ''free time'' to determine how play can become an intrinsic part of the curriculum, rather than a peripheral or enrichment part of the day.

Structure of the Environment   Regardless of the curriculum chosen, environment plays a key role. Curricula vary, however, in the way the environment is structured for the children. Some curricula provide environments and activities that facilitate interaction (toys, settings, and materials are made available to the child). The environment may even be intentionally arranged so as to promote a specific type of involvement. (For example, a play house may be set up with pots hanging in a sequence from large to small on matching shaded silhouettes. This arrangement encourages and facilitates practice with matching and size sequencing when the child hangs up the pots. The child chooses to play with the materials and is not necessarily corrected for not responding with the right sequence.) Or the environment may be structured in such a way that correct responses are virtually assured. (Montessori shape and size cylinders are examples of self-correcting materials; the pieces only fit properly in specific holes.)

The more structured the environment becomes, the more shaping of responses takes place. As the number of choices of stimuli the child is exposed to is reduced, the time allowed for stimulating a response becomes more definite, and the degree of specificity of response becomes more precise.

Role of the Staff   The role of the staff is directly related to the environment, as the staff are its organizers. Staff determine the choice of materials, the arrangement, the sequence and manner of presentation of materials, and the consequences for specific responses to the materials. The staff can play a facilitative role by providing opportunities for the child's interaction with the structured environment. They may also play a therapeutic or "training" role by structuring the environment to such a degree as to ensure a successful response, thus shaping desired behaviors. Of course, there are combinations of approaches, but curricula tend to promote a certain degree of environmental structuring throughout. Any curriculum can be modified as deemed necessary for a particular population or specific child; however, the role of the teacher in effectively structuring the environment is a key variable.

Role of the Child   The role of the child, as discussed in Chapter 3, depends to a great extent on the structure of the environment and the role of the staff. When staff see themselves as facilitators who structure experiences, then the child is given a more active role in his or her own learning. The child is free to select activities and skills and is afforded a broader range of acceptable responses within any one activity. When, on the other hand, staff view themselves as trainers of specific skills, the child has a less self-determining role. He or she then becomes a receptor of selective stimuli to ensure successful interaction at an appropriate level.

Role of the Parent   Depending on program philosophy, parents may be involved to varying degrees in their child's education. Because it is important to include parents as much as possible, the curriculum should be analyzed for adaptability by parents. Whether the parent's role is to be one of facilitator or trainer will determine the type of programs suggested for home. Activities should be amenable to home environments and not require specific equipment or skills, unless that equipment and skill training are provided to the parents (see Chapter 7).

Methodology

The curriculum methodology is closely intertwined with program structure. Elements of methodology that relate to curriculum implementation include: 1) source of activity initiation, 2) primary relationships, 3) motivational factors, 4) materials usage and sequence of presentation, 5) measurement of desired outcomes, and 6) behavior management. Analysis of each of these factors serves to further illustrate how curriculum utilization may vary.

Source of Activity Initiation Activities are either child-initiated or adult-initiated. As previously mentioned, the role of the child in the environmental structure can be active or more passive. Programs that allow children to choose activities and interactions will use teaching techniques different from those used in programs where the adult selects and initiates interactions. In child-initiated activities, the teacher may ask questions, focus attention on specific aspects of a problem or situation, make comparisons, or suggest solutions to problems. The parameters of the situation are broad, and the teacher can facilitate any number of interactions. Astute observational skills are necessary on the part of the teacher to discover opportunities for learning needed skills, and creativity is required to make the most of every event. Adult-initiated activities, in contrast, are more focused in their objectives, and the methods for achieving desired results are clearly outlined. Planned activities incorporate the teachers' selection of materials, methods, and outcomes.

Primary Relationships Child-initiated activities have as a philosophical justification the importance of developing independence, social interaction, and problem solving. Learning takes place through manipulation, experimentation, and imitation, with the primary relationships being child-environment interactions and child-child interactions to allow for maximum learning opportunities. Adult-initiated activities, on the other hand, place more importance on the relationship between teacher and child. Manipulation, experimentation, and imitation are still important, but environmental stimuli are selected and presented by the teacher. The adult, rather than peers, becomes the source of learning. Prompting, cueing, shaping, modeling, and scheduling of reinforcement are controlled by the teacher. The teacher in child-initiated activities may use some of these same techniques, but the approach is more informal and less structured.

Motivational Factors Internally and externally reinforcing factors are probably involved in every task. However, the degree to which a program adopts specific external reinforcement procedures to promote desired responses may differentiate one program from another. For example, two different programs may adopt the same goal from the same curriculum guide: ''The child recognizes and uses adjectives which describe properties that can be discriminated by touch'' (Coughran & Goff, 1976). In one program, this objective might be taught by arranging a tactilely stimulating environment and then observing the child in play and asking questions about the objects' characteristics: ''Is the block hard? Is it smooth?'' In the other program, the teacher may arrange a variety of objects with specific tactile characteristics and demonstrate these features by comparison and modeling: "Feel, these are smooth. These are rough." The response to "How does this one feel?" may be reinforced for accuracy. The question may be asked a set number of times in relation to various objects until the child has responded successfully enough times to meet criterion for that objective. In the first example, the involvement with the environment may provide the motivation for learning, while in the latter case, reinforcement from the teacher may provide the primary learning motivation.

Materials Usage The type and usage of materials is directly related to the above-mentioned elements. The kinds of materials employed in a program and the manner in which they are made available or presented to the child varies from program to program. Some programs have sets of materials for teaching specific objectives and other toys and materials for play experiences. Others use a variety of materials both for teaching and for play. It is recommended that for purposes of skill generalization, functionality, and the development of exploratory behaviors the following be considered:

1. Have a variety of toys and materials available for specific objectives.
2. Utilize materials also found in the home.
3. Utilize materials that can be applied in many different ways.
4. Utilize materials that are developmentally appropriate.
5. Encourage children to manipulate, explore, and use materials in non-conventional ways, without adult direction.

Measurement of Desired Outcomes The measurement of child progress is a requirement of all programs serving young handicapped children. As designated in PL 94-142, each child served must have written goals and objectives. The methods of documentation vary from program to program.

1. *Anecdotal records*, or brief narratives, may be kept on individual children in relation to specific objectives. Programs may also use this method of documentation as a supplement to other measurement techniques.
2. *Checklists*, or lists of objectives or skills, may be utilized in pre/post measurement at the beginning and end of the year or on an intermittent or continuous basis. The skills the child has accomplished are merely checked as "pass" or "fail." The spacing and range of developmental increments (small or large) and nature of the population served (severity) will determine how the checklists are used. For instance, a checklist that identifies only a few skills for each year may not provide small enough steps to enable teachers to select appropriate objectives for severely involved children. The teachers may need to provide supplementary substeps themselves. For example, in Figure 1, the child accomplished the task of naming three colors but was not able to name three shapes. For some children, the next task to be learned would therefore be the naming of shapes. For others, this task would be too high and a jump in the

Objective	Entry Behavior	Date Achieved
Names three colors on request	+	9/15/82
Names three shapes, ●, ■, and ▲	−	

Figure 1. The checklist as a measurement tool.

skill progression and would need to be broken down into more easily acquired steps.

3. *Probes* are devices used over a period of time to sample behaviors and assess change. White and Haring (1976) have identified certain elements of change that may be measured: *topography*, or behavior sequence; *force*, or magnitude of the behavior; *locus*, the direction or target or change; *duration*, or amount of time engaged in a behavior; *latency*, or the time between behaviors; and *frequency*, or rate of change. Probes can assess change in any of these factors by using 1) frequency of rate counts, 2) percentage statements, 3) ratio statements, or 4) criterion measures.

4. *Charting or graphing* the probes may be done on a regular basis to illustrate progress (see, for example, Figure 2). The frequency, percentage, or ratio may be stated on the vertical axis, and the probe period on the horizontal axis. Such graphs provide information on the rate, as well as the amount, of

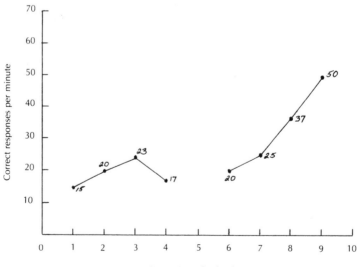

Figure 2. Graphing as a measurement tool.

growth. Behaviorally oriented programs tend to employ such measurement techniques.

5. *Criterion-referenced tests* may also be used as a probe to assess growth in relation to stated objectives (see Chapter 5). The rate of mastery can also be recorded, as in the example in Figure 3. Criterion-referenced tests can be used as ongoing or pre/post measures.

6. *Standardized testing* can also be used to measure growth from one time period to another (see Chapter 5). Normal testing is typically used along with other measures.

The type of curriculum a program uses and its philosophy in relation to structure and methodology will determine the type of measurement adopted. Measurement should be ongoing and capable of assessing the functionality of skills as well as the accomplishment of skills in specific situations.

Behavior Management Another aspect of methodology that varies across programs is behavior management. Depending on program philosophy, different techniques may be utilized. Hallahan and Kauffman (1978) have described the most common approaches:

Psychoanalytic approach—relies on psychotherapy for child and parents

Psychoeducational approach—emphasizes meeting individual needs of the child through educational and developmentally appropriate techniques

Humanistic approach—emphasizes a non-authoritarian, open, personal atmosphere

Ecological approach—involves all aspects of a child's life, including classroom, family, neighborhood, and community in teaching social skills.

Behavioral approach—involves measurement of responses and subsequent analysis of behaviors in order to change them. Emphasis is on reinforcement for appropriate behaviors.

As with other program aspects, behavior management techniques need to be consistent with program structure and methodology. Program staff should determine what approach is most appropriate for the population being served.

RECOMMENDATIONS

Program staff need to plan carefully not only what curricula will be adopted but how the curricula will be used. The following are additional questions for staff consideration in selecting curriculum materials.

Objective	Criterion	Begin	Accomplished
Names each of four objects—cup, ball, baby, shoe—when presented with real object	3 of 4	9/10/82	9/10/82

Figure 3.   The criterion-referenced instrument as a measurement tool.

1. For which development levels are the programs appropriate? Curricula should be broad enough in range to meet the needs of both the lowest functioning and highest functioning child in the population to be served. More than one curriculum may be necessary.

2. What skills does the program teach? Skills addressed in the curriculum should reflect needs identified in the assessment process.

3. Are the scope and sequence appropriate to the population? For severely impaired populations, specific content areas might need to include specific developmental sequences in feeding, dressing, toileting, and the like. Developmental progressions may need to be highly discrete. For higher functioning populations, broad curriculum areas that contain sequences in language, cognition, gross motor, fine motor, and social-emotional development may be adequate. The type of sequence is important as well. Task analyses provided in some curricula are not developmentally sequenced. For instance, a motor task analysis with the terminal objective "Child can stand on one foot for 10 seconds" may include the following steps:

   Stands on one foot for 1 second.
   Stands on one foot for 2 seconds.
   Stands on one foot for 3 seconds.
   Stands on one foot for 4 seconds.
   etc...

   This task analysis does not take into account developmental prequisites and sequences. A more developmentally oriented sequence might include:

   Balance in sitting
   Balance in standing
   Moves from standing to sitting without falling
   Stoops to retrieve objects from standing position
   Walks steadily
   Walks up and down stairs with assistance
   Walks up and down stairs without assistance

   Opportunities to demonstrate reflexive integration and appropriate body reactions, such as protective and righting reactions would be important.

4. How are the activities written? Many curricula are geared to specific disciplines and assume an understanding of terminology and "jargon" that may be meaningless to parents or laypersons involved in the program. The degree of specificity used to describe activities may also be important. Greater detail may be needed by parents, laypersons, or those from disciplines unfamiliar with certain techniques or methods.

5. For what types of handicapping conditions is this curriculum appropriate or inappropriate? An activity usually requires *input* on the part of the child and/or the teacher and *output* of some sort on the part of the child. Following are some aspects to consider: If visual, tactile, and auditory channels are heavily emphasized in a curriculum, the visually impaired, motorically involved, or hearing impaired child may be unable to receive information adequately.

Similarly, if specific verbal or motoric responses are demanded in an activity, the child who is handicapped in these areas may experience frustration. If activities are primarily geared to individual or group discovery approaches, the severely impaired child may end up watching other children or engaging in nonproductive or destructive activities. If activities require a high degree of didactic instruction, children must be cognitively able to understand the material and the style of presentation. Behavioral techniques, verbal instructions, and shaping and chaining procedures may be unduly limiting and educationally restrictive for a high level child. Precision teaching activities require a small staff-child ratio in order to accurately record a child's progress.

6. What teaching techniques are promoted? Staff will need specific skills, depending on the orientation of the curriculum and how detailed the instructions are. A cognitively oriented program will operate best when staff are capable facilitators of exploration and are able to ask questions to stimulate problem solving and language production. Behaviorally oriented programs, on the other hand, will need staff with skills in cueing, shaping, reinforcing, and other behavioral skills.

7. What amount of time each day is required for use of the curriculum? Many guides cover all areas of development and are sufficiently comprehensive for a full day's program. Others emphasize one area of development, or are inadequate for total program planning. Staff may need to utilize more than one curriculum to ensure a full day's activities.

8. Is the curriculum consistent with the philosophy of staff who will use it? Once again, it is important to examine the philosophical basis of the curriculum to ensure congruity with staff beliefs. Curricula may be modified and adopted, but staff need to discuss the changes that will be needed in content, methodology, and structure.

The Curriculum Evaluation Checklist provided on page 152 may be used to evaluate curricular materials currently being used or being considered for adoption. Systematic analysis of curricula may enable staff to select a variety of curricula that will be consistent with program goals and will meet diverse individual and group needs. Careful consideration of a range of materials will result in a more comprehensive and individualized program.

REFERENCES

Ainsworth, M.D.S. The development of infant-mother attachment. In: B.M. Caldwell & H.N. Ricciuti (eds.), *Review of child development research*, Vol. 3. Chicago: University of Chicago Press, 1973.

Bates, E. *Language in context*. New York: Academic Press, 1976.

Bloom, L. The accountability of evidence in studies of child language. Comment on everyday preschool interpersonal speech usage: Methodological, developmental, and sociolinguistic studies. In: F. Schacter, K. Kirshner, B. Klips, I.N. Friedricks, & K.

Sanders (eds.), *Monographs of the Society for Research in Child Development*, 1974, *39*(156).

Bobath, K. *Motor deficit in patients with cerebral palsy*. Lavenham, Suffolk, England: The Lavenham Press, 1974.

Bowlby, J. *Attachment and loss, Vol. 1: Attachment*. New York: Basic Books, 1969.

Bowlby, J. *Attachment and loss, Vol. 2: Separation: Anxiety and anger*. New York: Basic Books, 1973.

Brackbill, Y. Continuous stimulation and arousal level in infants: Additives effects. *Child Development*, 1971, *42*(1), 17–26.

Brazelton, T.B., Koslowski, B., & Main, M. The origins of reciprocity: The early mother-infant interaction. In: M. Lewis & L. Rosenblum (eds.), *The origins of behavior*. New York: John Wiley & Sons, 1974.

Bridger, W.H. Sensory habituation and discrimination in the neonate. *American Journal of Psychiatry*, 1961, *117*, 991–996.

Bruner, J. Poverty in childhood. In: R. Parker (ed.), *The preschool in action*. Boston: Allyn and Bacon, 1977.

Bruner, J.S., Olver, R.R., & Greenfield, P. *Studies in cognitive growth*. New York: John Wiley & Sons, 1966.

Campos, J.J., Langer, A., & Krowitz, A. Cardiac responses on the visual cliff in prelocator infants. *Science*, 1970, *170*, 196–197.

Cicchetti, D., & Sroufe, L.H. *The relationship between affective and cognitive development in Down's syndrome infants*. Paper presented at the biennial meetings of the Society for Research in Child Development, Denver, 1975.

Cohen, M., & Gross, P. *The developmental resource: Behavioral sequences for assessment and program planning* (2 vols.). New York: Grune & Stratton, 1979.

Connor, F.P., Williamson, G., & Siepp, J. *Program guide for infants and toddlers with neuromotor and other disabilities*. New York: Teacher's College Press, 1978.

Coughran, L., & Goff, M. *Learning staircase*. Boston: Teaching Resources Corporation, 1976.

Devoney, C., Guralnick, N.J., & Rubin, H. Integrating handicapped and nonhandicapped preschool children: Effects on social play. *Childhood Education*, 1974, *50*(6), 360–364.

Emde, R.N., Gaensbauer, T.J., & Harmon, R.S. *Emotional expression in infancy: a biobehavioral study*. New York: International Universities Press, 1976.

Engen, T., & Lipsitt, L.P. Decrement and recovery of responses to olfactory stimuli in the human neonate. *Journal of Comparative and Physiological Psychology*, 1965, *59*, 312–316.

Fantz, R.L., & Yeh, J. Configural selectives: Critical development of visual perception and attention. *Canadian Journal of Psychology*, 1979, *33*(4), 277–287.

Foley, G. *Attachment, separation, and individuation: The development bottom line*. Paper presented at the University of Denver, May 9, 1980.

Furth, H., & Wachs, H. *Piaget's thinking in practice: Thinking goes to school*. New York: Oxford University Press, 1975.

Garvey, O. *Play*. Cambridge, MA: Harvard University Press, 1977.

Guralnick, M.J. (ed.). *Early intervention and the integration of handicapped and nonhandicapped children*. Baltimore: University Park Press, 1978.

Haith, M.M. Visual competence in early infancy. In: R. Held, H. Leibowitz, & H.L. Teuber (eds.), *Handbook of sensory physiology*, Vol. VIII. Berlin: Springer-Verlag, 1980.

Hallahan, D.P., & Kauffman, J.M. *Exceptional children: Introduction to special education*. Englewood Cliffs, N.J.: Prentice-Hall, 1978.

Kessen, W. Sucking and looking: Two organized congenital patterns of behavior in the newborn. In: M. Klaus & J. Kennel (eds.), *Maternal-infant bonding*. St. Louis: C.V. Mosby Co., 1976.

Klaus, M., & Kennel, J. (eds.). *Maternal-infant bonding*. St. Louis: C.V. Mosby Company, 1976.

Korner, A., & Thoman, E.B. The relative efficacy of contact and vestibular-proprioceptive stimulation in soothing neonates. *Child Development*, 1972, *43*, 443–453.

Lillie, D.L. *Early childhood curriculum: An individual approach*. Chicago: Science Research Associates, 1975.

Linder, T. Pleasurable play: Its value to handicapped children and their parents. *Journal of the Colorado Speech-Language-Hearing Association*, 1982, *17*(1), 5–10.

Mahler, M. *The psychological birth of an infant*. New York: Basic Books, 1975.

Nowlis, G.H., & Keesen, W. Human newborns differentiate differing concentrations of sucrose and glucose. *Science*, 1976, *191*, 865–66.

Parten, M.L. Social participation among preschool children. *Journal of Abnormal Social Psychology*, 1932, *27*, 243–269.

Piaget, J. *The origins of intelligence in children*. New York: International Universities Press, 1952. New York: W.W. Norton & Co., 1963.

Piaget, J. The stages of intellectual development of the child. *Bulletin of the Menninger Clinic*, 1962, *26*(3), 120–145.

Piaget, J. *The child and reality*. New York: Penguin Books, 1973.

Pick, H.L., & Pick, A.D. Sensory and perceptual development. In: P.H. Mussen (ed.), *Carmichael's Manual of Child Psychology*. New York: John Wiley & Sons, 1970.

Shores, R., Hester, P., & Struin, P. The effects of amount and type of teacher-child interaction on child-child interaction during free play. *Psychology in the schools*, 1976, *13*(2), 169–175.

Van Etten, G., Arkell, C., & Van Etten, C. *The severely and profoundly handicapped. Programs, methods and materials*. St. Louis: C.V. Mosby Co., 1980.

Weikart, D.P., Epstein, A.S., Schweinart, L., & Bond, J.T. *The Ypsilanti preschool curriculum demonstration project. Preschool years and longitudinal results*. Ypsilanti, MI: High/Scope Educational Research Foundation, 1978.

White, O.R., and Haring, N.G. *Exceptional teaching*. Columbus, OH: Charles E. Merrill Publishing Co., 1976.

Curriculum Evaluation Checklist

____ The philosophical/theoretical approach is explained and justified for both content and methods.
____ The subcomponents are clearly identified.
____ The curriculum has a logical sequence.
____ The scope and sequence is appropriate to the population to be served.
____ How the curriculum is to be utilized is clear.
____ The skill level required of the person directing activities is addressed.
____ The structure is well conceived:
    ____ Time and space allocated to subareas are appropriate.
    ____ Time spent in functional versus structured practice activities is balanced.
    ____ Attempt is made to integrate other curricular areas (intra- or inter-).
    ____ The description of the necessary environment is clear.
    ____ The role of the staff is clear.
    ____ The role of the client is clear.
    ____ The role of the parents is clear.
____ The methodology is well defined:
    ____ Source of activity initiation is clear.
    ____ Roles are clearly defined.
    ____ Motivational factors are identified.
    ____ Type and usage of materials are adequately addressed.
        ____ Materials are chronologically appropriate.
        ____ Materials are developmentally appropriate.
        ____ The characteristics (color, size, concrete, interactive) of materials are appropriate.
        ____ Common as well as specialized materials are identified.
        ____ Independent problem solving is encouraged.
____ Means are provided for measurement of desired outcomes:
    ____ Anecdotal records.
    ____ Checklists.
    ____ Probes.
    ____ Charting or graphing.
    ____ Criterion referenced.
    ____ Standardized testing.
____ The assessment process reflects the skills addressed in the curriculum.
____ The activities use language appropriate to the persons who will use the curriculum.
____ The degree of specificity used to describe each activity is appropriate for the persons who will use the curriculum
____ The activities are appropriate for the population to be served:
    ____ Input required is appropriate.
    ____ Output or responses required are appropriate.
    ____ Individual or group activities are appropriate.
    ____ Activities reflect realistic consideration of staffing patterns.
    ____ The amount of time required for activities and/or units is clearly delineated and reflects consideration of the population.
    ____ The curriculum designates how to modify or individualize activities so as to adapt to different disabilities or developmental levels.
____ Regional, language, or other biases are taken into consideration.
____ Follow-up activities are provided.

chapter

7

Parent Involvement

A mother accompanies her son to his preschool class, then stays for a while to play with a group of children in the corner. A father brings his handicapped infant daughter to class on Saturday and proudly announces to the other parents that the child is now able to sit with just a little support. The sister of a handicapped child welcomes a developmental specialist into their home and helps her unload her toys and equipment, talking all the while of the skills her brother has practiced in the past week. A group of parents sit sipping coffee and watching a videotape of a cerebral palsied child in therapy. Afterwards the parents discuss the tape, their experiences with their own children, and their feelings about having a handicapped child.

These scenes are examples of the many ways in which parents are becoming increasingly involved with their handicapped child's program. In recent years there has been a growing emphasis on parental participation in the educational process (Fredericks, Baldwin, & Grove, 1975; Hofmeister & Reavis, 1974; Lillie & Trohanis, 1976; Quick, Little, & Campbell, 1973; Shearer & Shearer, 1972). This emphasis has occurred not only as a result of the requirements of funding sources, such as those of the federal government, but also as a consequence of research that shows the educational importance of parent participation. Bron-fenbrenner (1975) noted that evidence indicates that the family is both the most effective and economical "system" for fostering the development of the child. His review of early intervention studies found that the active involvement of the child's family was a critical factor in the success of the program. Without the parents' involvement, the positive effects of early intervention, at least in relation to cognitive achievement, seemed to decline once the program ended. Parents who regularly participated in their child's education, however, were able to conduct follow-through efforts at home, thus helping to sustain the effects of the program even after it ended.

RATIONALE

Parent involvement in its broadest context implies *shared responsibility* for the child's educational process. It also implies that as a member of a dynamic family unit, the handicapped child has as great an impact on the family as the family has on the handicapped child; it is a reciprocal relationship. The family is a critical factor in the child's environment, and thus, parent involvement implies an ecological approach to handicapped children. Morrison (1978) has defined parent involvement as the "process of actualizing the potential of parents; of helping parents discover their strengths, potentialities, and talents; and of using them for the benefit of themselves and the family" (p. 22).

The inclusion of the parent in the education process offers a new orientation to many children and families. The reasons for a parent component in early childhood programs are numerous, and there is abundant research to support the efficacy of parental participation. Among the benefits cited as resulting from active involvement of parents in early intervention programs for young handicapped children are the following:

1. The child's home environment can become more facilitative of learning. A child's first eight years have been documented as the period of most rapid intellectual growth (Bloom, 1964; Hunt, 1961). Because the parents are the child's primary teachers during this crucial period, early intervention programs can help parents work to create an optimal learning environment in the home.

2. Parents are given extra support and encouragement in coping effectively with the problems of having a handicapped child (Roos, 1978). Having a handicapped child can make the difficult job of parenting even more demanding. Parental reactions to having a handicapped child may also compound the situation by making the parents emotionally unavailable to the child. Roos, as both a professional (1963) and a parent (1978), has described these reactions as including: loss of self-esteem; shame over social rejection; ambivalence between love and anger for the child; depression, grief, chronic sorrow; self-sacrifice; defensiveness; disillusionment with being a parent; feeling of isolation; feeling of vulnerability or loss of control; feeling of inequity; feeling of insignificance; and withdrawal from planning for the future. Programs that offer support and encouragement to parents through counseling and parent groups have been shown to result in the parents attaining greater self-confidence and the ability to solve problems relating to their own personal growth and that of their handicapped child (Arnold, Rowe, & Tolbert, 1978; Johnson, 1979).

3. Parent involvement in the child's educational program enables greater continuity and coordination of learning between school and home. Objectives for the child that are developed as the result of parent-teacher exchanges, and that take

into account the parents' desires for the child at home, will be more effective than those developed without parental interaction. Furthermore, the skills that a child learns at school will be acquired faster and become more functional if they are also practiced at home. By involving parents in planning, implementing, and evaluating their child's program, parents gain a functional grasp of child development, an ability to work on specific skills, and the capacity to better judge appropriate activities for their child.

4. Parent education can provide parents with information that will allow them to improve their interactions with their handicapped child. Recent Gallup poll (1976) surveys have shown that a majority of parents in the general population feel they could benefit from parent education; this need is often magnified for parents of handicapped children. By providing information on a variety of topics of concern (for example, intervention techniques, behavior management, normal child development, medical aspects of handicapping conditions), parent education can be individualized to meet specific needs of families.

5. Parent involvement can help parents become aware of and learn to use existing community resources. Service delivery systems for handicapped children are often fragmented and confusing. For a parent, the "system" can be overwhelming and even contradictory (Selig, 1976). The agency providing services to young handicapped children can also serve as case manager for services to families involved in the program. Parental monitoring of service delivery is important, not only to ensure that the needs of the child and the family are met, but also to guarantee that service is consistent.

6. Parent involvement in planning and decision making ensures that needs are addressed at all levels of the program. When parents, for example, help to plan their child's individualized education program, they are more likely to comply with requests from the staff in regard to it. Parents, too, have the best insights into the needs of other parents. Thus, in numerous areas, whether it be deciding the content of the program newsletter, choosing speakers for a class, or preparing guidelines for classroom participation, parent involvement tends to make the program more meaningful to all parents. Parent participation in decision-making processes is essential to active, ongoing interest in the program (Powell, 1979).

7. Parent involvement can also be economically beneficial. By utilizing parent volunteers, program costs can be reduced (Stile, Cole, & Garner, 1978). The closer the ratio of adults to children, the more individualized the program can be. Parent involvement can thus provide needed human resources to expand the quantity and quality of services offered.

8. Parent involvement builds community support for early intervention programs. Parents who have observed their children's program and have worked closely with staff to provide follow-through at home gain a broader understanding of the goals and objectives of the total program and what it takes to accomplish them. Similarly, parents who have been helped to cope with the stresses of having a handicapped child can better appreciate the support systems that early inter-

vention programs provide. In addition, parents who have acquired better parenting skills and improved their interactions with their handicapped child and other children in the family have a keener understanding of the benefits the program offers to families as a unit. Parents who have thus benefited from the program often become vigorous proponents for program continuation and the development of other needed services. As consumers, parents will demand accountability for their tax dollars. Parents as program advocates and liaisons to other organizations and groups are therefore vitally important.

THE FAMILY AS A SYSTEM

In order to be most effective in working with handicapped children, staff must consider the needs of the family as a system. As with any system, many interrelated factors are involved. "Each family must be recognized as a unique system, with individual differences in its patterns of interaction, assignment of roles, developmental aspects, cultural orientation, environmental conditions, emotional climate and satisfaction of needs" (Klein, Bowser, Kater, & Waltraud, 1978, p. 33).

Families vary in the manner in which members interact. Some families are close, with strong mutual support systems within the nuclear family. Other families rely on extended family or outside support systems such as neighbors or friends. Communication within the family may range from open, direct, and honest to closed, self-concealing, or deceptive. Staff need to assess the patterns, levels, and types of interactions to ascertain how best to communicate with all family members.

The assignment of roles within the family system is also important. Roles within the home environment concerning housekeeping duties, parenting responsibilities, discipline, child care, and so on, reveal ongoing burdens and stresses as well as authority lines. The additional needs of a handicapped child may throw the traditional family equilibrium off balance. Individual family roles may need to be modified to take into consideration the additional responsibilities of a handicapped child.

Families also vary in their stage of family development. Barnard and Erickson (1976) state that role changes occur at different stages, depending often upon the growth and development of children. The family with no children, for example, functions differently than one with an infant. And the family with elementary school children assumes different roles than the family with children in college. Handicapped children, however, may not move through the normal patterns, and consequently, parents may get "stuck" in a developmental family level that is characterized by dependency. Families may therefore need assistance in moving to the next stage of family development.

Brown (1978) has described different developmental phases in family life:

1. *Establishing basic commitment.* Both partners disestablish from their families of origin and establish a commitment to each other.
2. *Creating a system for mutual nurturance.* Family structures are established for mutual support. Reciprocal nuturance is key.
3. *Defining mechanisms for mutual encouragement of individuation and autonomy.* Members of the family encourage individual initiative and exploration of personal goals.
4. *Facilitating ego mastery.* Family members establish positive identity in the various family roles.

The presence of a handicapped child may cause difficulty with mastery of tasks in each of these phases. Regression to earlier phases may occur. For example, a handicapped child may interfere with positive self-concept, may disrupt the existing support system, and may, in fact, threaten a couple's basic commitment to each other. Staff may be able to help families work through these difficulties.

In relation to these developmental phases, the emotional climate and satisfactions of needs are also important influences on the family system. Maslow's well-known hierarchy of needs (1954) is relevant here.

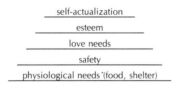

Individual family members may be at differing levels of satisfying their needs. A family at the level of needing to ensure continuing food and shelter may not see the provision of love and attention to a handicapped child as a priority. The presence of the handicapped child may also magnify an existing need. For example, a mother with a need to establish self-esteem in her career role may have an additional need for self-esteem as a ''good'' parent to her handicapped child.

Cultural orientations, too, influence attitudes toward handicapping conditions, as do religious beliefs. These divergent values should be recognized as affecting the family's ability to cope with the stresses associated with having a handicapped child.

The family as a system also must relate to a variety of other complex systems, including the neighborhood, community, society, the economy, and the school system. Arnold (1978) has pointed out that

input from any of these other systems or intervention within the parent-child system by doing or saying something to parents tends to have far-reaching reverberations throughout the parent-child system and other affiliated systems. Systems guidance makes use of this understanding by choosing points of intervention that are most likely to initiate constructive reverberation and by keeping in mind the likelihood of other components affecting the component being considered (p. 55).

The Effect of a Handicapped Child on the Family System

A handicapped child's effect on a family is significant. Exactly how the family is affected will depend on many variables, including the nature and severity of the handicap, the emotional climate within the family, the resources the family has to help cope with the problem, how the family defines the problems related to the child, and the family's values.

Research has revealed that many parents undergo similar feelings when they discover that they have a handicapped child. Rosen (1955) has described general stages that many such parents experience: first, the awareness that a serious problem exists; second, the recognition of what the problem means; third, a search for the cause of the problem; and fourth, a search for the solution.

Parents of handicapped children have stated that they have passed through stages of grief similar to the stages of mourning, identified by Kubler-Ross (1969), that are associated with one's own dying or the death of a loved one. These parents are mourning the "loss" of the expected normal child and the birth of a handicapped child.

Stage 1: Denial and Isolation   During Stage 1, disbelief predominates, and there is a refusal to accept the diagnosis. The parent may withdraw from friends and family and refuse to engage in social events. At this time, parents are often engulfed with feelings of guilt for the child's handicap. Mothers in particular worry that they did not take proper care of themselves during pregnancy. Others feel the child is punishment for previous sins. Both parents may search their family histories for evidence of similar problems that might show genetic causality.

There is also a sense of shame about the child. How will the relatives react? Other siblings? The neighbors? The self-imposed isolation of the parents is partially a withdrawal from the questions about the child that will inevitably arise. Our children are an extension of ourselves, and the birth of a handicapped child often makes parents feel that they have failed or that they are in some way inadequate or less than perfect themselves. Parents dream and plan for nine months (or longer) about the child—who it will look like, its sex, its characteristics, what it will be when it grows up. The birth of a handicapped child is the death of the hoped-for perfect child. It is natural that this loss should be mourned.

Fear is also experienced at this first stage. As the parents consider the future, questions about the meaning of the handicap loom large. What does this mean to me and my other chidren? Will there be large medical bills? Will the child be able to do the things other children do? Will he or she be able to go to college? What will happen to the child if something happens to me?

Guilt, shame, fear are all natural feelings, and the period of denial and isolation allows parents time to think and mobilize other defenses. During this time, they need support and the assurance that the feelings they are experiencing are not abnormal. Often talking to parents of similarly handicapped children is helpful, as other parents can identify with the pain and sorrow that the parents are feeling.

Stage 2: Anger   It is also not uncommon for parents to feel anger. Anger is often paired with a sense of injustice. The parents may lash out at many different targets, such as God, the doctors, or nurses. They may, for example, fault the doctor for the prenatal care or the delivery procedures, or for not telling them about the handicap in a sensitive manner. Anger may also be more indirect. A parent may begin to yell at other children in the family or the spouse for insignificant reasons. Or anger may be turned inward and the parent may experience feelings of self-hatred. Professionals working with parents need to recognize this anger as a natural feeling and not take it personally. Listening to the parent and allowing time for emotional release is important.

Stage 3: Bargaining   Bargaining often takes place with God. A promise is made that if the child gets better the parents will do things differently. Parents may expend all their energy working with the child, sacrificing their own goals in an attempt to make the child "better." It is as if they would trade their own growth and development for that of the child's. Such self-sacrifice may also reflect a subconscious wish on the part of the parents for punishment. Professionals working with parents at this stage need to help them focus on their own needs (not to mention those of other family members, such as other children), in addition to the needs of the handicapped child.

Stage 4: Depression   As the implications of the child's handicap begin to "sink in," it is natural for the parent to become greatly depressed. Often parents have conflicting feelings of love and hatred for the child. They may even wish the child were dead—and then feel guilty for thinking that. These periods of depression may come and go, but seem to intensify after experiencing or observing joyful moments for others. For example, depression may occur when a parent observes the neighborhood children happily racing off for the first day of school; or when the parent attends a friend's child's graduation or wedding. Such events serve as reminders of the discrepancies between what normal children have and what the future holds for their child. All parents want to feel pride in their child's accomplishments and share moments of happiness. For the parents of the handicapped child, these moments may be few and far between. Olshansky (1962) has described this recurring depression and sadness as "chronic sorrow," and states that this sorrow is present throughout the child's life. Professionals need to understand these periods of depression, as well as the chronic sorrow, and do their best to help parents share joyful moments with their child as well as help them recognize their child's strengths and accomplishments.

Stage 5: Acceptance   It is questionable whether any parent of a handicapped child every totally "accepts" his or her child's handicap (or whether he or she even should). However, parents can work through their feelings and come to a level of understanding of the child's abilities and limitations. They can develop realistic expectations for the future, and they can learn how to cope with each new problem systematically. Professionals should not expect, however, that parents will be reconciled to the point of always being positive. Depression, anger, guilt, shame, uncertainty, and sorrow may recur, and parents must learn how to deal with these feelings. The professional needs to be there to support, to encourage, and to provide direction and hope. It is an important role that demands much skill and perserverance.

Pearl Buck, in *The Child Who Never Grew* (1959) poignantly describes her sorrow over her handicapped daughter:

> To learn how to bear the inevitable sorrow is not easily done. I can look back on it now, the lesson learned, and see the steps; but when I was taking them they were hard indeed, each apparently insurmountable. For in addition to the practical problem of how to protect the child's life, which may last beyond the parent's, there is the problem of one's own self in misery. All the brightness of life is gone, the pride in parenthood. There is more than pride gone, there is an actual sense of one's life being cut off in the child. The stream of the generation is stopped. Death would be far easier to bear, for death is final. What was is no more. How often did I cry out in my heart that it would be better if my child died! If that shocks you who have not known, it will not shock those of you who do know. I would have welcomed death for my child and would still welcome it, for then she would be finally safe (p. 27).

Considerations in Working with Family Systems

Johnson (1979) recommends a family-centered approach in working with handicapped children. "Family-systems theory views the family as an interacting, reacting system which is delicately balanced and struggles to maintain that balance. A change or problem in one member of the system, thus, affects the entire system" (pp. 285–286). As previously discussed, the addition of a handicapped child to the family has a significant impact on the entire family. Professionals working with young handicapped children can provide better services to the child and the family by taking into consideration the following basic guidelines.

1. Communication with family members is facilitated when they feel valued and accepted. Professionals need to listen and not judge, be able to assure parents their feelings are normal, and be able to tolerate not being heard when they offer suggestions (Cansler, Martin, & Valand, 1975; Johnson, 1979).
2. Professionals need to be aware of societal expectations and pressures on parents to raise their handicapped child to conform to cultural patterns, to speak and to behave appropriately.
3. Parents who fail to discharge their cultural obligations are labeled as overprotective, rejecting, disinterested, apathetic, or guilt-ridden. These value judgments affect parents. Professionals should avoid unwarranted "diagnosing" of parents.
4. Professionals need to be aware of the conflicting opinions and advice with which parents must deal regarding their child. They must be able to help parents objectively evaluate information from varying systems.
5. Parents view their child differently than professionals. Whereas professionals operate from a background of general knowledge, parents have

specific knowledge about *their* child. Professionals need to utilize the parents' specific information and not overgeneralize.

6. Professionals need to be sensitive to the fact that parents' emotions and responses regarding their handicapped child may fluctuate. The ability to listen to, empathize with, and individualize for each family member is needed.

7. Parents need time to digest the significance of information presented them by professionals. They may need assistance in understanding the relevance of the information to their family system.

8. Siblings in the family tend to imitate the parents' (particularly the mother's) attitudes toward the handicapped child's role in the family (Banish, 1961). Professionals can influence children's attitudes by assisting the family in developing problem-solving skills relating to the child in the family system.

9. Professionals can help families by working to educate members of the extended family and immediate community about handicapping conditions.

10. Families need to be involved in assessing their strengths, setting goals, determining intervention methods, and evaluating success.

11. All parents need to experience a sense of adequacy in parenting. Professionals need to offer concrete suggestions and praise to help parents feel successful with their child.

Purposes of the Parent Component

In order to ensure individualization, the parent component needs to be carefully planned prior to intake of children. Because of parents' special perspective, their inclusion in the planning process is critical. As the program becomes operational, parents with children in the program can become involved in ongoing planning.

The purposes of parent involvement need to be identified. Although each early intervention program will have different expectations for its parent components, similarities among programs usually exist. Many early childhood special education programs have four dimensions to their parent involvement component (Amon, 1978; Lillie & Trohanis, 1976; Tidball-Strickler, 1975). Cansler et al. (1975) add a fifth. These five areas include 1) emotional support, 2) information exchange, 3) improving parent-child interaction, 4) parent participation, and 5) utilizing resources (see Table 1).

Steps in Establishing the Parent Program

In order to accomplish the intentions outlined in Table 1, it is necessary to follow the same process as in planning the total program. An important first step is to employ staff who support working with families. If staff feel threatened by parents and are not commited to working closely with them, parent involvement efforts are doomed. It is wise for the administrator to assess attitudes toward parents before hiring prospective staff.

Consider staff responses to such interview questions as:

Table 1.   Subcomponents and goals of a parent component

1. **Providing emotional support to parents**
   a.   Helping parents accept what it means to have a handicapped child
   b.   Helping parents reduce their anxieties caused by guilt and feelings of inadequacy in the family
   c.   Helping parents develop realistic expectations about their child
   d.   Providing stimulating activities to increase parents' feelings of self-worth

2. **Exchanging information**
   a.   Providing parents with an understanding of the rationale, objectives, and activities of the program in which their child is enrolled
   b.   Helping parents understand child growth and development and the impact of their child's handicap
   c.   Helping parents understand child behavior in the home
   d.   Maintaining consistency and reinforcement of training or educational concepts

3. **Improving parent-child interaction**
   a.   Providing information to parents on topics that will improve their knowledge of intervention and interaction strategies
   b.   Providing opportunities for parents to develop skills in childbearing practices
   c.   Providing opportunities for parents to develop skills in fostering growth and development of the child

4. **Increasing parent participation**
   a.   Involving parents in the ongoing activities of the program
   b.   Giving parents an opportunity to express their needs and to develop programming around them

5. **Facilitating the use of community resources**
   a.   Assisting parents in referral to and coordination of educational, medical, financial services
   b.   Increasing parents' knowledge of community resources

Do you see the family as a focus of the program?
How do you see the parents functioning with the training team?
What alternatives do you feel must be made available to families?
How do you react to families whose value systems are different from yours?
How will you react to families who do not want to be involved at the level at which you would like to see them involved?
How do you feel about parents gaining skills in teaching their child effectively? (adapted from Cansler et al., 1975).

Staff who are committed to parent involvement can work with parents to assess needs, to plan, implement, and evaluate the parent involvement component of the program. In Chapter 3, several goals, objectives, and activities were suggested for the parent component. These may, of course, be altered or expanded to meet the needs of a specific target population, including needs associated with: varying socioeconomic status; minority and ethnic populations; urban populations; rural populations; "exceptional" parents (for example, mentally retarded, deaf); single parents; working mothers; working fathers; and very young mothers.

Consideration of the nature and needs of the parents being served is important to ensure the development of appropriate objectives and viable activities. The needs assessment should be ongoing, with new information compiled with each new family and reevaluated as appropriate.

Meeting the Needs of Families

A family's needs come to the attention of educators as a result of the needs of the handicapped child. The child is referred to the school for further assessment, an evaluation is completed, and the child's needs are identified (see Chapter 5). In the course of this evaluation, staff must interview parents and obtain information about the child's developmental history, family situation, and parental concerns. From these interviews, staff may form some idea of family needs; in fact, some provisions for services to families may be designated in the staffing.

After the child has been evaluated and the IEP determined, it is important for the staff to work closely with the child's family to implement the child's program. At this time, it is important that further family assessment be done to clarify family strengths and needs. Klein et al. (1978) suggest that family needs be explored in an informal discussion rather than in a question-and-answer format. The parent/ family worker or designated staff member should make an effort to visit with both parents in their home. Barnard and Erickson (1976) and Bradley and Caldwell (1979) also recommend observations of the home environment to judge the level of home stimulation. Identification of the professional's role and establishment of rapport is an important beginning. General issues about which parents may have concerns can then be discussed.

1. *Parenting issues*—problem behaviors of children (i.e., discipline); understanding their handicapped child's individual developmental stages; stressful times for the family; concerns about the family's teaching roles; provisions for play activities; parental expectations of the child's performance

2. *Family maintenance*—special survival needs (food, clothing); health and safety concerns; distribution of roles and responsibilities; satisfaction with roles and responsibilities

3. *Communication*—communication patterns among family members; support systems within the family; handling stress and conflicts; meeting special needs of family members

4. *Leisure time*—things the family enjoys doing together; special interests or hobbies of family members; private time for parents; social outlets outside the family (adapted from Klein et al., 1978, p. 37).

Informal discussion allows staff to identify areas of parental concern, patterns of family interaction, and family value systems. It is important to look at how the family is already dealing with their problems, rather than automatically imposing on the family an external process; family strengths should be used to advantage. A more formal questionnaire or written needs-assessment may be done after the informal discussion. As comprehensive an approach as possible to family needs should be taken; even if the agency cannot meet all identified needs, other resources can be coordinated to assist the family.

After gathering information, the staff member should summarize the family's concerns and record the needs and strengths. The home visitor can later help the family place the needs in order of priority and develop two or three realistic, long-term (annual) goals. The home visitor then takes these goals back to the team to determine specific objectives that will aid families in accomplishing their goals. Alternative activities for each objective can then be listed. For example, a family may identify as one of its priorities the improvement of their skills in working with their handicapped child. The team might list the following short-term objectives for the family under this goal:

1. To teach the parents five techniques for encouraging Mary's language.
2. To teach the siblings six toys they can use with Mary.
3. To reduce the time it takes mother to feed Mary to 30 minutes.

Alternative means for accomplishing objective number 1 might be: to have family members observe the speech and language therapist working with Mary; to have the home visitor make weekly visits to observe the family working with Mary; to have family members use videotapes of language techniques; or to provide the family with materials, books, and articles of language techniques appropriate for Mary.

Alternatives should be selected or developed for each of the identified objectives. As the program develops, the team can add to the list of objectives and alternative activities, which serve, in essence, as a curriculum guide for parent involvement. As with curricula designed for working with children, goals, objectives, and activities for parents should be organized into logical areas that may serve as a guide and resource for future work with other families. These curricular areas may parallel the children's curricular areas (for example, cognitive, language), or may represent areas of need common to parents (for example, obtaining support, information). In seeking appropriate activities, the staff may then refer to the guide.

After listing all the possible alternatives, the family should be allowed to select those activities that are most feasible for them. A schedule for implementation can be determined and methods for evaluation of progress outlined. Coordination with other agencies to meet family needs, as appropriate, should also be undertaken. The level and type of involvement for each family will vary, and consideration should be given to the emotional readiness of parents to participate. Gradual involvement is often the best approach. Programs often make the mistake of offering only one or two parent involvement options (for example, parent groups or home visits). The result is often limited involvement or high parent attrition because the program is not individualized to meet their needs.

DELIVERY OF SERVICES TO PARENTS

The following section analyzes the types of services that are often delivered to parents and a variety of alternative methods for accomplishing the previously stated goals. Sharing information with parents, counseling parents, working with parents in the home, working with parents in the classroom, and parent education are addressed.

Sharing Information with Parents

Staffings The staffing process (a joint meeting of staff and parents to assess a child's needs and develop the child's IEP) has been discussed in Chapter 5; however, parent involvement in staffing merits further discussion. For many parents, the child's staffing is the first time they are presented information relating to their child's difficulties. Naturally, it is a highly stressful occasion. Staff need to have an idea before the staffing of the parents' knowledge level about their child, and their related feelings.

Parents need to be involved throughout the staffing. They have valuable information to contribute and should not be considered mere observers. If possible, parents should be invited to be present during various aspects of the assessment. This will make information shared at the staffing and references to specific assessment procedures more relevant. A case manager or staff person (one who will be working with parents in the future) can act as a support person and advocate for the parents. This individual should meet with parents prior to the staffing to explain the staffing purpose and process—the testing that was done, how to interpret profiles, who will be present at the staffing, and the staffing agenda.

Information concerning assessment results can be shared with parents before the staffing. If parents are given an opportunity to absorb, integrate, and express feelings prior to the staffing, they will be able to participate more fully during the staffing. This also allows parents time to formulate questions for the staffing. During the staffing, the case manager can ask questions that the parents may be hesitant to ask in front of numerous staff. He or she can also define unfamiliar terminology or jargon used in the staffing to ensure that parents do not become confused. Parents should also be encouraged to bring along a friend or another parent for support.

The assessment data presented during the staffing need to be related to behaviors that parents see at home, thus making the information much more relevant. The assessment data should also be used to emphasize the child's needs rather than for the purpose of a diagnostic label. Emotion-laden diagnostic labels can be all that parents remember from a staffing, and can hamper objective discussion.

Parents should be allowed to express their feelings. As noted previously, it is natural for parents to deny the handicap, demonstrate anger toward professionals, or grieve openly. It is important for professionals to be supportive of parents and listen without becoming defensive.

Another critical, but frequently overlooked, aspect of staffings is follow-up. Parents need to be contacted several days after the staffing in order to answer questions that may not have been answered during the staffing. This is also an appropriate time to offer emotional support, to arrange for further contacts with parents, provide additional information, or put parents in touch with other parents in the program.

Conferences Parent conferences with school-age children are usually scheduled once or twice a year to examine the child's progress. With young handicapped children, these conferences should be more frequent. In many programs, conferences are informal, with much information exchanged in home visits or in casual conversations with the parent before or after class. When scheduling more structured parent conferences, there are several points to consider:

1. Establish objectives or decide what you want to accomplish before the meeting.
2. Use concrete or graphic examples to report on the child's progress: skills the child has accomplished; skills on which the child is working.
3. Be positive. Obtain feedback from parents on how they perceive the child's progress at home.
4. Ask the parents' opinion on what skills they feel are important to stress in the future.
5. Ask parents to evaluate the child's program and to appraise their child's progress.
6. Provide follow-up activities for the child at home. Demonstrate specific techniques.
7. Discuss other child or family needs. Be flexible; if parents have important additional concerns, staff should be able to adapt their agenda.
8. Before ending the conference, have parents summarize the information presented as they have understood it; this helps to avoid misunderstandings and misinterpretation.
9. Keep records of parent conferences including: objectives of the meeting; information covered; parental concerns; and arrangement for follow-up.

Counseling Parents

Counseling is a helping relationship between a knowledgeable professional and parents of an exceptional child, working toward a better understanding of their unique concerns, problems or feelings. It is a learning process focusing upon the stimulation and encouragement of personal growth by which parents are assisted in acquiring, developing, and utilizing the skills and attitudes necessary for satisfactory resolution to their problem or concern. Parents are helped toward becoming fully functioning individuals who are assets to their children and value harmonious living as members of a well-adjusted family unit (Stewart, 1978, pp. 21–22).

Although there are many definitions of counseling, Stewart's definition underscores the importance of understanding, learning, and acquiring skills, and is particularly relevant to staff working with parents of handicapped children. Although the social worker or parent/family worker is often given the responsibility for counseling troubled families, *all* staff members working with young handicapped children need to have counseling skills to enable them to deal with family concerns as they arise. Persons who have daily contact with the parents are most likely to develop a trusting relationship that is essential to effective communication. The development of good communication skills is an important goal that should be addressed in the staff development component of the program (see Chapter 8). Regarding counseling techniques, staff should be skilled in three approaches: 1) nondirective counseling, 2) behavioral counseling, and 3) problem-solving.

Nondirective Counseling Nondirective counseling (Benjamin, 1974; Brammer, 1973; Rogers, 1951) is used to gain greater understanding of a problem. Counseling skills inherent in this approach are important for all staff to acquire. The intent of nondirective counseling is for parents to come to understand their feelings and arrive at solutions to problems on their own. The staff's role is to provide support and aid parents in clarifying their own strengths and abilities. The ability to *listen* to parents' concerns is paramount.

Specific skills that are important in nondirective counseling include:

1. Allowing parents to discuss topics of their own choosing, rather than staff directing the conversation.
2. Using open-ended questions (i.e., questions that elicit alternative and complete responses rather than short answers or "yes" and "no") to encourage parents to decide what information is important.
3. Using paraphrases, or rephrasing statements made by parents. Paraphrasing lets the parents know they are being heard and gives them an opportunity to correct misconceptions.
4. Using reflection of feelings. Emotions are seen as important. Staff state how they think the parent is feeling at a particular moment. Often this helps parents to focus on and express their feelings without fear of judgment.
5. Clarifying or asking for more information; this allows the listener to check perceptions.
6. Using indirect leads, including nodding the head, saying "mm-hmm," and allowing silence. Silence gives the parents time to think and lets them know you want to hear more.
7. Interpreting information that is being stated; this may allow parents to pinpoint and express subconscious thoughts or feelings.
8. Confronting parents with crucial information that they may not want to hear.
9. Summarizing for the parents the feelings they have expressed, and aspects of content and process that the counselor feels are most important.

10. Supporting and reassuring parents by letting them know that their thoughts and feelings are important.

The skills involved in nondirective counseling are useful when the staff want to better understand parents' feelings about a particular situation. Use of these techniques is valuable at the beginning of any session with parents, because it helps establish a sense of trust and mutual understanding. These techniques can also be woven into any session with parents when a better understanding is desired.

Behavioral Counseling Behavioral counseling (Bergan, 1977; Patterson, 1975) is beneficial for crisis intervention and for bringing positive action. When change is needed quickly, behavioral counseling can be effective. Behavioral counseling is much more structured than nondirective counseling, with the counselor guiding the counseling session. The counselor may ask many direct questions requesting information or closed questions requiring "yes" and "no" short responses. It is a step-by-step process to which parents contribute, with the final course of action planned by the counselor:

1. Initial analysis of the problem situation. Determination is made of which behaviors are problematic, either because they occur with excess frequency, intensity or duration, or because they do not occur often enough. Also, determination is made of which behaviors are done well.
2. Clarification of the problem situation. The counselor explores with the parents the situations in which the behaviors occur, the consequences of the behaviors, and the probable effects of changing the behaviors.
3. Motivational analysis. The counselor explores with the parents what events are rewarding and punishing to the child and their effects in different situations.
4. Developmental analysis. The counselor explores any physiological limitations, earlier behavioral problems, or recent changes in the child's environment.
5. Analysis of self-control. Determination is made of behaviors the child can control and in what situations.
6. Analysis of social relationships. The counselor determines what social relationships the child has and how behavior varies within these relationships.
7. Analysis of the socio-cultural-physical environment. Exploration is made of the norms, limitations, and expectations of the child.
8. Specification of behavioral objectives. The counselor and parents pinpoint a behavior to change.
9. Development of plan. Antecedents and consequences are selected. Specific procedures for implementation are outlined, including reinforcement, schedule of reinforcement, time-line, and record-keeping.
10. Evaluation of change. The counselor follows the progress and works with the parents to modify the program as necessary.

11. Development of plan for maintenance. A schedule of reinforcement is developed to maintain the desired behaviors.

Behavioral counseling is most frequently used to modify problem behaviors of children. It can also be used, however, to change parents' counter-productive behaviors.

Problem-solving Counseling Problem-solving counseling (Carkhuff, 1969; Gordon, 1970) combines nondirective and behavioral counseling skills with some added components. Nondirective skills are used to define and explore the problem, while behavioral skills in the form of closed and directed questioning may also be applied. An important difference with problem-solving counseling is the involvement of the parents in identifying and evaluating alternative solutions.

Carkhuff (1969) has outlined a seven-stage process for problem-solving, as summarized below:

1. Define and describe the problem situation. This includes exploring the parents' feelings about the situation.
2. Define and describe the direction(s) and/or goals dictated by the problem areas. This allows the parents and the counselor to work together to determine the changes they would like to see.
3. Describe existing conditions related to the problem and hindrances to the accomplishment of goals.
4. Discuss all the possible alternatives to solving the problem (i.e., brainstorm). Judgments should be withheld at this time.
5. Consider the advantages and disadvantages of alternative courses of action. Parents should be actively involved in determining a plan of action most feasible for them.
6. Develop physical, emotional-interpersonal, and intellectual means for achieving the selected alternative. Parents need to determine the course of action and support systems that will allow them to follow through on the plan.
7. Delineate progressive steps in the plan, including evaluating the outcome and making future plans.

Problem-solving counseling can be used to deal with a variety of family-related problems. It is also an effective way of teaching parents to deal with new problems as they arise. Home visitors find the process particularly effective for encouraging parents to think of new alternatives for working on a child's objectives. As parents gain more confidence in their abilities to solve problems, the counselor can become more of a resource and support person.

The goal of each of these counseling approaches is to help parents become more confident and self-sufficient. Different approaches may be needed for different problems, and counselors should build on the family's strengths. It is also important that counselors know their own strengths and limitations and know when to refer families for more intense professional counseling.

Parent Groups   There are many types of parent groups, the most common being a support group that derives the content of its discussions from the interests and concerns of parents. By sharing their knowledge and experiences, parents help each other to "examine, clarify and understand a specific aspect of their life situation—their role as parents—and use the dynamics of group learning to help them become more capable and self-assured" (Brown, 1978, p. 2).

Parents gain a sense of mutuality and identity from the supportive environment of parent groups. By seeing themselves mirrored in the actions and concerns of others, parents can pinpoint their feelings and develop a deeper awareness and understanding of themselves and their relationships with other family members. They may gain knowledge and information in a nonthreatening, nonauthoritative setting, and acquire methods for approaching problems, exploring alternatives, and making decisions. Parents can also discuss and evaluate difficult upcoming choices with others who have faced similar situations. In addition, the new friendships gained and opportunities to socialize provide important outlets to parents who may feel isolated.

The success of parent groups depends in large measure on the skills of the staff member who acts as group facilitator. This person needs good individual counseling skills as well as skills in conducting group sessions. The group needs to identify specific concerns or problems the parents are having. The group leader can help focus the group by asking open-ended questions (not theoretical, but about real life situations) and then narrowing the topic to one of mutual concern. The facilitator needs to be able to create a relaxed environment and set parents at ease. Respect should be shown for the parents' individual values and ideas.

According to Barnard and Erickson (1976), the group leader also:

1. Keeps the purpose of the meeting clear, collects the agenda, checks with all group members to be certain of priority topics for consideration.
2. Teaches and models clear communication.
3. Encourages expression of opinions on both sides of an issue.
4. Encourages expression of feelings when painful experiences are evident.
5. Supports individuals in their efforts to express themselves.
6. Helps assess problem-solving abilities of the group as a whole.
7. Gives verbal feedback regarding approaches.
8. Aids progress by always offering to summarize major points or topics covered in each session.

The group facilitator must be able to keep the meeting within its time limit, attend to the needs of all group members, control the process and level of interaction, and confront, when necessary—discouraging, for example, gossip, "super-mothering," and invasion of privacy. The group leader must be a model of good communication and a catalyst for interaction. He or she helps the group to find their own answers, but adds information, summarizes, and underlines healthy attitudes and strengths.

It should be recognized that not all parents want or need to belong to a parent group. Participation may be needed only to help a parent through a particular crisis or difficult time. Husbands and wives may move through crisis at different levels, and therefore have different needs. Also, single parents often feel uncomfortable in a group of couples. In planning for parent groups, staff need to be aware of these individual differences and plan a variety of types of individual and group opportunities.

Working with Parents at Home

The home is the child's natural setting, and parents the child's primary teachers; therefore, the home is a natural learning environment. Home visitors play different roles depending on the needs of the family and the program's philosophy and goals. In any one home visit the developmental specialist may:

Work directly with the child while parents watch
Work directly with parents, who then work with the child
Work with child and parent by modeling techniques for the parent who then tries the techniques
Talk to the parent and give suggestions about what to do
Leave printed materials for the parents to read
Practice problem-solving strategies with the parent that relate to child, family, and personal matters
Leave toys and materials for the family to use

The primary purpose of home visits is to increase the family's ability to cope with and interact with their handicapped child. As a result of the previously discussed reactions to the birth of a handicapped child and as a consequence of the child's lower level of interaction, attachment bonds may not be as strong as between a normal child and parents. Fraiberg, Smith, and Adelson (1969) and Klaus and Kennel (1976) have noted that promotion of love bonds between parent and child is paramount to educational success. Therefore, the continual promotion of positive, pleasurable interaction between parent and child is as important as the development of motor and cognitive skills. The home visitor needs to work with the child to facilitate acquisition of behaviors that will allow the child to interact maximally with the family. As the child interacts increasingly with the environment and begins to use gestures, sounds, and words to communicate with others, parents receive greater reinforcement and their desire to interact with the child increases. The more positively the parents interact with their child, the more opportunity the child has for continued growth, and a positive cycle thus replaces a negative cycle that is reinforcing to neither parents nor child. It is the home visitor's role to work on improving the child's skills, improving the parent-child interaction, and helping families to develop a facilitative learning environment.

In order to accomplish these tasks, the home visitor must win the trust and respect of the family. This trust and respect often develops over time, so it is important to spend time with the family just listening and establishing rapport. It is also advisable to make arrangements for both parents (in two-parent families) to be involved in some way. It is not always wise for the mother to continually be in a position of transferring information to the father. This can set up a difficult situation in which the mother feels she has all the answers and tries to tell the father what to do. It is better either to come to the home when both parents are present or to make some visits when the father can be there. Flexibility in scheduling is important.

Whether the child is in a home-based or a home- and center-based program, the emphasis on both family and child should be strong. Many center-based programs provide home visits only for the purpose of teaching parents how to follow through on skills learned at school. The emphasis in any home visit should be the child's functioning in the home environment and the interaction among the family members and the child.

One of the important tasks of the home visitor is to help parents develop good observation skills. This may be done by sharing observation checklists and criterion-referenced assessment tools with parents. Through such observation, parents can understand their child's different rates of developmental growth, understand the steps and usual sequences in acquiring skills, develop realistic expectations, provide data for recording progress, and start to generate suggestions for appropriate activities (Cansler et al., 1975). Observation skills can also help parents in 1) pinpointing problem behaviors, 2) establishing the frequency, duration, and intensity of behaviors, and 3) determining the relationship between behaviors and the consequences they produce (White & Haring, 1976).

After helping parents to determine where and how the child is functioning, it is *imperative* that the home visitor demonstrate intervention strategies and work with the parents in developing alternatives for them to implement immediately at home. A good place to begin is to focus on behaviors that will improve the interaction level between parent and child. For example, if the child is difficult to feed, and every meal is a frustrating 2-hour struggle, then it is appropriate to begin working on feeding skills. The priorities that parents have at home may be different from those at school. The home visitor also needs to focus on play behaviors and to help parents engage in pleasurable interactions with their child. Often, handicapped children come to be seen as "therapy objects" and parental interactions revolve around "working" with the child (Linder, 1982). Parents may need help in learning how to *play* with their child, thus also facilitating the child's development.

By following a home visit self-evaluation, such as that shown in Figure 1, the home visitor can ensure that the important tasks of the visit are accomplished. (For a detailed model of the home visitation process, the reader is referred to Morrison, 1978).

Working with Parents in the Classroom

Observations   As with the home visitor, it is important for the classroom teacher to help parents to observe and assess their child's growth and development.

Home Visit Self-Evaluation Form

Child: _____ Date _____

1. What did I do to prepare for the visit?

2. The objectives for the visit were:

3. The activities to accomplish these objectives were:

4. The materials and methods I used in the visit included:

5. I provided opportunities for the parents to try activities by:

6. Types of feedback I provided to the parents included:

7. I ensured that the parents experienced success by:

8. I monitored progress by:

9. I am helping the parents to observe progress by:

10. I am individualizing for this family by:

11. Siblings who were present were included by:

12. I listened to the parents' concerns about:

13. I dealt with these concerns by:

14. I need to discuss the following with other team members:

15. I need to know more about the following in order to deal more effectively with this family:

16. The most positive aspect of this visit was:

17. The following things should be done differently next time:

18. On the next visit I plan to:

Figure 1.   A sample home visit self-evaluation form.

Classroom observations, with guidance from the staff, can help parents see how their child behaves with other children and adults and also observe how the team handles specific behaviors. Often, the child's strengths and weaknesses are more apparent to parents in the classroom setting. Use of intervention techniques may also be informally acquired through observation, thus facilitating follow-through at home.

Guidelines for classroom observation should be developed by staff with input from parents in the program. It is also important for staff and parents to meet before the observation to discuss program objectives and activities geared to individual programs. Teaching methods and behavior management techniques should also be explained. After the observation, staff should meet again with parents to discuss their observations and their child's strengths and progress. Staff need to be willing to answer parents' questions, but must keep information on other children confidential. This is also an appropriate time to focus on the need for consistency between home and school. The staff and parents may practice problem-solving activities that can be done at home. With some parents, an observation checklist or an open-ended form with spaces for notations under specific categories can be devised; the parent can then observe with a purpose.

Parents as Aides or Volunteers Parents who act as classroom aides can benefit from the above-mentioned activities, and also have the advantage of learning over an extended period of time. There are many classroom aide roles that parents can assume, and whenever possible, parents should be allowed to choose the activities they prefer. Some parents feel uncomfortable working directly with the children, while others prefer to work with children other than their own. Parents can work on a one-to-one basis with child or with small groups. They may be responsible for supervising specific activities, or they may prefer to help out in nonteaching roles. In the latter case, parents can help by creating new materials, performing clerical duties such as record-keeping, or maintaining classroom materials. Whatever tasks are assigned should be meaningful and selected by parents as tasks they would enjoy.

Regardless of the role that parents play, two important points should be noted: First, *staff attitudes toward parents in the classroom must be positive to work effectively*. And second, *parents should be trained for the functions they perform*. The first issue needs to be addressed when staff are hired and during inservice training. To accomplish the second, it is necessary to provide parents with inservice training (this can be done by other experienced parents or by including parents in staff inservice training sessions).

Morrison (1978) has discussed the benefits of having parents involved in the classroom as extending to the parents themselves, the teachers, and the children. Benefits for the parents can include increased self-esteem and the development of a better understanding of the educational process. The teachers gain a better understanding of parents' concerns and also benefit from the variety of talents the parents can share. An increased efficiency may also result from the "extra pair of hands.'' The children benefit from the opportunity for additional individual attention as well as the exposure to other adult figures. If carefully planned, having parents (and even siblings) in the classroom can be worthwhile for all involved.

Parents who have been involved in a program for some time or who are in combination home- and center-based programs may become more autonomous in working with children. They may be able to help with evaluations, planning, and teaching. After observing staff working with the children, parents can perform many of the same activites. While the parents are working with the children, staff can give them feedback, reinforcement, and ideas for working with the child at home. Parents can also be useful as teachers of other parents and volunteers who come to the program. Given meaningful involvement, parents can contribute greatly to the effectiveness of the program and to their child's growth.

Parent Education

Parent education involves providing parents with information that will increase their knowledge and skills in parenting. For parents of normal children, parent education classes have become very popular. For parents of handicapped children, who have additional parenting responsibilities, parent education is all the more valuable. There are many different forms of parent education, from informal discussion in meetings with parents, to formal courses. As previously discussed, working with parents during home or classroom visits can provide parents with much parenting information. It is often desirable, however, to provide a more structured approach to content. At the beginning of the year, an assessment of parent's needs can be completed, usually as part of the initial interview. In developing this assessment, staff should attempt to be as specific as possible in addressing topical areas. For example, a commonly used form lists topical areas with blanks after them to be checked (see Figure 2).

In examining the items, one can see they are too vague. There are many different types of behavior management approaches, and the term itself may be confusing. The term "child development" is also too general. Another problem with this assessment approach is that it does not give staff any notion of priorities if more than one item is checked. Staff are also not provided any idea of how parents would like to receive the information or at what level.

```
                        Needs Assessment

        Please check those items you are interested in learning about.

        Behavior management
        Child development              _____
        Handicapping conditions        _____
```

Figure 2. Sample items from an inadequately detailed needs assessment form for parent education.

Needs Assessment

Parent's name: _____

Child's name: _____

Topic	Priority (put 1 by your first choice, 2 by your second choice, etc.)
How can I help improve my child's language?	_____
What can I do when my child misbehaves?	_____
What kinds of toys are appropriate for my child?	_____
[Include other topics as appropriate]	_____
	_____

Preferred Format for Information:

Films, tapes	_____	Role play	_____
Group discussion	_____	Lecture	_____
Panel discussion	_____	Demonstration	_____
Workshop	_____		

	Yes	No
I would be willing to help plan the meeting.	_____	_____
I would like to car-pool to the meeting.	_____	_____
It would help if child care were provided.	_____	_____

Time preference: _____ morning _____ afternoon _____ evening

Preferred day: _____ M _____ T _____ W _____ Th _____ F

I would also be interested in the following kinds of informal meetings with other parents in the program:

	Yes	No
Parent group discussions	_____	_____
Potluck	_____	_____
Picnics	_____	_____
Field days	_____	_____
Learning a craft	_____	_____
Other (specify):	_____	_____

Comments:

Figure 3. Sample items from a comprehensive needs assessment form for parent education.

Figure 3 is an example of a needs assessment form that takes into account these problems. The items are phrased in questions to help the parent see the relevance of the topic to their family. The priority listing gives staff some idea of individual parent priorities and also enables staff to rank topics for presentation to a general group. The preferred format section enables staff to plan meaningful activities. Also a variety of other options are made available to parents, thus helping to meet a wider range of needs.

Once the staff have completed a needs assessment of parents' interests, they may also want to assess what staff feel are important parent education topics. After the information has been collected, planning can take place. Parents should be represented on a parent education planning team to develop the format and specific activities.

As with programs planned for children, educational programs for parents need to be based on well-defined, measurable objectives. The curriculum should consider the cultural, ethnic, and economic diversity of the parents. Motivational strategies are important both to involve parents initially and to keep them involved. Continuity from topic to topic is important. Formal and informal evaluation throughout the program is necessary in order to document the success of the educational efforts (Love, 1979).

The range of topics that parents may desire is infinite. Table 2 includes some

Table 2. Suggested topics for parent education classes

After Conception
Psychological, physiological, and sociological changes of pregnancy and parenthood, including real life experiences with children in their homes
Prenatal health, genetics, nutrition, and the ramifications of diet and medication
Intrauterine development of the fetus
Labor and delivery—different methods of childbirth, the hospital, what to expect
Selection of a good obstetrician and pediatrician; medical decisions that may arise

Infant Care
Infant care techniques—bathing, feeding, sleeping, playing, illnesses, developmental patterns of growth, safety
Child development fundamentals—physical, perceptual, cognitive, emotional, behavioral
Infant play and learning—how to stimulate movement and language
Needs of infants
Nutritional needs for nurturance—creating early trust in environment, feelings of love, and self-esteem
Disciplining toddlers—behavior management and socialization techniques
Community resources—where to go for help

Preschool Years
Behavioral patterns
Preschoolers' needs; developmental tasks
Physical, motor (fine and gross), cognitive and language, psychological, and social development as manifested in behavior
Play activities
Appropriate toys and books
Family dynamics
Handling crisis situations
Discipline and behavior management
Community resources
Peer relationships
Acceptance of children's feelings and attitudes

Adapted from Lane (1975).

suggestions in the areas of prenatal, infant, and preschool care that may be particularly appropriate. Although prenatal topics may seem "after the fact," keep in mind that parents of young handicapped children may want to have additional children, and one of their natural fears is about having another handicapped child; programs can play a significant *preventive role* by providing parent education on prenatal topics. In addition to the topics in Table 2, parents may also want information on medical terminology, legislation for handicapped children, how to plan for their child's care if something happens to them, or other concerns.

Depending on the topic chosen and the level of information desired, the format for parent education will vary. Options include: group discussion of ideas, panel discussions, small group discussions, lectures, symposia or workshops, debates, role playing or brainstorming, field trips or observations, and inservice training. Audiovisual aids, resource room materials, filmstrips, videotapes, movies, books, newsletters, and reaction sheets can all be used to supplement or enhance the meetings. In order to ensure maximum participation, provisions should be made to take care of basic needs (refreshments), transportation, and child care. Parents will not continue to attend if programs do not meet their needs by providing information that is immediately relevant.

Guidelines for Parent Education The following suggestions should be taken into consideration when planning parent education programs.

1. Work with school administrators, staff, resource people, and parents to plan the parent education program.
2. Needs assessments should be done by interview if possible.
3. Work with community agencies to help meet the total needs of parents.
4. Provide opportunities for informal communication as part of the parent education sessions.
5. Hold meetings on convenient days and times, using the parents' preferred format.
6. Design and distribute attractive flyers or announcements.
7. Ask parents to develop a "telephone chain" or other mechanism to remind one another of upcoming sessions.
8. Have parents organize a car pool.
9. Arrange for child care.
10. Use the news media to help publicize activities.
11. Do evaluations of all sessions to provide for program improvement.
12. Provide follow-up to parents who desire it.

OTHER PARENT INVOLVEMENT OPTIONS

Resource Center

In addition to formal meetings, parent education can be accomplished through many informal means. For parents who enjoy reading materials, books, pamphlets, articles, and journals may be made available on topics of interest.

A resource room for parents can become an active "parent room." A comfortable room with a couch, overstuffed chairs, and a coffee pot can provide a "place" for parents that is all their own. After they drop off their child, after a meeting, or while waiting for a class session to end, parents can enjoy an informal opportunity to talk to other parents or just sit and relax. Books and journals on such topics as exceptionalities, parenting, and development should be available for parents to peruse or check out. Toys, materials, and activities can also be available in this room. A parent room can also provide an informal, comfortable setting for discussions with a parent or group of parents. A resource room can contain such materials as: books, games, records, pictures, manipulatives for use with children at home; materials on parenting, child development, nutrition, community agencies, and organizations; suggestions for use of household items in teaching children at home; materials for parents to make for use at home (staff can conduct toy-making workshops while educating parents on developmental aspects of play and learning); and a parent bulletin board with a calendar of events, community resource information, current legislation, pictures of children and parents, and information on parenting issues.

Newsletters

Newsletters can be very effective in both increasing communication with parents and providing parents with information on parenting and educational topics. Because producing a quality newsletter can take a great deal of effort, forming a "parent press corps" can greatly assist staff responsible for the publication. Possible topics for inclusion, suggested by Cansler et al. (1975), include:

> Reports of children's learning experiences, opportunities for parent and staff training, announcements of group meetings, and special activities
> Suggestions for helping children at home and printed instructions for making inexpensive toys or teaching materials
> Facts concerning community services and organizations for families, and discussions of local, state, and national issues related to handicapped children
> A "meet the staff" section to introduce parents to the persons working with their children
> Recognition and thanks for parents' contributions to the school program
> Descriptions of specific tasks that require the assistance of volunteer workers
> Descriptions of books and toys available in a lending library as a way of encouraging the use of such a service
> A "Parent Exchange" section to help families locate others interested in exchanging services (child care or transportation) or goods (p. 40).

Parent Handbook

A handbook providing information on the program and on school policies and procedures is also important. Information in the handbook should be clear and concise. A description of the philosophy and goals of the program, examples of school forms and their purposes, and a delineation of program services are chief features to include. Following are specific suggestions of items for a handbook:

1. Philosophy of the program
2. Admissions procedures
3. Assessment and placement procedures
4. Health care policies—medication, illnesses, communicable diseases, accidents and emergencies, absences, clothing
5. Program—classes and schedules, home visits, therapy services, consultation
6. Parent involvement opportunities—parent groups, conferences, parent education, volunteering
7. Parents' rights
8. Miscellaneous

Parent Advisory Committee

Most grant-funded early intervention projects have as a mandate the inclusion of a parent advisory group to work with school administrators in planning and evaluating the program. The reasoning behind the mandate is the recognition that parents are the "consumers" of early childhood programs, and, as such, deserve a voice in decision-making processes related to services for their children. The success of these advisory committees justifies the need for early childhood programs to continue to involve parents at this level. Parent advisory committee members can discuss their feelings and offer opinions about policies, procedures, and current issues that relate to program decisions; they can provide a needed perspective in developing program goals and objectives and in recommending curricular content; they can assist with long-range planning and help maintain liaisons with other community agencies and organizations; and they can form subcommittees to help evaluate program components. An active parent advisory group can give valuable guidance and advice on administrative decisions, as well as provide an advocacy base in the community.

GENERAL CONSIDERATIONS FOR PARENT INVOLVEMENT

"Parents of handicapped children need assistance, support, acknowledgement, and objective feedback in their decision-making, problem solving, and planning for alternatives of care for their children" (Barnard & Erickson, 1976). Staff who keep in mind these needs will be able to plan and implement programs with families as the intervention focus. Buscaglia (1975), in his discussion of the basic rights of the family of a handicapped child, nicely summarizes the responsibilities of professionals to respect these rights:

> The right to sound medical knowledge regarding their child's physical or mental problem
> The right to some form of continual reevaluation of their child at definite periodic intervals and a thorough, lucid explanation of the results of the findings
> The right to some helpful, relevant and specific information as to their role in meeting their child's special physical and emotional needs

The right to some knowledge of the educational opportunities for a child such as theirs and what will be required for later admission for additional formal schooling

The right to a knowledge of the community resources available for assistance in meeting the family needs, intellectual, emotional, and financial

The right to knowledge of the rehabilitation services in the community and the resources available through them

The right to some hope, reassurance, and human consideration as they meet the challenge of raising a child with special needs

The right to some help in seeing their child's potentials instead of forever concentrating upon his imperfections

The right to good reading material to help them acquire as much relevant information as possible

The right to some interaction with other parents who have children with disabilities

The right to actualize their personal rights as growing unique individuals, apart from their children (p. 109).

As professionals who care about handicapped children and their families, we have a responsibility to ensure that these rights are protected. The parent component of every early intervention program should provide mechanisms to guarantee that the needs of families will be respected.

REFERENCES

Amon, C. *Colorado parent book*. Denver: Colorado Department of Education, 1978.

Arnold, L.E. Helping parents beat the system. In: L.E. Arnold (ed.), *Helping parents help their children*. New York: Brunner/Mazel, 1978.

Arnold, L.E., Rowe, M., & Tolbert, H.A. Parent groups. In: L.E. Arnold (ed.), *Helping parents help their children*. New York: Brunner/Mazel, 1978.

Banish, R. Explanations offered by parents and siblings of braindamaged children. *Exceptional Children*, 1961, *27*, 286–291.

Barnard, K.E., & Erickson, M.L. *Teaching children with developmental problems. A family care approach*. St. Louis: C.V. Mosby Co., 1976.

Benjamin, A. *The helping interview*. Boston: Houghton Mifflin Co., 1974.

Bergan, J.R. *Behavioral consultation*. Columbus, OH: Charles E. Merrill Publishing Co., 1977.

Bloom, B. *Stability and change in human characteristics*. New York: John Wiley & Sons, 1964.

Bradley, R.H., & Caldwell, B.M. Home observation for measurement: A validation study of screening efficiency. In: R. Piazza & R. Rothman (eds.), *Readings in preschool education for the handicapped*. Guilford, CO: Special Learning Corporation, 1979.

Brammer, L. *The helping relationship: Process and skills*. Englewood Cliffs, N.J.: Prentice-Hall, 1973.

Bronfenbrenner, U. Is early intervention effective? In: J. Hellmuth (ed.), *Exceptional infants*, Vol. 3. New York: Brunner/Mazel, 1975.

Brown, S. Functions, tasks and stresses of parenting: Implications for guidance. In: L.E. Arnold (ed.), *Helping parents help their children*. New York: Brunner/Mazel, 1978.

Buck, P. *The child who never grew*. New York: John Day Co., 1959.

Buscaglia, L. *The disabled and their parents: A counseling challenge*. Thorofare, NJ: Charles B. Slack, 1975.

Cansler, D.P., Martin, G.H., & Valand, M.C. *Working with families.* Winston-Salem, NC: Kaplan Press, 1975.

Carkhuff, R.R. *Helping and human relations: A primer for lay and professional helpers. Selection and training,* Vol. 1. New York: Holt, Rinehart and Winston, 1969.

Fraiberg, S., Smith, M., & Adelson, E. An educational program for blind infants. *Journal of Special Education,* 1969, *3*(2), 121–139.

Fredericks, H.D.B., Baldwin, V.L., Grove, D.N., & Associates. *A data-based classroom for the moderately and severely handicapped.* Monmouth, OR: Instructional Development Corporation, 1975.

Gallup, G.H. Eighth annual Gallup poll of the public's attitudes towards the public schools. *Phi Delta Kappan,* 1976, *58*(2), 187–200.

Gordon, T. *Parent effectiveness training.* New York: P.H. Whyden, 1970.

Hofmeister, A., & Reavis, H.K. Learning packages for parent involvement. *Educational Technology,* 1974, *14*(7), 55–56.

Holfing, C.K., & Lewis, J.M. *The family: evaluation and treatment.* New York: Brunner/ Mazel, 1980.

Hunt, J. McV. *Intelligence and experience.* New York: The Ronald Press Co., 1961.

Johnson, S.H. *High-risk parenting: Nursing assessment and strategies for the family at risk.* Philadelphia: J.B. Lippincott, 1979.

Klaus, M., & Kennel, J. *Maternal-infant bonding.* St. Louis: C.V. Mosby Co., 1976.

Klein, D.L., Bowser, M.A., Kater, W.L., & Waltraud, L.E. *Families first: a program and staff development system.* York, PA: Individual and Family Development Services, 1978.

Kubler-Ross, E. *On death and dying.* New York: Macmillan Publishing Co., 1969.

Lane, M.B. *Education for parenting.* Washington, DC: National Association for the Education of Young Children, 1975.

Lillie, D., and Trohanis, P.L. *Teaching parents to teach.* New York: Walker and Co., 1976.

Linder, T. Pleasurable play. *Journal of the Colorado Speech-Language-Hearing Association,* 1982, *17*(1), 5–10.

Love, R.B. Parents and public schools: Needed characteristics and necessary concerns. In: D.R. Powell (ed.), *Families and schools: Implementing parent education.* Report No. 121 from the Education Commission of the States, Denver, CO, January, 1979.

Maslow, A.H. *Motivation and personality.* New York: Harper & Row, 1954.

Morrison, G.S. *Parent involvement in the home, school and community.* Columbus, OH: Charles E. Merrill Publishing Co., 1978.

Olshansky, S. Chronic sorrow. *Social Casework,* 1962, *43*(4), 190–193.

Patterson, G.R. *Families.* Champaign, IL: Research Press, 1975.

Powell, D.R. Organizational problems in institutionalizing parent education in the public schools. In: D.R. Powell (ed.), *Families and schools: implementing parent education.* Report No. 121 from the Education Commission of the States, Denver, CO, January, 1979.

Quick, A.D., Little, T.L., & Campbell, A.A. Early childhood education for exceptional foster children and training of foster parents. *Exceptional Children,* 1973, *40*, 206–208.

Rogers, C. *Client-centered therapy.* Boston: Houghton Mifflin Co., 1951.

Roos, P. Psychological counseling with parents of retarded children. *Mental Retardation,* 1963, *1*, 345–350.

Roos, P. Parents of mentally retarded children—misunderstood and mistreated. In: A.P. Turnbull & H.R. Turnbull, III (eds.), *Parents speak out: Views from the other side of the two-way mirror.* Columbus, OH: Charles E. Merrill Publishing Co., 1978.

Rosen, L. Selected aspects in the development of the mother's understanding of her mentally retarded child. *American Journal of Mental Deficiency,* 1955, *59*, 522–528.

Selig, A.L. The myth of the multi-problem family. *American Journal of Orthopsychiatry*, 1976, *46*(3), 526–532.

Shearer, M.S., & Shearer, D.E. The Portage Project: A model for early childhood education. *Exceptional Children*, 1972, *36*, 210–217.

Stewart, J.C. *Counseling parents of exceptional children*. Columbus, OH: Charles E. Merrill Publishing Co., 1978.

Stile, S.W., Cole, J.T., & Garner, A. *How to get parents involved and keep them involved: Strategies for regular and special education personnel*. Paper presented for the Colorado Special Education Resource Center, Denver, December 7, 1978.

Tidball-Strickler, K. *Parent Involvement*. Pierre, SD: State of South Dakota, Department of Education and Cultural Affairs, Divisions of Elementary and Secondary Education, 1975.

White, O.R., & Haring, N.G. *Exceptional teaching*. Columbus, OH: Charles E. Merrill Publishing Co., 1976.

8

Staff
Development

Once staff are hired and the program becomes operational, how can the early childhood special education (ECSE) coordinator ensure continued improvement and refinement of the program? How can he or she assist in the interchange of ideas and skills among staff? What can be done to prevent staff "burn-out"? The solutions to questions such as these may depend, in part, on the provision of a substantive and responsive staff development component.

IMPORTANCE OF STAFF DEVELOPMENT

The *Handbook for Facilitators of Staff Training*, compiled by the Department of Special Education at the University of Texas at Austin, states:

> Staff training is a planned sequence of experiences designed to foster a) continuing development of the understanding, skills, and knowledge of each staff member and b) cooperation, interaction, and integrated activity among the disciplines represented in a program. Thus staff training contributes to both individual and group development. Such development is necessary if the staff is to offer a high quality of services to preschool handicapped children and their families (p. xi).

When staff development is viewed as an integral part of the early childhood special education program and, as such, is carefully planned and implemented, the benefits to the program are numerous. As early childhood special education is a relatively new field, there has not been a sufficient number of preservice training programs to meet the growing demand for qualified, capable personnel to work with young handicapped children. Early childhood special education programs have, by necessity, hired personnel trained to work with *normal* young children or *older* handicapped children. These persons are often unprepared to assume the multiple responsibilities involved in working with children who are both young *and* handicapped (Karnes, 1975). Staff development can provide supplementary training to enable personnel to acquire additional background and skills needed to carry out their responsibilities.

Just as level of training may vary, so, too, may the philosophical orientation of the institutions from which staff received their original training. Depending on their background, for example, staff may be more familiar with a behavioral approach, a psycholinguistic approach, a sensorimotor integration approach, or a cognitive developmental approach. They may therefore need training in the theory and/or application of a particular approach to an early childhood special education program. Often, it is beneficial to have staff with differing backgrounds; by examining problems relating to handicapped children and their families from different perspectives, they can expand the problem-solving capabilities of the staff. The importance, however, of a staff whose members understand each other and can demonstrate consistent approaches must not be neglected. If various personnel are using different terminology and making recommendations that reflect inconsistent methodologies, the consequence may be confusion and frustration for the family and the child.

Staff development can improve program consistency and reduce tension arising from diverging philosophies. It can also increase communication among the various disciplines on the staff. Transdisciplinary training can increase the effectiveness of all staff members. As the subtle boundaries formed by various backgrounds are eliminated, staff are increasingly able to learn from and communicate with each other. Team coordination is thus enhanced.

Knowledge of early childhood special education is expanding continuously. Staff development therefore plays an important role by helping staff keep informed of new developments and findings—for example, changes in theories and intervention strategies in the areas of language, motor, cognitive, and social-emotional development, and in family involvement and program modification. Programs have a responsibility to children and families to keep their staff apprised of research developments and to incorporate changes that will provide more effective services.

Staff development can also increase the skills of paraprofessionals, parents, and volunteers who work directly with children. With broadened knowledge and strengthened skills, parents and aides may assume greater responsibilities in the program, thereby allowing staff members to increase the amount of individual attention given children and families. Staff development for paraprofessionals, parents, and volunteers also helps ensure that these persons will be able to provide quality services.

Staff development can enhance staff members' self-confidence in performing their various roles. By providing the means by which staff can expand their knowledge and skills, staff job satisfaction is likely to increase. People who feel they are capable and competent in their jobs are also better able to handle the pressures of working closely with families and other team members.

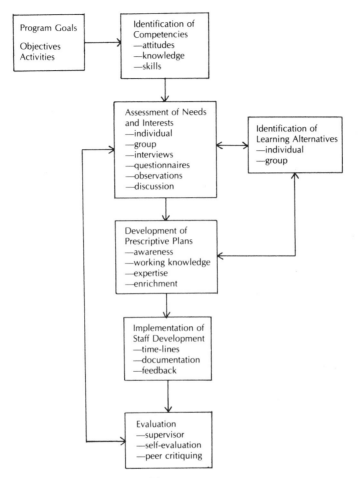

Figure 1.   Staff development process model.

Legislators recognized the importance of staff development when they specified in PL 94-142 that a comprehensive system of personnel development be a component of each state plan. The primary purposes of this staff development are to: change attitudes, increase knowledge, and improve performance and interpersonal skills. To accomplish these purposes, a competency-based inservice planning process that is well known to special educators may be used to advantage in early intervention programs (see Figure 1). The major features of this process are the following:

1.   The knowledge, attitudes, and skills needed by staff are identified.
2.   Staff members are assessed to determine their strengths and weaknesses in relation to the identified standards.

3. Prescriptions for growth and development are written to improve areas of weaknesses.
4. Learning alternatives that will enable staff to acquire requisite competencies are identified.
5. The process is evaluated to determine whether objectives have been met and what directions future training will take.

Competency-based education has become popular in recent years. A competency-based (or performance-based) preparation is one in which "performance goals are specified, and agreed to, in rigorous detail in advance of instruction. The student must either be able to demonstrate the abilities or perform job tasks. . . . Emphasis is on demonstrated produce or output" (Elam, 1973, pp. 1–2). Competency-based inservice planning can provide a fundamental reference for individualizing staff training, as well as aid in determining priorities for such training. It can also serve as the basis for active, practical application of knowledge by individual staff (Falkenstein, 1977).

The issue of teacher competencies was addressed by many researchers during the 1970s (Altman & Meyen, 1974; Bullock, Dykes, & Kelley, 1974; Fredericks, Anderson, Baldwin, Grove, Moon, Moore, & Baird, 1977; Rosner, 1974). The question of which competencies are important for working with young handicapped children has been studied more recently (Garland, 1978; Klein, Bowser, & Kater, 1978; Linder, 1982). The competencies that have been identified derive from three basic sources: 1) expert opinions from professionals in early childhood special education and experienced teachers and support staff, based on observation, experience and research; 2) evaluation data from parents and program supervisors regarding what attitudes and skills contribute to a successful program; and 3) the literature on important concerns and successful methods and practices in early childhood special education.

Review of information from all of these sources reveals consensus regarding general areas of significance for training. Messick (1975) identifies these areas as: *evaluation, planning instruction, managing instruction, communication, human relations, instructional resources,* and *institutional administration.* The unique nature of early childhood special education programs also necessitates that inservice training take into consideration: 1) a noncategorical approach to children; 2) the wide range of ability levels among children; 3) a need for transdisciplinary training; 4) a need for training professionals to work with families as well as children; and 5) a need for training professionals to work with social service systems. The latter two concerns have been viewed as areas that demand special attention in inservice training.

Klein et al. (1978) have identified six competency areas for training staff to work with families: self and human relations; communication and group process; individual development and exceptionalities; family systems and family involvement; crisis intervention and problem solving; and work environment and human service systems. Many universities have developed competency-based preservice training programs. The competencies they identify can serve as a foundation for planning an inservice program. A suggested set of competencies (see pages 205–216) is offered at the end of this chapter. Competencies can be added or deleted as necessary to meet individual program training needs.

ASSESSMENT OF STAFF NEEDS

After determining appropriate targets for inservice training, it is necessary to ascertain the functional level of staff competence in relation to the desired level of competence. A system needs to be devised to assess objectively the knowledge, attitudes, and skills of staff and others receiving training. Ideally, inservice training should be individualized and based on singular personnel needs. Perrone (1976) has noted that problems with traditional inservice activities include the fact that they are too general, they are geared for groups rather than individuals, and they address perceived rather than actual needs. For inservice activities to be meaningful, it is important for staff to be involved in identifying their own needs and in structuring alternatives for growth. Yeatts (1976) states, "teachers will take reform most seriously when they are, at least partially, responsible for defining their own educational problems, delineating their own needs, and receiving help on their own terms" (p. 417). By developing a system that takes into consideration subjective self-evaluation as well as objective supervisory evaluation, staff development can become more meaningful.

Methods for obtaining information about staff levels of competence may come from various sources. Background, experience, and training should be discussed with each staff member in an interview. Questionnaires may be used to enable personnel to express their interest in training in specific areas. In addition, the coordinator and other team members can observe staff performance in the program with the aid of checklists relating to competencies. The assessment should provide a method for determining strengths as well as weaknesses. Utilization of team strengths not only enables the supervisor to develop more efficient training but also provides a means of reinforcing quality performance.

The Needs Assessment for Staff Development included at the end of this chapter allows the supervisor, the staff member, or colleagues to assess levels of competence in specific areas. The competencies may be modified as necessary for individual programs. The needs assessment also can function as a formative and summative evaluation measure. Different colored pens or pencils are used at mid-year and end of year conferences. Thus, improvement, lack of growth, or even loss of skills is clearly visible. The usefulness of program planning and evaluation in connection with needs assessment becomes clearly apparent; the instrument can be adapted and modified as the program is altered or staff needs change.

Skills are rated on the needs assessment on a scale of 1 to 5: 1 or 2 indicate areas of weakness needing further development; a 3 represents average ability and, depending on the skill, may indicate adequate competence or need of additional work; ratings of 4 or 5 indicate strengths, with 5 denoting expertise. Skills can also be rated by the level of competence needed. Depending on the staff member's position, training at a level of awareness (A), a working knowledge (K), or functional expertise (E) may be necessary (Illinois Department of Specialized Educational Services, 1979). Particularly in a transdisciplinary model, the level of competence (and subsequent) training needed by each team member may vary. For instance, in an early intervention program with motorically involved or delayed children, it is imperative that the occupational or physical therapist have *expertise* in reflexes, motor development, and intervention techniques for young handicapped children. The other members of the transdisciplinary team need a *working knowledge* of reflexes, motor development, and intervention techniques so that they can follow through on recommended strategies. The principal of the school needs an *awareness* of the importance of reflexes, motor development, and intervention techniques so that he or she can justify hiring an occupational or physical therapist for the program.

After the skills have been rated, the competencies ranked 1 or 2 are put in order of priority in relation to immediacy of need for training. Competencies that are ranked 5 are noted as particular strengths in column 3. Column 4 in the form, "Methods for Staff Development," is used to list possible options for increasing knowledge and skills. The items that have been identified as priorities should be addressed first. The number of skills selected for professional development should be kept to a manageable number.

UTILIZING DATA

When a supervisor or colleague uses an assessment instrument, care should be taken that several observational opportunities are planned prior to filling out the forms. Being rated by one's peers can be extremely threatening. A wise alternative may be to have individuals assess themselves, in addition to having a supervisor assess them.

After the self-assessments and supervisory assessments are completed, Garland (1978) recommends constructing needs assessment grids. A grid can be developed for each competency area, listing each competency vertically and the rating horizontally across the top. The supervisor then tabulates how many staff members have been rated at each level for each competency. An excerpt from a sample needs assessment grid is provided in Figure 2. It may be desirable to develop separate grids for information obtained from self-assessments and for ratings done by the supervisor; this may help the supervisor to see patterns of variant perceptions.

In the section of the grid shown in Figure 2, it can be seen that there is some need for training in each of the competencies. The ECSE coordinator can look at the overall grid and decide where there is a need for group training and where individual activities are appropriate. For example, from Figure 2 the ECSE coordinator could determine that most of the staff, with one exception, can plan activities for children based on assessment findings and can task analyze skills. The coordinator can work singly with the one staff member (represented as a 1 in the grid square) on options to develop this skill. The coordinator can also see that four persons have deficient skills in assessing the accomplishments of children during a lesson. Group learning experiences can then be planned to help staff develop these observational and record-keeping skills. Planning for staff development is discussed in more detail in the following section.

Prescriptive Planning

Once the needs assessments and the summarizing grids are prepared, planning for individual and group staff development activities can begin. The ECSE coordinator, in consultation with each staff member, discusses that individual's self-assessment form. The coordinator's perceptions of the staff person's strengths and weaknesses can also be discussed; objective data obtained through observation should be used whenever possible. Together the coordinator and staff member determine competency areas on which to focus in the coming year. Priorities for individual training may be selected by examining priority rankings marked on the needs assessment form. If the supervisor's and staff member's lists of needs and priorities differ, negotiation should follow. It is often wise to let the staff member select an area on which to concentrate first—self-determination often enhances motivation to change. Some competencies are sequential, however, and prerequisites must be addressed first. Also, program priorities may dictate the sequence.

After targeting the priority competencies for professional growth, the staff member and the ECSE coordinator can collaborate to determine the best methods for accomplishing the objectives. A suggested time-line should also be discussed and at least tentatively planned.

Competency	NO	NA	1	2	3	4	5
Can develop lesson plan based on assessment findings.				1	3	2	
Can task analyze skills to be taught to the child.			1		1	4	
Can evaluate activities to assess how well lesson objectives have been met.				4	1		1

Figure 2. Excerpt from a sample needs assessment grid. (NO = no opportunity to observe; NA = not applicable.)

The ECSE coordinator can also summarize data from the strengths column of the needs assessment form. It is important that staff members get recognition from the supervisor to reinforce their demonstrated knowledge and skills. Information on staff strengths also proves useful as a basis for coordinating training resources—by utilizing internal staff as resources whenever possible, self-confidence is strengthened and training money can be used for needed external resources, thereby expanding training potential.

Group Needs

The staff as a whole, or a subcommittee of staff representatives, may be used to help analyze the assessment grid for group training needs and to assist in planning more global concerns. They can look for sets of skills that may best be addressed in combination and make sure that planned activities are relevant. Priorities for group training efforts can be determined by scanning the needs assessment grid for competencies in which many staff are rated in the 1 and 2 columns, and then selecting those areas that are most important for effective program functioning. For example, certain assessment needs may be more vital to fulfill at the beginning of the program than others.

Planning Learning Alternatives

The accumulation and coordination of a variety of resources for staff development is an important function of the ECSE coordinator, whose job becomes one of "matching the identified prioritized staff development needs with appropriate and available experiential and educational resources" (Klein et al., 1978, p. 27). Provocative and challenging experiences will help motivate staff. The coordinator needs to be able to provide aid, resources, and materials to encourage continued growth. The entire community may be utilized as a resource. The possibilities for learning alternatives are limited only by the creative imaginations of the coordinator and staff.

In choosing methods for accomplishing staff development objectives, it is important to consider a training hierarchy. Particularly in a trandisciplinary program model, not all staff members need the same level of competence. The three levels of competence suggested by the Illinois Department of Specialized Educational Services (1979) and mentioned earlier in the needs assessment process, are helpful in planning for training. The levels are: 1) awareness, 2) working knowledge, and 3) functional expertise. The implications for training at these various levels are obviously different. The staff development coordinator needs to plan for the various levels of training required. In addition, those individuals with demonstrated levels of expertise need enrichment opportunities (thus, a fourth level of competence) through staff development. By offering a diverse range of options for individuals and groups to acquire competence at levels of awareness, working knowledge, functional expertise, or enrichment, the coordinator can personalize staff development. Figure 3 lists various learning alternatives, designates whether an alternative is appropriate for an individual or a group, indicates what level of training can be accomplished by the method, and designates appropriate evaluation methods (the latter are discussed below under "Evaluation").

Seminars, lectures, courses, and conferences are appropriate for group training efforts or for an individual to attend. They can provide basic, current information; follow-up application of information, however, is usually lacking. Discussion groups, simulations, demonstrations, and workshops are usually more active and involve application of knowledge to specific situations. Again, however, they tend to be short, "one-shot" activities usually lacking follow-up. Other group activities, such as curriculum and materials development, may be long-term projects.

Falkenstein (1977) recommends that whenever possible, community resources should be used in an "action learning model." Internships in professional, business, political, or civic situations can provide valuable learning experience that may also have the added benefit of building community awareness and support. Staff exchanges and other on-the-job training experiences can be very effective in terms of planning, support, and follow-up. "Learning by doing" as utilized in demonstration and practice workshops, simulations, tapings, and in-classroom consultation can also provide opportunities for immediate feedback that is important to learning.

Classroom research is an infrequently used approach to staff development that can assist staff in determining effective training techniques. Such individual activities as reading specific materials, keeping goal-directed journals, working at teacher centers, or observing and discussing new methods with colleagues can be rewarding under facilitative guidance.

For those with a high level of expertise in most competency areas, enrichment activities and involvement in leadership roles can be valuable. Conducting workshops, planning conferences, holding professional office, publishing articles, and assisting with staff development can provide means for continual growth and professional development.

The most commonly used staff development alternatives such as lectures, courses, workshops, and conferences are primarily for developing "awareness" and a working knowledge of a topic. They can be made more effective by being combined with other activities to develop the needed "expertise." For example, in an inservice workshop in which staff are learning about reflexes and positioning techniques, staff might also 1) be provided with relevant readings, 2) observe an occupational or physical therapist doing an individual assessment and working with a child, 3) do simulations with dolls, or 4) help keep a journal of their observations of their children's performance when in different positions in the classroom or at home. Follow-up is also essential if actual transfer and generalization are to take place. It is suggested that some type of follow-up consultation take place to provide feedback and reinforcement to the staff. This can be done

Learning Alternatives	Appropriate for Individual	Appropriate for Group	Level of Competence Acquired				Evaluation Methods									
			Awareness	Working Knowledge	Expertise	Enrichment	Pre/posttest	Interaction Analysis/Observation	Discussion	Staff Journal	Report	Product	Data	Video/Audiotape	Peer Critique	Other
Holding organizational office	X			X	X	X			X		X	X	X			
Conducting workshop	X				X	X			X				X			
Publishing articles	X	X			X	X						X	X			
Developing materials	X	X		X	X	X						X				
Lecture series	X	X	X	X	X		X		X	X	X					
Travel	X	X	X	X		X				X	X					
Readings	X	X		X	X	X	X		X	X	X					
Classroom research	X	X		X		X		X		X			X			
Classroom journal	X			X					X		X	X	X			
Work sessions at Teacher Center	X	X		X	X			X				X				

On-the-job training	X			X	X		X	X	X	X	X	X	X	X	X	
Internship	X			X	X		X	X	X	X	X	X	X	X	X	
Teacher exchange	X			X	X		X	X	X	X	X	X	X	X	X	
Seminar	X	X	X	X		X	X		X	X						
Lecture	X	X	X			X	X		X	X						
Discussion		X	X	X				X		X						
Conferences	X	X	X			X			X	X	X					
Workshops	X	X	X	X		X	X	X	X	X	X	X	X			
Audiovisuals	X	X	X	X			X	X	X					X	X	
Demonstrations	X	X		X	X		X	X	X				X	X	X	
Site visits	X	X	X			X			X	X	X					
Role play/simulation	X	X	X	X	X			X	X					X	X	
Consultation	X	X		X	X		X	X	X				X	X	X	
Curriculum development	X	X		X	X	X						X	X			
Courses	X	X	X	X	X	X	X	X	X	X		X	X			

Figure 3. **Staff development alternatives and evaluation methods.**

through direct consultation in the classroom, or by videotaping staff working with children and families and reviewing the tapes later in individual or group problem-solving sessions.

An effective personalized staff development plan can be developed by carefully assessing the level of staff needs and then working with staff to determine what combinations of activities will lead to the achievement of stated objectives. It should be emphasized that staff development activities should be viewed holistically rather than as fragmented, isolated events. A transdisciplinary, ecological approach to training is recommended.

There are advantages and disadvantages to each training option, so in fulfilling individual staff needs, each option should be carefully discussed. The specifics of what is to be accomplished and how it will be accomplished should be put into writing. For group efforts, careful planning with staff input is necessary.

In determining which alternatives are the most appropriate, consideration should be given to the following:

1. Efficiency and effectiveness
2. Cost-effectiveness
3. Interest level
4. Motivational factors/reinforcement
5. Necessary prerequisite knowledge or skills
6. Support needed
7. Time involved
8. Need for follow-up
9. Scheduling problems
10. Whether generalizable
11. Staff supervision time required
12. Special equipment or materials necessary
13. Individual learning styles
14. Available resources

EVALUATION

Since application of knowledge and skills is the ultimate goal of staff development, most planned activities should result in some observable change in behavior. Demonstration and verbalization of new or improved competence on the part of staff members is an indication of successful staff development.

When the coordinator and staff member meet to discuss the needs assessment and to plan learning options, it is also important to decide how growth will be evaluated. Each staff member needs to be responsible for recording his or her own progress toward the mutually determined objectives. Regularly scheduled supervisory sessions may also be outlined. These sessions may involve observation of the staff member while on the job, followed by a review meeting. Informal, ongoing discussions of progress can also be effective. The coordinator/supervisor must maintain an atmosphere supportive of growth, rather than one that is demanding or threatening.

Figure 3 lists a variety of evaluation methods that might be used to assess progress for each of the learning alternatives presented. Again, various combinations of techniques may be desirable. One of the most commonly utilized methods of evaluation is the pre/posttest. This type of assessment is effective in measuring change in the level of knowledge on a particular subject, but usually does not reveal whether the staff member is able to apply the information in work situations. Pre/post tests are given shortly before and after a training session and are usually limited to brief answer responses that do not adequately assess integration of information or long-term retention of information. They are quick and easy to administer, and criteria for success are easily established. Most staff however, do not like taking tests.

Another method of assessing a group is by follow-up discussion. New awarenesses and application of principles can be shared informally in problem-solving sessions. The coordinator can observe changes in attitude and application of knowledge by directing discussion of issues relevant to the program. For example, after an inservice session on the importance of parent involvement, the coordinator might follow up with a staff discussion on parent involvement in the program. Staff could be called upon to apply new knowledge by planning for changes in the existing program. The coordinator can thus informally assess each staff member's attitudes and ability to apply the new information. Additional staff development activities on parent involvement may then be added as needed.

Individual or small group discussions with the coordinator can also provide informal assessment of staff when the total staff is not participating in the inservice activities. Discussions can be quite supportive and can allow for application of knowledge. They are also less threatening than tests.

When specific skills are being learned, an interaction analysis model is often helpful. The coordinator uses a checklist or observational guide to assess the behaviors the staff member is demonstrating. Interaction analysis is particularly useful for evaluating interactions between a child and a staff member, a staff member and a parent, or two or more staff members. For example, after a series of inservice workshops on communication skills in which participants have read materials, listened to lectures, viewed videotapes, and simulated conferences, the coordinator should evaluate staff members' acquired "expertise." By observing actual conferences between staff members and parents, viewing a videotape of the conference, or listening to an audiotape, the coordinator can assess the degree to which staff members demonstrate the necessary skills. The staff member can then either be congratulated for utilizing good communication skills or, if inadequate skills are demonstrated, be channeled into further staff development activities.

Use of logs or staff journals is an effective way for staff members to be involved in their own assessment. By keeping a journal of daily activities, staff can document growth toward developing a particular process or skill. Often staff do not realize the changes that occur over time. A journal can help a staff member conduct a self-analysis of strengths and weaknesses as well as a self-assessment of progress toward objectives. It is important that the staff member be given enough information and guidelines on what to document. If, for instance, a staff member is working on improving behavior management techniques in the classroom, the coordinator might provide guidelines on the types of information to include in the journal—for example, size of groups, constellation of groups, time of group activities, antecedents to and consequences of negative behaviors, and so on. Ongoing conferences with the supervisor to discuss the material in the journal is important to facilitate problem solving and continued growth.

Much information can be gained through site visits, job-related travel, conferences, external lecture series and workshops, seminars, and university course work. Whenever possible, this information should be shared with other staff members. When making site visits or traveling to other locations to observe different programmatic approaches, it is useful to develop beforehand the objectives of the visit, a list of questions, and an observation guide. The information gained is then easily summarized. Knowledge acquired through external, structured formats can either be assessed by observation of new skills or through informal seminars on-site. It is appropriate for staff to demonstrate their new "working knowledge" in some meaningful way. Preparation of an inservice workshop on the topic can help staff to consolidate and integrate new information more fully. Staff evaluation of the workshop or training session can constitute assessment of competence.

The development of products for use in the program is another means of evaluation. Depending on the knowledge and skills that have been targeted, the following examples of products might serve to evaluate growth:

Curricula
Specialized toys, games, or materials
Specialized equipment
A slide/tape show or film strip
A videotape
Parent information packets
Parent education modules

The effectiveness of the product when used within the program can serve as the measure of success.

The ongoing collection of data with respect to a particular staff development objective is another method for evaluating professional change. Many different forms of data collection can take place. Gathering baseline data and charting increases or decreases in behavior can be done by staff on themselves as well as on their children. Other forms of data can be collected with regard to: time spent with individual children, time spent with groups, number of skills developmentally sequenced or task analyzed, number of contacts with parents, amount of communication with team members, time spent on various activities, and so on.

The coordinator/supervisor can help staff to select program facets that can be measured and analyzed. After desired changes are determined and plans for change implemented, continuous or probe data collection methods can be instituted to record progress. Involving staff in the data collection process makes the information more meaningful and also serves as a motivational factor.

Videotapes or audiotapes can serve as pre- and posttest measures as well as training methods. Audiovisual methods are invaluable and whenever possible should be utilized in conjunction with other methods for planning, implementing, and evaluating professional growth. The entire staff team should also be used in much the same way. Its members can act as a support system and also provide clinical evaluation through peer critiquing of specific skill areas. For example, the speech therapist on the team can help identify targets for improvement for other team members in the areas of speech and language. He or she can also help plan and carry out inservice training activities. At appropriate times the speech therapist can also help team members evaluate their professional growth in this area. Often the use of videotapes by team members during various phases of staff development is an excellent method of strengthening both individual growth and team functioning. Videotapes can also be used to record valuable inservice sessions for future use with other team members or other community agencies.

The optimal staff development assessment plan will incorporate supervisor evaluation, self-evaluation, and colleague critiquing. The appropriate use of each of the previously discussed methods of evaluation by these various program personnel will contribute to a comprehensive evaluation system. Both formative and summative measures of staff development will contribute greatly to the overall program evaluation.

The assessment, planning, implementation, and evaluation phases should comprise an ongoing cycle. Evaluation, for example, may reveal the need to return to the planning phase. In addition, in order for the staff development process to be viewed as continuous, incremental, and responsive to individual and group needs, staff need an opportunity to evaluate the staff development component on a regular basis. The form shown in Figure 4 is an example of an evaluation instrument that can facilitate this feedback process.

GUIDELINES FOR STAFF DEVELOPMENT

1. Staff development needs to be a fundamental component of the program, not an extraneous activity, with a person responsible for coordinating training who has sufficient time and skills to do a quality job.
2. Staff development should be viewed as a supportive, rather than critical, approach to individual and group growth.
3. Competency-based staff development lends itself to individualization and measurement.
4. Competencies should reflect all the areas of the program and include

Evaluation of Staff Development

1. Indicate the inservice activities in which you have participated.
   In column 1, indicate the frequency of your participation:
   1 = at least once a week, 2 = at least once a month, 3 = at least once a year, 4 = never
   In column 2, indicate the usefulness of this activity to you:
   0 = not useful, 1 = not very useful, 2 = useful, 3 = very useful
   In column 3, include any comments you may have.

Staff Developmental Activity	Frequency	Usefulness	Comment
Seminars			
Lectures			
Discussions			
Conferences			
Workshops			
Audiovisuals			
Demonstrations			
Site visits			
Role play, simulations			
Curriculum development			
Courses			
Conducting workshops			
Holding an office			
Publishing articles			
Travel			
Readings			
Classroom research			
Work session at Teacher Center			
On-the-job training			
Teacher exchange			

(continued)

Figure 4. Sample staff development evaluation form.

Evaluation of Staff Development
(continued)

2. What have you gained from inservice training activities?

   1) Awareness (list attitudes or topics about which your awareness is now greater)

   2) Knowledge (list topics or areas about which you now have some working knowledge that is greater than the awareness level)

   3) Skills (list types of skills you have gained)

   4) Expertise (list areas in which you feel you have sufficient expertise to be able to share your knowledge or skills with others)

   5) Other:

3. Indicate your overall satisfaction with inservice activities (circle the one closest to your opinion):

1	2	3	4	5	6
Totally inadequate	Superficial/ insufficient	Met some needs but not enough	Was pretty good, but not individualized	Was pretty good but not indepth	Comprehensive and individualized

4. How could inservice activities be improved? (check (√) those with which you agree)

   _____ More variety
   _____ More applicability
   _____ More individualized
   _____ More incentives
   _____ More time for activities

   _____ More recognition of growth and improvement
   _____ Higher level activities
   _____ More internal staff exchange
   _____ Other (list):

Figure 4. *(continued)*

attitudes, knowledge, and skills commensurate with program philosophy and objectives.

5. A wide variety of alternatives should be available for individual and group learning at the levels of awareness, working knowledge, functional expertise, and enrichment.

6. Staff needs should be identified by a variety of methods, including interviews, questionnaires, and observations, as well as group discussions and team observations.

7. Staff should be involved in developing a written plan of learning alternatives appropriate to their needs that will result in professional growth.

8. Staff should be involved in planning evaluation methods as well as documenting their own growth.
9. Provision should be made for debriefing sessions after training, and feedback to staff on a regular basis.
10. Time and compensation should be considered in planning for staff development.
11. Staff development needs to meet the needs of paraprofessionals, volunteers, and parents, *in addition to* professional staff.
12. Utilization of community resources as well as internal resources can maximize training efforts.
13. An adequate training budget is needed for ongoing staff development.
14. Competence should be rewarded.
15. Staff development should be viewed as a continuous, responsive process.
16. Professionals serving children and families should be involved in training whenever possible.
17. Effectiveness is best evaluated by demonstrated competence.

REFERENCES

Altman, R., & Meyen, E.L. Some observations on competency based instruction. *Exceptional Children*, 1974, *40*(4), 260–265.
Bullock, L.M., Dykes, K.M., & Kelley, T.L. Competency based teacher preparation in behavior disorders. *Exceptional Children*, 1974, *41*(3), 192–194.
Elam, S. *Performance based teacher education: What is the state of the art?* Washington, DC: American Association of Colleges for Teacher Education, 1973.
Falkenstein, L.C. Action learning: A model for inservice teacher education. *The Clearinghouse*, 1977, *50*, 188–191.
Fredericks, H.D., Anderson, R.B., Baldwin, V.L., Grove, D., Moon, W.G., Moore, M., & Baird, J.H. *The identification of competencies of teachers of the severely handicapped.* Monmouth, OR: Teaching Research, 1977.
Garland, C.W. *Skills inventory for teachers.* Williamsburg, VA: Child Development Resources, 1978.
Illinois State Board of Education, Department of Specialized Educational Services. *Early childhood education for the handicapped: Recommended practices and procedures.* Springfield, IL: Illinois State Board of Education, 1979.
Karnes, M.B. *Education of pre-school age handicapped children.* In: W.P. McLure, R.A. Burnham, & R.A. Henderson (eds.), *Special education: needs, costs, methods of financing. Report of a study.* Urbana, IL: Bureau of Educational Research, College of Education, University of Illinois, 1975.
Klein, D.L., Bowser, M.A., & Kater, W.L. *Families first: A program and staff development system.* York, PA: Individual and Family Services, 1978.
Linder, T. A competency-based needs assessment for personnel in early intervention programs. *Educational and Psychological Research*, 1982, *2*(1), 31–42.
Messick, R.G. Competency-based education: In-service implications. *Thrust for Educational Leadership*, 1975, *5*(2), 16–18.
Perrone, V. An in-service program for teachers: The teacher as a student of teaching. *Today's Education*, 1976, *65*(4), 50–52.

Rosner, B. Response to Dr. Broudy's critique. In: W.R. Houston (ed.), *Exploring competency based education.* Berkeley, CA: McCutcham Publishing Corp., 1974.

University of Texas at Austin, Department of Special Education. *Handbook for facilitators of staff training: Early education for handicapped children.* University of Texas at Austin, n.d.

Yeatts, E.H. Staff development: A teacher centered inservice design. *Educational Leadership,* 1976, *33*(6), 417–421.

Needs Assessment for Staff Development

Staff Member: _____

Person Completing Scale: _____

Initial Assessment Date: _____ Color: Green

Mid-year Assessment Date: _____ Color: Blue

End-of-year Assessment Date: _____ Color: Red

Column 1: *For each of the competencies listed below, circle the appropriate skill rating for the staff member being assessed (or for yourself) according to the scale outlined below:*

1 = *a very weak skill (observed less than 25% of the time)*
2 = *a weak skill (observed 25%–50% of the time)*
3 = *an average skill; could use some improvement (observed 50%–70% of the time)*
4 = *something the person does well (observed 75%–90% of the time)*
5 = *a skill that is a real strength (observed 90%–100% of the time)*
NA = *Not applicable*
NO = *No opportunity to observe*

Column 2: *After each competency marked 1, 2, or 3, indicate with a check (√) whether there is a need for training at the level of A = awareness, K = working knowledge, or E = functional expertise. After ranking all competencies, go back through the instrument and place in order of priority (with 1 the highest priority) those items marked as 1 or 2, according to the need for immediacy of training.*

Column 3: *Indicate with a check any items marked as 5 that you feel are skills the person could use to assist in training.*

Column 4: *After discussion with the supervisor, fill in the Staff Development column with the planned activities for increasing knowledge or skills, along with the projected amount of time that will be needed.*

Competency	Skill Rating							Level of Training Needed and Priority of Need				Strengths for Team Sharing	Methods for Staff Development and Time Required
								A	K	E	Priority		
												Column 3	Column 4
		Column 1							Column 2				

Screening/Assessment

Competency													
1. Demonstrates ability to identify different methods of locating children for screening.	NA	1	2	3	4	5	NO						
2. Demonstrates knowledge of screening methods.	NA	1	2	3	4	5	NO						
3. Demonstrates knowledge of current research on screening.	NA	1	2	3	4	5	NO						
4. Demonstrates skill in interviewing parents during screening.	NA	1	2	3	4	5	NO						
5. Demonstrates skill in recording observations of children during screening.	NA	1	2	3	4	5	NO						
6. Demonstrates ability to accurately record and analyze screening data.	NA	1	2	3	4	5	NO						
7. Demonstrates ability to review screening data with an interdisciplinary team.	NA	1	2	3	4	5	NO						
8. Demonstrates knowledge of normal development in observing and assessing the functioning of children from birth through 8 years.	NA	1	2	3	4	5	NO						
9. Demonstrates knowledge of etiologies and psychoeducational implications of various handicapping conditions.	NA	1	2	3	4	5	NO						

(continued)

205

Competency	Column 1 Skill Rating							Column 2 Level of Training Needed and Priority of Need				Column 3 Strengths for Team Sharing	Column 4 Methods for Staff Development and Time Required
								A	K	E	Priority		
10. Demonstrates knowledge of terminology used by other disciplines.	NA	1	2	3	4	5	NO						
11. Demonstrates knowledge of the impact of environmental and cultural factors on a child's development.	NA	1	2	3	4	5	NO						
12. Demonstrates ability to assess a child's level of functioning using nonstandardized assessment techniques (birth through 8 years).	NA	1	2	3	4	5	NO						
13. Demonstrates ability to assess a child's level of functioning using standardized assessment instruments (birth through 8 years):													
gross motor	NA	1	2	3	4	5	NO						
fine motor	NA	1	2	3	4	5	NO						
language	NA	1	2	3	4	5	NO						
cognition	NA	1	2	3	4	5	NO						
social-emotional	NA	1	2	3	4	5	NO						
14. Demonstrates ability to integrate findings derived from 1) interviews and records, 2) observation, 3) formal assessment, and 4) informal assessment; and to state conclusions in written form.													
15. Demonstrates ability to coordinate and conduct a staffing in	NA	1	2	3	4	5	NO						

	NA	1	2	3	4	5	NO						
a manner that is comprehensive, comfortable, and practical.	NA	1	2	3	4	5	NO						
16. Demonstrates ability to share assessment information in a manner that can be understood by all present at the staffing (uses functional examples of behaviors).	NA	1	2	3	4	5	NO						
17. Involves parents in all stages of the staffing, including the development and approval of the IEP.	NA	1	2	3	4	5	NO						

Program and Strategies

	NA	1	2	3	4	5	NO						
18. Demonstrates ability to plan educational programs, both long-term (annual) and short-term (weekly), based on assessment, environmental data, and parental input.	NA	1	2	3	4	5	NO						
19. Demonstrates ability to write instructional objectives in which outcome criteria are specified.	NA	1	2	3	4	5	NO						
20. Demonstrates ability to develop and modify daily lessons based on assessment and observational findings.	NA	1	2	3	4	5	NO						
21. Demonstrates ability to write instructional sequences and activities so that parents and paraprofessionals can follow them.	NA	1	2	3	4	5	NO						
22. Demonstrates ability to task analyze skills to be taught to the child when necessary.	NA	1	2	3	4	5	NO						
23. Demonstrates awareness of and utilizes appropriate curricula in planning appropriate strategies.	NA	1	2	3	4	5	NO						

(continued)

Competency	Column 1 Skill Rating							Column 2 Level of Training Needed and Priority of Need				Column 3 Strengths for Team Sharing	Column 4 Methods for Staff Development and Time Required
	NA	1	2	3	4	5	NO	A	K	E	Priority		
24. Demonstrates ability to evaluate activities to assess how well lesson objectives have been met.	NA	1	2	3	4	5	NO						
25. Demonstrates ability to incorporate input from other disciplines into the child's program.	NA	1	2	3	4	5	NO						
26. Demonstrates ability to modify lessons, response mode, and difficulty level to accommodate the handicap of the child, interests, and unexpected events.	NA	1	2	3	4	5	NO						
27. Demonstrates ability to define a rationale and implement procedures for remediation of deficits or delays in the following areas:													
gross motor	NA	1	2	3	4	5	NO						
fine motor	NA	1	2	3	4	5	NO						
oral motor	NA	1	2	3	4	5	NO						
self-help	NA	1	2	3	4	5	NO						
cognition	NA	1	2	3	4	5	NO						
receptive language	NA	1	2	3	4	5	NO						
expressive language	NA	1	2	3	4	5	NO						
social-emotional	NA	1	2	3	4	5	NO						
health and nutrition	NA	1	2	3	4	5	NO						
28. Demonstrates ability to locate, develop, and/or construct materials													

	NA	1	2	3	4	5	NO
for use with a specific child or group of children to achieve given instructional objectives.	NA	1	2	3	4	5	NO
29. Demonstrates ability to develop and implement a contingency reinforcement system for use with individual children as needed.	NA	1	2	3	4	5	NO
30. Demonstrates ability to record complete, concise data on the child's progress toward stated objectives.	NA	1	2	3	4	5	NO
31. Demonstrates ability to include parents as an integral part of the child's program.	NA	1	2	3	4	5	NO
32. Demonstrates ability to coordinate individual educational and therapeutic programs and activities of the various team members into a comprehensive and consistent plan.	NA	1	2	3	4	5	NO
33. Demonstrates ability to develop and implement activities that are appropriate for home- and center-based programs.	NA	1	2	3	4	5	NO
34. Demonstrates knowledge of and ability to plan and implement formative and summative program evaluation.	NA	1	2	3	4	5	NO
35. Demonstrates ability to monitor the progress of children and staff toward meeting program goals.	NA	1	2	3	4	5	NO

(continued)

Competency	Column 1 Skill Rating							Column 2 Level of Training Needed and Priority of Need				Column 3 Strengths for Team Sharing	Column 4 Methods for Staff Development and Time Required
								A	K	E	Priority		
36. Demonstrates ability to plan safe, appropriate early childhood environments using space, equipment, and materials to foster cognitive, language, self-help, social-emotional, and motor development to meet individual goals.	NA	1	2	3	4	5	NO						
37. Demonstrates ability to articulate criteria for selecting curricula, methods, and materials appropriate for infants and/or preschool children.	NA	1	2	3	4	5	NO						
38. Demonstrates ability to write plans for activities, lessons, and units for groups of children in appropriate development areas at the infant and/or preschool levels.	NA	1	2	3	4	5	NO						
39. Demonstrates ability to individualize for children within a group.	NA	1	2	3	4	5	NO						
40. Demonstrates ability to group children according to appropriate criteria.	NA	1	2	3	4	5	NO						
41. Includes cross-cultural considerations in devising and implementing plans.	NA	1	2	3	4	5	NO						
42. Maintains appropriate records and adheres to confidentiality policies.	NA	1	2	3	4	5	NO						

	NA	1	2	3	4	5	NO			
43. Demonstrates skill in utilizing a variety of behavioral and affective approaches to the management of children's behavior at the infant and/or preschool levels.	NA	1	2	3	4	5	NO			
44. Demonstrates understanding of and skill in interpersonal communication dynamics with children, parents, professionals, and others.	NA	1	2	3	4	5	NO			
Working with Parents										
45. Demonstrates skill in discussing with parents:										
the needs of the family	NA	1	2	3	4	5	NO			
the functioning levels of their handicapped child	NA	1	2	3	4	5	NO			
specific problems or deficits	NA	1	2	3	4	5	NO			
remediation strategies	NA	1	2	3	4	5	NO			
46. Listens to parents' responses and demonstrates empathy for parents' feelings and problems.	NA	1	2	3	4	5	NO			
47. Demonstrates skill in offering parents appropriate suggestions for facilitating their handicapped child's growth and development through play activities.	NA	1	2	3	4	5	NO			
48. Provides written home programs for parents that are appropriate in level and function for both the child and the parents.	NA	1	2	3	4	5	NO			
49. Demonstrates ability to instruct parents in developmental, nutritional, and health related aspects of education.	NA	1	2	3	4	5	NO			

(continued)

211

Competency	Column 1 Skill Rating							Column 2 Level of Training Needed and Priority of Need				Column 3 Strengths for Team Sharing	Column 4 Methods for Staff Development and Time Required
	NA	1	2	3	4	5	NO	A	K	E	Priority		
50. Demonstrates skill in counseling parents and/or siblings regarding problems related to having a handicapped child in the family; and can deal effectively with crises.	NA	1	2	3	4	5	NO						
51. Individualizes the program for families depending on their needs and desires, strengths and limitations.	NA	1	2	3	4	5	NO						
52. Demonstrates ability to guide parents in the selection or creation of materials and toys for their handicapped child.	NA	1	2	3	4	5	NO						
53. Demonstrates ability to conduct parent discussion groups.	NA	1	2	3	4	5	NO						
54. Demonstrates ability to provide parent education information to parents through a variety of channels.	NA	1	2	3	4	5	NO						
55. Demonstrates ability to conduct home visits in a manner that takes into consideration the total family's needs.	NA	1	2	3	4	5	NO						
56. Demonstrates ability to refer parents to appropriate community services when necessary.	NA	1	2	3	4	5	NO						

Leadership

57. Demonstrates ability to train parents, professionals, and paraprofessionals in educational procedures, such as observing and assessing the child, and planning, implementing, and evaluating a program.	NA	1	2	3	4	5	NO
58. Demonstrates understanding of regular preschool classroom operation.	NA	1	2	3	4	5	NO
59. Demonstrates ability to plan and conduct effective inservice training activities for regular preschool teachers.	NA	1	2	3	4	5	NO
60. Demonstrates skill in interacting and consulting with regular preschool teachers.	NA	1	2	3	4	5	NO
61. Uses appropriate techniques—such as modeling, prompting, assisting, cueing—to train others in new skills.	NA	1	2	3	4	5	NO
62. Uses effective measures to provide feedback and reinforcement to persons being taught new skills.	NA	1	2	3	4	5	NO
63. Demonstrates skill in acting as a liaison between persons, groups, or agencies regarding problems relating to handicapped children.	NA	1	2	3	4	5	NO
64. Demonstrates understanding of the total service delivery system and is able to work effectively within the system as a change agent.	NA	1	2	3	4	5	NO

(continued)

213

Competency	Column 1 Skill Rating							Column 2 Level of Training Needed and Priority of Need				Column 3 Strengths for Team Sharing	Column 4 Methods for Staff Development and Time Required
	NA	1	2	3	4	5	NO	A	K	E	Priority		
65. Demonstrates ability to evaluate staffing needs with regard to the number and type of children being served and the type of program model being implemented.	NA	1	2	3	4	5	NO						
66. Demonstrates ability to define and describe various roles within the program.	NA	1	2	3	4	5	NO						
67. Demonstrates ability to define criteria for hiring staff.	NA	1	2	3	4	5	NO						
68. Demonstrates ability to develop formative and summative evaluation measures for children, staff, and the total program.	NA	1	2	3	4	5	NO						
69. Demonstrates ability to plan for individualized staff development, establishing criteria for determination of needs and value of training.	NA	1	2	3	4	5	NO						
Knowledge													
70. Demonstrates knowledge of the rationale for early intervention.	NA	1	2	3	4	5	NO						
71. Demonstrates knowledge of agency goals, funding sources, services, and personnel.	NA	1	2	3	4	5	NO						
72. Demonstrates knowledge of community services, agencies, and resources important to early childhood special education programs.	NA	1	2	3	4	5	NO						

73. Demonstrates knowledge of state and federal legislation and litigation regarding education of exceptional children.	NA	1	2	3	4	5	NO			
74. Demonstrates knowledge of alternative models, program designs, curricula, methods, and materials appropriate for young handicapped children.	NA	1	2	3	4	5	NO			
75. Demonstrates knowledge of research relevant to the development and education of handicapped children.	NA	1	2	3	4	5	NO			
76. Demonstrates knowledge of sociology of the family, family development, and family relationships.	NA	1	2	3	4	5	NO			
Affect										
77. Demonstrates enthusiasm when working with children and families.	NA	1	2	3	4	5	NO			
78. Demonstrates confidence and composure in maintaining the learning environment.	NA	1	2	3	4	5	NO			
79. Demonstrates patience and understanding toward children and families.	NA	1	2	3	4	5	NO			
80. Assumes initiative and responsibility for accomplishing necessary program tasks.	NA	1	2	3	4	5	NO			
81. Utilizes constructive feedback for personal growth and development.	NA	1	2	3	4	5	NO			

(continued)

215

Competency	Column 1 Skill Rating							Column 2 Level of Training Needed and Priority of Need				Column 3 Strengths for Team Sharing	Column 4 Methods for Staff Development and Time Required
								A	K	E	Priority		
82. Recognizes and expresses need for skills and information and staff development activities.	NA	1	2	3	4	5	NO						
83. Shares ideas and skills with other staff.	NA	1	2	3	4	5	NO						
84. Exhibits honest respect for:													
children	NA	1	2	3	4	5	NO						
families	NA	1	2	3	4	5	NO						
staff	NA	1	2	3	4	5	NO						
85. Accepts responsibility for own actions.	NA	1	2	3	4	5	NO						

chapter 9

Evaluation

In periods of economic distress, human service programs often are among the first to come under attack. Innovative projects or programs that are not "traditional" components of education—such as early intervention programs—are frequently targeted for reduced budgets, or even elimination. Unfortunately, programs so threatened are often essential. That they should be continued can only be justified to legislators and others if well-planned and comprehensive evaluations have documented their worth and effectiveness. Indeed, evaluations have become a crucial defensive tool as concern has grown throughout education for greater accountability to justify expenditures.

Evaluation can be described as the objective judgment of the worth of something, usually in terms of its adequacy, effectiveness, or costs. Products, processes, or individual performance are usually evaluated in educational programs. Renzulli (1975) states that

> the general purpose of evaluation is to gather, analyze, and disseminate information that can be used to make decisions about educational programs. Evaluation should be directed toward *action* that hopefully will result in the improvement of services to students through the continuation, modification, or elimination of conditions which affect learning (p. 2).

Anderson, Ball, and Murphy (1975) have identified major purposes for program evaluation as first, that program evaluation can contribute to decisions relating to program initiation, continuation, expansion, endorsement, or modification; second, information from evaluation can be used to rally support for or opposition to a program; and third, evaluation information can contribute to greater understanding of related educational, psychological, social or other processes, that may, in turn, lead to more effective programs.

Program evaluation can be considered analogous to child evaluation. It should be "diagnostic," indicating the strengths and weaknesses of the program, as well as providing the basis for decisions leading to positive growth. To this end, the specific purposes of program evaluation as outlined by Renzulli (1975) include:

1) to discover whether and how effectively the objectives of a program are being fulfilled
2) to discover unplanned and unexpected consequences that are resulting from particular program practices
3) to determine the underlying policies and related activities that contribute to success or failure in particular areas
4) to provide continuous in-process feedback at intermediate stages throughout the course of a program
5) to suggest realistic, as well as ideal, alternative courses of action for program modification (p. 6).

THE PROCESS OF EVALUATION

The evaluation design should flow logically from the stated objectives of the program. The evaluation procedures can be incorporated into activities developed to accomplish program goals (Bourgeois, 1971). Two basic types of information are needed: *formative* evaluation information, which is gathered in an ongoing manner or at intermediate stages in order to discover deficiencies and successes; and *summative* evaluation information, which is concerned with looking at overall program effectiveness. Formative evaluation data are used to measure both the students' and the program's progress toward accomplishing their objectives. Summative evaluation data, on the other hand, measure the end of the students' and the program's growth and are used to determine the fate of the program. Table 1 compares the characteristics of these two types of evaluation.

When to Evaluate

Throughout the life of a program, both formative and summative evaluation are necessary. In early childhood special education, it is recommended that program components be examined using both formative and summative evaluation techniques. Services to children, services to parents, and staff development are all important components for evaluation (Suarez & Vandivier, 1978). In addition, coordination of community services and demonstration and dissemination (for grant-funded projects) may also be worthy aspects to be evaluated. For each component, various models have been recommended for structuring the analysis of data (Eash, 1972; Provus, 1971; Stake, 1967; Stufflebeam, Foley, Gephart, Guba, Hammond, Merriman, & Provus, 1971; Suarez & Vandivier, 1978). Regardless of the terminology employed, however, most models examine 1) what resources and conditions contribute to program objectives, 2) what events take place to accomplish necessary objectives, and 3) what takes place as a result of the program.

Table 1. A comparison of formative and summative evaluation

Feature	Formative Evaluation	Summative Evaluation
1. Principal purpose	Developmental improvement of a program or product	Judgment of the overall worth of program or product
2. Schedule of use	Continual; data fed back into developmental cycle	Normally, when program is completed or product finished; or at go/no-go, fund/no-fund decision
3. Evaluative style	Rigorous, systematic diagnosis	Rigorous, systematic, comparative, or using absolute standards
4. Normal evaluators	Internal staff or supportive consultants hired by program or product developers	External, non-partisan personnel or internal staff
5. Consumers of evaluation	Program designers and staff, product developers, "insiders"	Market consumers, funding agencies, "outsiders"

Reprinted with permission from: Goodwin, W.L., & Driscoll, L.A. *Handbook for Measurement and Evaluation in Early Childhood Education*. San Francisco: Jossey-Bass, 1980, p. 355. Based on Scriven's model.

Stake (1967) suggests that at the various levels of evaluation (for example, antecedents, transactions, and outcomes) observations should be compared to the initial purposes of the program. The resulting comparative data, when analyzed in relation to accepted standards, provide the basis for judgments concerning program decisions. The types of data gathered will vary, depending on the stage of evolution of the program—that is, whether the program is in the "initiatory" stage, when it is being planned and conceptualized; the "developmental" stage, when the program is actually implemented; or the "integration" stage, when the program becomes an internal part of the existing program (Eash, 1972). Table 2 depicts examples of questions (evaluation concerns in question form) that might be raised at each level of evaluation according to the stage of program development. Information is needed in relation to input, processes, products (or results), and efficiency of each stage. Again, note that at different evolutional stages, the evaluation questions and data needed are different.

Program evaluation is an integral part of the program and should *always* be planned prior to project implementation. Several key questions need to be asked at the time of planning for evaluation:

1. Why is the evaluation being conducted?
2. Who will receive the evaluation information? (Who are the decision makers?)
3. What kind of information do the decision makers need? (In what evolutionary stage is the program?)
4. What type of formative evaluation data are needed?

Table 2. Evaluation according to program development stages for each level of evaluation

Level	Initiatory	Developmental	Integrated
Input	What community agencies have been involved in program planning? What have been the contributions to planning of the various agencies?	What are the program objectives? Where has financial support for the program emanated?	What data are available to document the effect of the program on existing program components? What data are available to assist in long-range planning?
Process	What formal and informal mechanisms have been initiated to ensure comprehensive programs? What have been the impediments to organizing the program?	What activities have been utilized to meet objectives for children? What activities have been organized to provide support to parents?	What ongoing mechanisms have been established to ensure quality programs? What plans have been implemented to expand dissemination of program information?
Product	Does the planning committee have an action plan with a time frame for activities?	What have been the effects of the program on the children served? What have been the effects of the program on families served?	Is any provision made for studying long-term effects? Have there been any unanticipated effects?
Efficiency	Given the amount of time and money invested, has a useful product emerged?	How does the cost per child compare to comparable programs in the state?	What is the projection for maintenance of the program?

Adapted from Eash (1972).

5. What type of summative evaluation data are needed?
6. What instruments are needed to gather necessary data?
7. When should the data be gathered?
8. How will data be analyzed?
9. Who will do the evaluation?

The responses to these questions will determine the structure of the evaluation.

Why Evaluate

The question of *why* the evaluation is being conducted is vital. Administrators, staff, parents, and outside agencies working with the project will all be called upon to provide data, and it is important that all parties concerned understand the rationale for evaluation and perceive its usefulness to them individually. A commitment to follow through on conducting the formative and summative measurements is necessary, or the entire evaluation design, and consequently the program, could be jeopardized for lack of sufficient data. Equally important is a commitment by all parties, particularly administrators and staff, to *utilize* information gained from evaluations to *modify* programs accordingly. It is human nature for administrators to want to see evaluation data that are favorable to the existing systems. However, an openness to self-examination, which may point out deficiencies or service gaps, is essential to the development of an effective program.

Who are the recipients of the evaluation information, why are they interested in the information, and what will they do with it? The major groups concerned with evaluation results include: parents, staff, administrators, the school board, state and/or federal agencies, and community agencies and organizations. Different types of information appeal to the various groups: Parents, for example, are not only interested in how much their child has progressed, but may also want to know how other parents view the program or what modifications are planned to address unmet needs. Teachers may want to know what environmental changes would enhance their classroom's effectiveness, while speech therapists may want information about aspects such as the effectiveness of individual versus group instruction. Administrators may be concerned with cost efficiency and program effectiveness as well as staff training needs. The school board may want information on continuation of the program, the implications for long-range planning, as well as consumer satisfaction. Other community agencies may want information relating to overlaps or gaps in service and the impact of agency involvement.

By analyzing the nature of the groups who will receive evaluation data, a comprehensive evaluation design can be planned to encompass the needs of all interested persons and groups. The lack of thoughtful planning may lead to information collected for one group only (the funding agency) to the exclusion of others who might be important advocates and support groups when the critical question of program continuation arises.

COMPONENTS TO EVALUATE AND TYPES OF DATA NEEDED

As previously mentioned, several critical components need to be addressed in evaluation:

Services to children
Services to parents
Staff development
Coordination of community resources
Demonstration/dissemination (for grant-funded projects)

Documentation in each of these areas is crucial. Documentation refers to

> the process of recording the design, activities, and accomplishments of a program. Documentation forms the foundation of a project's evaluation in that it provides both the description of the program and many of the results. It also substantiates the contents of progress reports and continuation proposals. Finally, documentation provides the substance for products, demonstration and information materials which include brochures, speeches, workshops, and the like (Suarez & Vandivier, 1978, p. 3).

Recommended documentation in each area includes: 1) the *rationale*, or the framework for selection of strategies; 2) a *description* of services provided and their outcomes; 3) the *reaction* of people to the services, their perceptions of and satisfaction with the quality and quantity of activities; and 4) the *changes* that have occurred in people and/or activities after participation in the project (Suarez & Vandivier, 1978). Table 3 indicates the types of documentation that may be needed in each area.

The types of formative and summative data needed can be determined by addressing the needs of the decision makers and potential "advocacy" groups. Mayer (1982) indicates that evaluation to meet local, state and federal requirements should include a) program information indicating programs, components, pupil, and personnel data, b) fiscal status and budget control information, c) nonduplicated child count, d) program description, e) program quality, and f) legal compliance.

Each of the stated objectives of the program also needs to be addressed in the evaluation plan. A variety of methods may be needed to assess adequately the program's effectiveness in accomplishing its objectives. For example, an objective might state: "Ninety percent of the children served will accomplish seventy percent of the stated objectives in their IEPs within 1 year." To evaluate this objective, both formative and summative measures would be needed. During the year, staff should maintain ongoing assessment data to enable them to modify the child's program as needed to increase the rate of growth. Summative measures will address the child's total growth at the end of the year.

Important additional information, however, should also be gained in relation to the above objective. For instance: What strategies seemed most effective in intervention? Did the parents see the same growth at home as the staff did at

Table 3. Types of documentation needed in evaluation

Component	Rationale	Description	Reaction	Changes
SERVICES TO CHILDREN	1. Document the rationale on which the services to children are based.	1. Document the criteria for selection of children.	1. Document the parents' degree of satisfaction and/or their reaction to project services for their children.	1. Document the progress of children receiving project services using the most reliable and valid measure available.
		2. Provide evidence that the children served are handicapped.		
		3. Describe the project children, including their ages and type and severity of handicap.		
		4. Document the existence, implementation, and results of an IEP for each child.		
		5. Describe the services that were provided.		
		6. Document the extent to which the stated goals and objectives were attained.		

(continued)

Table 3. *continued*

Component	Rationale	Description	Reaction	Changes
SERVICES TO PARENTS	1. Document the rationale for services to parents.	1. Describe the services that were provided to parents.	1. Document the parents' reactions to the program for their children.	1. Document changes in parents' knowledge and/or behavior during and after participation in the program.
		2. Document the extent to which stated goals and objectives for parents were attained.	2. Document the parents' reactions to the program for themselves.	
STAFF DEVELOPMENT	1. Document the rationale for the specified staff roles needed to carry out the project activities.	1. Document the responsibilities of the staff and their particular training and experience for those responsibilities.	1. Document the staff development activities in which they participated.	1. Document the change in staff members' knowledge competencies and/or behavior after participation in the staff development program.
	2. Document the existing staff development needs on which the staff development program is to be based.	2. Document the activities and outcomes of the staff's orientation of the project.	2. Document other persons' reactions to the staff in areas targeted for staff development.	
		3. Describe the staff development activities.		

224

	4. Document staff involvement in staff development activities.		
	5. Document the extent to which stated goals and objectives for staff development were attained.		
COORDINATION OF COMMUNITY RESOURCES[a]	1. Document the rationale for interagency coordination and cooperation.	1. Describe the various agencies that are involved in coordinating services to children in the project.	1. Document the reaction of the community agency staff who have been involved in interagency coordination.	1. Document the services that have been provided as a result of interagency coordination.
		2. Describe the various roles and responsibilities of the agencies involved.	2. Document the reaction of the program staff who have been involved with coordination efforts.	2. Document other changes that may have occurred as a result of the coordination of services.
		3. Document the formal and informal agreements that have been developed among agencies to provide comprehensive services to children.		
		4. Describe the activities that have taken place in ongoing coordination.		

(continued)

Table 3. *continued*

Component	Rationale	Description	Reaction	Changes
COORDINATION OF COMMUNITY RESOURCES[a] (*continued*)		5. Document the extent to which stated goals and objectives have been met.		
DEMONSTRATION/DISSEMINATION[b]	1. Document the rationale for demonstration/dissemination.	1. Specify the target audiences for each demonstration/dissemination activity.	1. Document the reaction of demonstration/dissemination audiences as appropriate for specific activities.	1. Document change in knowledge or action of audiences as appropriate for specific activities.
		2. Specify what project or projects are to be demonstrated or disseminated.		
		3. Describe demonstration/dissemination activities.		
		4. Document the extent to which the goals and objectives of the demonstration/dissemination component were attained.		

Adapted, with permission, from: Suarez, T.M., & Vandivier, P., (eds.). *Planning for Evaluation. A Resource Book for Preschool Handicapped Children: Documentation.* Chapel Hill, NC: Technical Assistance Development System, 1978. p. 4.

[a]Not included in the discussion presented by TADS, but included here because of its importance to program planning and evaluation.

[b]May not be a component of nongrant funded projects.

school, in other words, did the skills generalize? What problems occurred to hinder growth? What environmental conditions most facilitated growth? Was input from other agencies helpful? Did parents' efforts at follow through affect the rate of growth? Obviously, the questions asked and information gathered to supplement the formative and summative measurements will vary with the objective or program aspect being evaluated.

If only the accomplishment per se of a program objective is evaluated, much valuable information will not be obtained. The variables and parameters related to each objective need to be studied to determine important interrelationships among inputs, processes, and outputs, and, thus, their implications for program improvement.

EVALUATION INSTRUMENTS AND DATA ANALYSIS

The instruments used to gather evaluation data are extremely important. Use of poorly designed or inappropriate devices may yield inadequate data (at best) or even worthless data. The program evaluator needs an extensive background in tests and measurement. Whenever possible, existing reputable instruments should be used. As in the case of individual child assessment, instruments should be valid, reliable, appropriate to the population, and practical (in administration and interpretation).

Established instruments, however, do not need to be used for every aspect of evaluation. Many instruments may need to be constructed to obtain information that is unique to the evaluation needs of the program. Questionnaires, rating scales, checklists, interview schedules, logs, anecdotal recording systems, inventories, and observational systems are all frequently used tools in both formative and summative evaluation.

Analysis of data involves breaking down the information gathered into areas so that relationships can be seen between and among program variables. Two types of data analysis are commonly used: logical analysis and statistical analysis (Renzulli, 1975).

Logical analysis involves taking descriptive data and looking for patterns, trends, and implications. Anecdotal records or information from open-ended questionnaires are often analyzed in this fashion.

Statistical analysis can be used to describe characteristics of groups in relation to particular variables. Means, standard deviations, medians, percentiles, and stanines are examples of statistical data that may be used to describe a population. Inferential statistics are then used to ascertain whether the differences between scores are significant. Tests of statistical significance include t-tests, analysis of variance and covariance, and multiple regression.

It is important that the evaluator have a working knowledge of the uses and limitations of such statistical devices, so as to plan appropriately for what information needs to be obtained. Statistical analysis is most useful in summative evaluation, and in trying to isolate variables that may affect certain outcomes. Again, the audience should be kept in mind in presenting statistical data. These data may need to be described in lay terms, but supported by the statistical methodology.

In planning for both formative and summative evaluation, decisions need to be made concerning when data will be collected. It is wise to plan key formative evaluations early in the program so that information obtained can be used to make program improvements *within* that school year. As stated earlier, formative evaluations are done for the purpose of providing an ongoing basis of decision making concerning the services being provided to children and their families. By spacing evaluations carefully, knowledge gained may lead to important changes.

For example, after the first quarter of the year, information on the parent component could be gathered: a) parents might be surveyed to determine their level of satisfaction with program options; b) counts could be made of parental involvement in program options; c) and data on parent follow-through examined. In this way, factors might be identified that would allow for changes to be made to increase participation of *both* parents. The analysis of data may reveal the need for transportation, day-care, or evening and weekend options that may necessitate changing staff patterns and service delivery options. If these checks are not performed early in the year, the information will end up in summative evaluation—and thus changes will not be made until the following year, with the possible consequence that children and families might not progress as rapidly as they would have had the changes been made earlier.

CONDUCTING THE EVALUATION

The question of who should do the evaluation is important because it is most desirable that the evaluator be involved from the beginning of program planning. In this way, the evaluation can incorporate a comprehensive evaluation system suited to the program objectives, with appropriate formative measurement instruments ready to be implemented at the outset of the program. Depending on the budget, an outside evaluator may be hired. Usually, however, the program coordinator or administrator is responsible for planning the evaluation, supervising data collection and compilation, and interpreting the results.

Summative Evaluation

A sample summative evaluation plan for early childhood special education programs is included at the end of this chapter (pages 232–240). The format used examines 1) evaluation questions, 2) sources of data that might answer the question, 3) methods to be used for data collection, 4) how data will be analyzed, and 5) when the information will be gathered, across five areas of concentration. These areas of concentration—services to children, services to parents, staff development, coordination of community resources, and demonstration/

dissemination—represent the components of evaluation discussed earlier, and are subdivided as necessary to allow for comprehensive evaluation. Services to children is broken down into Child Find, assessment, and program considerations. Services to parents is examined in the areas of due process, parent support, parent involvement, and parent education. Staff development is subdivided into preservice/inservice and staff evaluation.

This evaluation design is offered as a starting point for programs, and is meant to provide examples of major concerns that deserve attention in planning for evaluation. Specific instruments are not recommended; these should be selected according to individual needs of programs. The data gathered in this summative evaluation should provide information concerning overall program effectiveness as well as areas for program modification.

Formative Evaluation

The majority of evaluation concerns included in the plan at the end of the chapter are summative in nature, providing an overview of the strengths and weaknesses of the program. But even more essential, perhaps, are the evaluation data gathered by staff throughout the year. This ongoing formative evaluation can provide the data necessary to make decisions concerning daily practices that affect children and their families (Caldwell, 1977). Howell, Kaplan, and O'Connell (1979) have identified the advantages of formative evaluation. Ongoing formative evaluation allows a means for evaluating growth in children as it occurs, and thus enables teachers to detect problems more quickly. By providing the teacher with up-to-date feedback, program changes may be made as needed, and more rapid growth may result.

Perhaps the most important type of formative evaluation is that which measures the handicapped child's day-to-day progress. There are many instruments available to provide growth information. These include criterion-referenced tests, teacher-made task analyses, and precision teaching instruments. (For additional information, see Chapter 6.) Use of such instruments facilitates observation of the child's progress. If progress is not occurring at an expected rate, then something is wrong and modifications are needed. Ongoing child assessment can serve to alert staff to re-examine what is happening within the child's environment (or perhaps within the child in the case of a degenerative disorder).

Many other program aspects are worthy of formative evaluation. Program effectiveness can be strengthened through staff analysis to determine the relationships between program variables and the effects of these variables on program outputs (in other words, child, parent, and staff behaviors). At the classroom level, for example, numerous environmental parameters affect the final behavioral results seen in the child, the parents, and the staff. Characteristics of the physical environment, interpersonal environment, curriculum, schedule, children, parents, staff, therapies, and specialized training strategies have an effect on one another and, in turn, influence program results.

It is extremely important that teachers understand that they make formative evaluation decisions almost every day. Child, parent, and staff behaviors—the program outputs—are strongly influenced by these evaluation decisions. Any changes made in the child's environment or program should be made only after evaluating the relevant variables. Staff should be encouraged to conduct "mini" research projects to determine how different variables can have an impact on the program to achieve more effective results.

GUIDELINES FOR EVALUATION

1. The evaluation design should flow logically from the stated objectives of the program.
2. Measurements obtained should be appropriate to the stated needs and objectives.
3. Procedures for data collection should be carefully delineated.
4. Both formative and summative evaluation measures should be incorporated from the beginning of the program.
5. With formative evaluation measures, systematic feedback mechanisms must be developed so that information reaches decision makers in time to make changes.
6. Personnel at each level of decision-making responsibility must make a commitment to incorporate needed changes, based on evaluation data.
7. Methods of data analysis should be outlined.
8. Avoid logical and statistical errors in design or interpretation by utilizing personnel or consultants who are knowledgeable in tests and measurements, or by utilizing established instruments.

REFERENCES

Anderson, S.B., Ball, S., Murphy, R.T., & Associates. *Encylopedia of educational evaluation.* San Francisco: Jossey-Bass, 1975.

Bloom, B.S., Hastings, T.J., & Madaus, G.F. *Handbook of formative and summative evaluation of student learning.* New York: McGraw-Hill Book Co., 1971.

Bourgeois, M.M. *Grantsmanship: How to develop and write proposals.* Cheyenne, WY: State Department of Education, 1971.

Caldwell, B.M. Evaluating program effectiveness. In: B.M. Caldwell & D.J. Stedman (eds.), *Infant education: A guide for helping handicapped children in the first three years.* New York: Walker & Co., 1977.

Eash, M.J. *Issues in evaluation and accountability in special programs for gifted and talented children.* Chicago Circle: University of Illinois, 1972.

Goodwin, W.L., & Driscoll, L.A. *Handbook for measurement and evaluation in early childhood education.* San Francisco: Jossey-Bass, 1980.

Howell, K.W., Kaplan, J.S., & O'Connell, C.Y. *Evaluating exceptional children. A task analysis approach.* Columbus, OH: Charles E. Merrill Publishing Co., 1979.

Illinois State Board of Education, Department of Specialized Education Services. Appendix A: Evaluation of early childhood programs. In: *Early childhood education for the* handicapped. *Recommended procedures and practices manual.* Springfield: Illinois State Board of Education, September, 1979.

Mayer, L.C. *Educational administration and special education: A handbook for school administrators.* Boston: Allyn and Bacon, 1982.

Provus, M.M. *Discrepancy evaluation.* Berkeley, CA: McCutchen, 1971.

Renzulli, J.S. *A guidebook for evaluating programs for the gifted and talented* (working draft). Ventura, CA: Office of the Ventura County Superintendent of Schools, 1975.

Stake, R.E. The countenance of educational evaluation. *Teacher's College Record,* 1967, *68,* 523–540.

Stufflebeam, D.L., Foley, W.J., Gephart, W.J., Guba, E.G., Hammond, R.L., Merriman, H.O., & Provus, M.M. *Education evaluation and decision making in education,* Itasca, IL: F.E. Peacock Publishers, 1971.

Suarez, T.M., & Vandivier, P. (eds.). *Planning for evaluation. A resource book for programs for preschool handicapped children: Documentation.* Chapel Hill, NC: Technical Assistance Development System, 1978.

**Sample Summative Evaluation Plan for an
Early Childhood Special Education Program**

Evaluation Question	Sources of Data	Data Collection Methods	Data Analysis	When Gathered
I. Services to Children **A. Child Find** Has joint planning taken place among agencies serving children and their families?	Child Find Coordinator	Documentation of meetings, delineation of roles and responsibilities, formal and informal commitments	Descriptive analysis	Ongoing collection plus annual summary
Have procedures been implemented to inform the community about: 1) the importance of early intervention, 2) availability of programs, 3) parent/child rights, 4) early warning signs?	Child Find Coordinator	Documentation of newspaper articles, film clips, TV and radio announcements, meetings, brochures and their distribution	Descriptive analysis	Ongoing collection plus annual summary
How effective have the awareness efforts been?	Parents in the community; Agencies serving families	Survey of parents by telephone, random questionnaire survey; Survey of community agencies; Summary data of number of referrals and source of referral	Descriptive and statistical analysis	Annually
Have procedures for locating all preschool children been implemented?	Child Find Coordinator	Documentation of procedures	Analysis of percentage of population found	Documentation at the conclusion of activities
How effective are the location procedures?	Hospital birth rates; Kindergarten records; Screening results	Comparison of numbers of children screened with birth rate and school records	Descriptive plus percentage estimates	Annually
Is the identification/referral process effective?	Child Find Coordinator; Program Coordinator	Comparison of number of children referred with the number diagnosed	Statistical analysis	Annually
B. Assessment Have procedures been established for conducting individual assessments?	Program Coordinator; Teachers; Parents	Documentation of procedures, numbers of children evaluated, types of instruments, staff, etc.	Descriptive	Ongoing collection plus annual summary

232

Are assessment procedures in compliance with federal, state and local requirements?	Program Coordinator	Comparison of procedures with federal, state, local guidelines	Descriptive	Annually
How effective are assessment procedures?	Program Coordinator; Teachers; Parents	Interviews, questionnaires (post-staffing) to determine if information was helpful; Comparison of assessment data to classroom	Descriptive	Intermittent (quarterly) checks
Have procedures for conducting a staffing been implemented?	Program Coordinator	Documentation of procedures, who is involved, amount of time spent, records, etc.	Descriptive	Annually
Are staffing procedures in compliance with federal and state requirements?	Program Coordinator	Comparison of procedures with federal and state guidelines	Descriptive	Annually
How effective are the staffing procedures?	Program Coordinator; Teachers; Parents	Interview or questionnaire distributed to participants of staffings; Tally the number of appeals; Follow-up with teachers to ascertain if placement was appropriate	Descriptive plus percentages	Ongoing collection plus annual summary
Are the IEPs developed for each child appropriate?	Program Coordinator; Teachers; Parents	Survey of parents and teachers; Number of changes made after staffing	Descriptive. What changes are necessitated? Satisfaction with IEPs	Annually
C. Program				
Has a full range of services been implemented?	Program Coordinator	Documentation of range of options available, number of children participating in each option, staff allocations	Descriptive	Annually
Is there evidence that the learning environment is maximally effective?	Staff; Parents; Program Coordinator; Outside evaluator	Survey staff and parents through interview and questionnaire; On-site review by coordinator or expert using observation guide	Descriptive data from observation tools; Descriptive data summarizing surveys	As needed when questions arise; Once mid-year and end of year

(continued)

233

Sample Summative Evaluation Plan for an
Early Childhood Special Education Program
(continued)

Evaluation Question	Sources of Data	Data Collection Methods	Data Analysis	When Gathered
Are the methods and activities used by staff maximally effective in achieving children's goals and objectives?	Staff	Test of performance of child based on CRT and norm-referenced instrument	Descriptive and statistical analysis	Ongoing collection plus annual summary
Is there evidence that the content and sequence of the curriculum are developmentally appropriate?	Staff	Documentation of child progress and documentation that the curriculum is sequential and based on learning theory	Descriptive	Beginning of program, revised as needed
Have procedures for ordering equipment been developed that require justification that materials are developmentally appropriate and geared to the needs of handicapped children?	Program Coordinator	Documentation of procedures inventories, forms; when used, etc.	Descriptive	Prior to beginning of program, and end of year
How effective are the materials and equipment used in the program?	Staff	Frequency-of-use survey with inventory check	Descriptive	Annually
Is there evidence that the instructional groupings are based on need rather than disabilities?	Program Coordinator	Child progress and documentation of procedures for determining groupings; Policy statement	Descriptive	Beginning of program
Is there evidence that the staff utilization model is trans-disciplinary?	Program Director; Staff	Job descriptions, staff assignments, time-activity records, staff log	Descriptive	Annually
Is there evidence that the staff/child ratio is optimal?	Program Director; Staff; Parents	Time/work sheets; Survey of staff, parents	Descriptive	Annually

234

Question	Responsible party	Method	Analysis	Frequency
Do the staff possess necessary skills to intervene in all necessary aspects of the child's program?	Program Coordinator	Staff evaluation through output and interview	Descriptive	Ongoing but at least annually
Do teachers, administrators, support personnel and parents have a positive attitude about the program?	Administrators; Staff; Parents	Survey of these groups through interview and/or questionnaire	Statistical analysis of results	Annually or every 2 years
Is there evidence that the overall program is making a significant difference in children's learning?	Staff; Assessment team	Group progress on standardized instruments; Group tally of numbers of objectives attained	Pretest/posttest design, statistical analysis	Annually
Have procedures for the smooth transition from one program to another been implemented?	Program Coordinator	Documentation of procedures, forms, flowcharts, meetings, etc.	Descriptive	Every 2 years
Are the transition procedures effective?	Staff; Teachers	Attitude survey; Follow-up of child progress via IEP	Descriptive	Every 2 years
Have procedures for integration with nonhandicapped children been implemented?	Program Coordinator	Documentation of procedures, number of handicapped and nonhandicapped integrated and participating, length or frequency of contact, nature of interaction	Descriptive	Every 2 years
II. Services to Parents **A. Due Process** Is information on due process procedures made available to parents prior to assessment and staffing?	Program Coordinator	Documentation of information given to parents delineating their rights	Descriptive	Beginning of the program: This information should be made available to parents upon referral for evaluation

(continued)

Sample Summative Evaluation Plan for an
Early Childhood Special Education Program
(continued)

Evaluation Question	Sources of Data	Data Collection Methods	Data Analysis	When Gathered
Is there evidence that parents understand their rights?	Parents; Program Coordinator	Survey by interview, questionnaire; Document number of parents who appeal staffing decision	Descriptive	Annually
Are parents actively involved in staffings and the development of IEPs?	Parents; Program Coordinator; Staff	Documentation of parental input into IEP; Survey of staff to determine parents' attitudes after staffing their child	Descriptive	Annually
Are there procedures for informing parents of their child's progress?	Program Coordinator	Documentation of scheduling and procedures for parent-staff counseling meetings	Descriptive	Annually
Is there evidence that parents understand the methods of measuring the progress?	Parents	Survey parents by interview and questionnaire	Descriptive	Annually
B. Parent Support Are options available for parents to obtain support and counseling?	Program Coordinator	Documentation of nature of services available to parents, number of parents served in each	Descriptive analysis	Annually
Are parent support and counseling efforts effective?	Parents	Attitude of parents measured through interviews, questionnaires, or rating scales; Staff observations of growth and change	Descriptive analysis	Intermittent
C. Parent Involvement Are options available for parent participation?	Program Coordinator	Documentation of options available, number of parents participating	Descriptive	Annually

Are parents involved in decision making, program planning, and operation?	Program Coordinator	Documentation of the types of decision-making activities, number of parents involved	Descriptive	Annually
Is there evidence that parent participation is meaningful to the parents?	Program Coordinator	Survey of parents to determine their perception of their participatory role	Descriptive	Annually
D. Parent Education				
Are options available to parents for obtaining information concerning issues related to their handicapped child?	Program Coordinator; Staff; Parents	Document options available: classes, workshops, library, videotapes; counseling sessions, etc.	Descriptive	Annually
Is there evidence that parents have increased their knowledge about issues related to their handicapped child?	Program Coordinator; Staff; Parents	Document numbers of parents utilizing each option: Pre/posttest in courses and workshops; Questionnaire, ratings	Descriptive and percentage analysis	Ongoing analysis, evaluate each class or workshop at the time of presentation; End-of-year summary of total effectiveness
Are the parents given opportunities to increase their skills in working and playing with their handicapped children?	Staff	Documentation of processes used to teach parents intervention skills and outcomes	Descriptive	Annually
Is there evidence that parents are effectively interacting with their children and providing a stimulating environment for growth?	Staff; Parents	Document numbers of programs planned and/or completed by parents, types of changes made in home environments, pre/posttests; Survey of parents by interview and questionnaire to determine their comfort level in interacting and working with their handicapped child	Descriptive and statistical analysis	Annually

(continued)

**Sample Summative Evaluation Plan for an
Early Childhood Special Education Program**

(continued)

Evaluation Question	Sources of Data	Data Collection Methods	Data Analysis	When Gathered
III. Staff Development **A. Preservice/Inservice** Have role descriptions been written delineating responsibilities, background and experience desired?	Program Coordinator	Documentation of job descriptions	Descriptive	Prior to hiring program staff
Have persons been hired with philosophy and skills needed in the program?	Program Coordinator	Documentation of criteria for selection of staff, job applicants	Descriptive	Annually
Has a needs assessment been implemented to determine training needs prior to (if possible) or after program initiation?	Program Coordinator	Documentation of needs assessment procedures, who was surveyed, when, how, with what results	Descriptive	Beginning of year and ongoing
Have systematic procedures for inservice training been implemented?	Program Coordinator	Documentation of procedures, i.e., identification of objectives, format, dates, attendance, etc.	Descriptive	Ongoing
How effective are the procedures for inservice training?	Staff involved in training	Evaluation questionnaire on content, organization, presentation, etc. given to participants of training	Descriptive and statistical analysis	Ongoing collection plus annual summary
Have the client groups acquired the awareness, knowledge, or skills targeted in training?	Program Coordinator; Staff	On-site observtion of skills, development of product or pre/posttest	Descriptive and statistical analysis	Ongoing, plus annually
B. Staff Evaluations Are there procedures for evaluation of individual staff members?	Program Coordinator	Documentation of procedures, forms, interviews, observation scales	Descriptive	Prior to beginning of program

Are the procedures for staff evaluation effective and acceptable to staff?	Program Coordinator; Staff	Documentation of results of evaluation, staff development, reassignment, etc.; Survey of staff attitudes toward evaluation procedures	Descriptive	Annually or every 2 years
Are there procedures for determining effectiveness of staff utilization?	Program Coordinator	Documentation of time scheduling, staff/child ratios, meeting times, planning time, etc.	Descriptive	Annually
Are the staff utilization procedures effective?	Program Coordinator; Staff	Survey of staff	Descriptive	Annually
IV. Coordination of Community Resources Has a system for coordinating contacts between various public and private agencies been implemented?	Program Coordinator	Document interagency network development—logs, matrices, diagram of interrelationships	Descriptive	Prior to initiation of program
Have procedures been established for coordinating services to children and their families?	Program Coordinator	Document procedures for coordination of services, i.e., services summary, duplication and gaps, formal and informal agreements, objectives, responsibilities	Descriptive	Prior to initiation of program; Ongoing as needed for specific children
Are the interagency coordination efforts effective?	Program Coordinator; Other agencies	Survey of representatives of cooperating agencies to ascertain degree of satisfaction with cooperative efforts; Document number of children and/or families receiving cooperative services and/or fundings	Descriptive	Ongoing and annually

(continued)

239

**Sample Summative Evaluation Plan for an
Early Childhood Special Education Program**
(continued)

Evaluation Question	Sources of Data	Data Collection Methods	Data Analysis	When Gathered
V. Demonstration/ Dissemination				
Have materials, strategies, products to be demonstrated or disseminated been identified?	Program Coordinator	Documentation of objectives of demonstration and dissemination	Descriptive	Beginning of program
Have procedures and timelines for the development of materials, products, strategies, etc. been developed?	Program Coordinator; Staff	Documentation of plans, timelines, outlines, etc., related to each demonstration/dissemination project	Descriptive	Beginning of program.
Have a variety of demonstration/dissemination efforts been implemented?	Program Coordinator	Documentation of speeches, workshops, presentations, articles, publications, final products, etc., with dates, audiences, and presentor	Descriptive	Ongoing
Have demonstration/dissemination efforts been effective?	Program Coordinator; Staff	Evaluation questionnaires after presentations; Document change in knowledge of audiences; Number of publications; Number of replication sites and number of children served	Descriptive and statistical analysis	Ongoing

Some aspects of this chart adapted from Illinois State Board of Education, Department of Specialized Education Services. Appendix A: Evaluation of early childhood programs. In: *Early Childhood Education for the Handicapped: Recommended Procedures and Practices Manual*, pp. 34–44. Springfield: Illinois State Board of Education, 1979.

chapter
10

Funding
Alternatives

Traditionally, concern for funding has been an administrative responsibility. Today, however, as funding is becoming more competitive and program continuation increasingly problematic, it is imperative that all personnel understand the fiscal process. If early childhood special education programs are to be sustained and, indeed, augmented, it will require the efforts of all those involved in the field. The more information staff have about budgets and funding options, the greater their contribution can be toward solving fiscal problems.

HISTORICAL TRENDS

The growth of early childhood special education programs has post-dated the development of school-age special education programs, but has generally utilized parallel funding sources. Special education programs have historically been a local responsibility. Prior to 1975, mildly handicapped children were usually served in the public schools and moderately to severely handicapped children, if served at all, were to be found in private or not-for-profit programs. Many severely and profoundly handicapped children were placed in state institutions where maintenance, but little education, was provided. As a result, however, of both litigation and legislation, state and federal governments have assumed an ever increasing role in providing funds for adequately serving all of our handicapped children. At the same time, though not at the same level, both state and federal governments have become more involved in the funding of early intervention programs for the handicapped.

FUNDING PATTERNS

Public Schools

Federal Funds   Special education programs in public schools have traditionally been funded through a combination of federal, state, and local outlays. Funds from the federal government have come through one of two channels. The first is through formula or *entitlement* programs, which authorize money according to a specific formula that takes into consideration the number of pupils enrolled in a program. PL 94-142 funds, for example, are distributed according to the number of children enrolled in special education programs. Funds flow through the state education agency (SEA) to the local education agency (LEA). Programs may receive extra dollars for each preschool handicapped child from a second entitlement program, the Preschool Incentive Grants program. The amount of this entitlement varies from year to year, depending on the fiscal authorization from Congress.

The second channel for federal funds is through *competitive* funds. These are available through application for grants. Depending on the type of grant, the SEA or LEA might apply to the federal government for funding. Another source of funding is the State Implementation Grants, which are awarded on a competitive basis to state education agencies. The Handicapped Children's Early Education Program (HCEEP) projects (model demonstration projects funded by the office of Special Education Programs) are awarded on a competitive basis to LEAs or private agencies. Funds may also be given to states, and the LEAs must then apply to the state agency on a competitive basis. Some Title I (of the Elementary and Secondary Education Act) grants may also be awarded in this manner.

State Funds   State funds also contribute greatly to the support of special education programs. The general education funding formula serves as a base, with a special additional funding formula calculated into it. The increased cost of special education may be determined by different formula approaches. Mayer (1982) describes those formulas as:

1. *Unit funding*—the LEA receives a given sum of money for each designated unit (for example, classroom or special service unit)
2. *Personnel funding*—the LEA receives a varying amount for each personnel classification (for example, teacher, psychologist)
3. *Weight funding*—categories of children (for example, mentally retarded or blind children) receive a weighted amount (for instance, 2 or 3) times the base amount for regular education, depending on their increased educational costs
4. *Excess cost*—the excess cost of educating the handicapped child over the cost of educating regular students is fully or partially reimbursed at a certain rate per child
5. *Straight sum formula*—a sum is designated in advance, on the basis of category or service, and the LEA receives that amount per pupil
6. *Percentage formula*—the LEA is reimbursed for a special program cost

7. *Differentiated*—different services (for example, assessment, special class-room) are funded at specified rates

Local Funds   Local property tax levies are a significant source of funding for both general and special education. LEAs frequently have assessed a special tax to help pay the excess of special education.

In 1979, an analysis of the average percentage of contribution to special education revealed funds from the federal government averaged about 14%, while state funds accounted for 55%, and local funds were approximately 31% of the total special education budget (U.S. Department of Health, Education and Welfare, 1979, p. 113).

Private and Not-for-Profit Schools

Not-for-Profit Schools   Although not-for-profit programs frequently have some of the same federal, state, and local funding sources, there are also some differences. If the not-for-profit program is part of a comprehensive statewide education system, the state and local general revenue base dollars may be available to the program. For example, some states have programs for severely handicapped children operated under the auspices of an agency other than the state education agency. In this case, agreements may be made to allow per-child entitlement dollars, in addition to excess cost dollars that are available to public schools, to flow to the not-for-profit organizations. This is also the case if the LEA determines that the most appropriate placement for the handicapped child is in a non-public program. The costs of the child's program must be assumed by the local education agency.

In addition to "flow-through" funds from the LEAs, not-for-profit organizations may obtain money through special programs authorized by other federal and state agencies. Departments of health, social or human services, and developmental disabilities may have funds available for the education, therapy, or training of handicapped children. Programs such as Title XX of the Rehabilitation Act of 1973, the Early Periodic Screening, Diagnosis, and Treatment (EPSDT) program of Medicaid, the Supplemental Security Income (SSI) program, the Work Incentive (WIN) program, and the Maternal and Child Health programs, including the Handicapped Children's Program, have contributed in a variety of ways to the funding of special education programs.

Not-for-profit agencies may also affiliate with country commissions or other area-wide government agencies that may have discretionary funds available. Fund raising projects such as bake sales and car washes have added dollars, as have benefits, endowments, trusts, and donations. Not-for-profit agencies can also apply for a range of grants to enable them to provide specialized or innovative services. If the programs are providing a free appropriate public education at no cost to the parent, then these preschool children may also be counted by the LEA and consequently by the state for the Preschool Incentive Grant moneys.

Private Agencies   Private agencies normally charge tuition or fees. In many cases, agencies receiving federal funds are not allowed to charge for services, so private agencies may be restricted from using certain types of federal dollars. They may, however, apply for grants.

CHANGING FUNDING PATTERNS

Federal Changes

Before discussing the changes that may be occurring in relation to funding patterns, it is necessary to define several terms. Sugarman (1981) examines the types of grants that have been authorized by the federal government. The three types of grants that have significant implications for future funding are categorical, block, and consolidated grants. Sugarman defines these as:

> *Categorical grant*: 1) includes a number of closely related activities focused on a specific set of purposes; 2) is subject to a relatively large number of Federal regulations including definitions of eligibility and required services; 3) requires some sort of Federal pre-approval of plan before money is spent; and, 4) is subject to relatively extensive reporting requirements and program audits.
>
> *Block grant*: 1) includes a broader range of related activities with less precise purposes; 2) is subject to relatively few Federal regulations; 3) requires *no* Federal approval of a plan before money is spent; and 4) permits a state to do its own program auditing and to establish its own reporting system.
>
> *Consolidated grant:* generally combines several formerly categorical grants. They retain many of the program requirements in prior legislation. They often limit the authority of Federal agencies to issue program regulations and provide greater authority to states in administrative matters (p. vii).

Categorical grants have, in the past, provided substantial support for special education. An advantage of such grants is that they have built into them a form of "insurance" to guarantee that federal guidelines are met. Requirements for accountability and reporting thus provide a means of quality control. Categorical grants were initiated in 1965 with the Title I programs in response to problems of national scope, often regarding the needs of a particular subgroup in the population. Since then, the federal government has provided ever-increasing amounts of money through "ear-marked" funds to guarantee rights and to assist in solving major social problems.

For handicapped children, landmark legislation in the form of categorical grants came in 1975, with the passage of PL 94-142, which guaranteed the right to a free appropriate education for all handicapped children. It was felt that without federal mandate, schools would not and *could* not provide the necessary services. There is no doubt that since 1975, thousands of handicapped children have been provided rights and services under the law that they would not have enjoyed had it been left to the states. An oft cited disadvantage of categories grant programs, however, likens the federal funding to federal control of local programs. Compliance with federal regulations often entails expenditure of time and money that state and local officials feel could be more judiciously spent. Local agencies believe that the establishment of priorities and standards by the federal government is an infringement upon their rights.

President Reagan reiterated this latter view of government responsibility in his State of the Union message on January 26, 1981, in which he stated that the federal government has gone too far in its efforts to solve social, health, and educational problems through federal funding; that in the effort to protect human rights, state and local rights have been usurped. The New Federalism that the President has proposed would transfer many previously federally funded programs to the states. The government's role in priority-setting would also be de-emphasized, and state and local governments would be asked to establish priorities. Hundreds of regulations would also be repealed, again for the purpose of allowing greater decision making at the state and local levels.

Under Reagan's plan, the number of categorical grants is to be greatly reduced, and many programs consolidated into block grants, with funding greatly decreased. The result is that all of the special programs previously supported through categorical funds will now have to compete for the same diminished dollars. In education, many programs affecting early childhood special education are included in the Education and Consolidation Improvement Act of 1981. Chapter 1 of the act continues the allotment formula in Title I of the Elementary and Secondary Education Act. Chapter 2 consolidates into block grant form Titles II, III, IV, V, VI, VIII, and IX (except the Women's Educational Equity Program) of the Elementary and Secondary Education Act. The Education and Con-solidation Improvement Act also restricts the regulations related to planning, implementing, or evaluating programs. Great discretion is given to local education agencies for distributing the funds.

Although this 1981 act may have some impact on the funding of early childhood special education, additional funds come from other sources. As of this writing [September, 1982], PL 94-142, which includes programs affecting young children, remains intact, although it had been proposed for inclusion in the Education Block Grant. Other programs that affect the funding of various aspects of early childhood special education are listed in Table 1, along with the programs' proposed authorization states. As can be seen by a quick scan of the right-hand column of the chart, many programs are slated to be absorbed into block grants; many will have their funds reduced; some will be maintained at the same funding level, and others will increase slightly and then be maintained at the same level until 1984. Authorization for 1984 and beyond is not known. It is not difficult to deduce that the present administration is currently not interested in increasing its support of these programs. (For further discussion of the proposed legislative and funding changes, the reader is referred to Jule M. Sugarman's *A Citizens Guide to Changes in Human Service Programs*, 1981.)

State Changes

With the shifts that are taking place at the federal level, one might expect that the states would be gearing up to assume a larger role in funding important social,

Table 1. Proposed status of programs affecting young handicapped children

Code number of programs from Federal Catalogue of Domestic Assistance	Title of program	Authorization status
13.211	Crippled Children's Service	1982—block grant
13.224	Community Health Centers	1982—decrease 1983—block grant
13.232	Maternal and Child Health Services	1982—block grant
13.233	Maternal and Child Health Training	1982—block grant
13.600	Administration for Children, Youth and Families—Head Start	increases yearly
13.608	Administration for Children, Youth and Families—Child Welfare and Research and Demonstration	such amounts as necessary—determined by Congress
13.628	Child Abuse and Neglect, Prevention and Treatment	1982—maintained 1983—maintained 1984—0
13.630	Administration on Developmental Disabilities—Basic Support and Advocacy Grants	1982—decrease 1983—maintained 1984—maintained
13.632	Administration on Developmental Disabilities—University Affiliated Facilities	1982—increase 1983—maintained 1984—maintained
84.003	Bilingual Education	1982—decrease 1983—maintained 1984—maintained
84.009	Program for Education of Handicapped Children in State-Operated or Supported Schools (PL 89-313)	1983—block grant
84.010	Educationally Deprived Children—Local Education Agencies (Title I, ESEA: Part A, Subpart 1, Basic Grants; Subpart 2, Special Grants)	1983—block grant
84.011	Migrant Education Program State Formula Grant Program	1983—block grant
84.012	Educationally Deprived Children—State Administration (Title 1, ESEA: State Administration)	1983—block grant
84.013	Educationally Deprived Children—in state-administered institutions serving neglected or delinquent children (Title 1, ESEA: Neglect and Delinquent	1983—block grant
84.023	Research on the Education of the Handicapped	1982—increase 1983—maintained

Table 1. (*continued*)

Code number of programs from Federal Catalogue of Domestic Assistance	Title of program	Authorization status
		1984—no authorization of appropriation
84.024	Handicapped Early Childhood Assistance (Early Education Program)	1982—increase 1983—maintain 1984—no authorization of appropriation
84.025	Handicapped Innovative Programs Deaf-Blind Centers	1982—maintained 1983—maintained 1984—no authorization of appropriation
84.027	Handicapped Preschool and School Programs (Part B, Education of the Handicapped Act)	
	State Grants	1982—increase 1983—increase 1984—maintained
	Preschool Incentive Grants	1982—decrease 1983—maintain 1984—no authorization of appropriation
	Evaluation	1982—maintained 1983—maintained 1984—no authorization of appropriation
84.028	Handicapped Regional Resource Centers	1982—increase 1983—maintained 1984—no authorization of appropriation
84.029	Handicapped Personnel Preparation	1982—increase 1983—maintained 1984—no authorization of appropriation
84.086	Innovative Programs for Severely Handicapped Children	1982—increase 1983—maintained 1984—no authorization of appropriation
84.133	National Institute of Handicapped Research	1982—increase 1983—maintained 1984—no authorization of appropriation

Chart compiled from information presented in Sugarman, J.M. *A citizen's guide to changes in human services programs.* Human Services Information Center, 1981. (Address: 1408 N. Fillmore Street, Suite 7, Arlington, VA 22201.)

health, and educational programs. Unfortunately, this has not been the case. Many states have reduced their income taxes or have set limits on the percentage of increase in expenditures that will be allowed. Very few new programs are being initiated if a dollar authorization is necessary. As a consequence, programs that have been eliminated, reduced, or transferred from the federal budget may *not* find support at the state level. Taxes will need to be raised in order to increase revenues, and competition for limited funds is inevitable. Priority setting will be imperative but difficult.

Local Changes

Local tax levies have constituted an important educational funding source. But as with the federal and state levels of government, the issue of taxes has caused a crisis in school funding at the local level in many areas. The rising costs of personnel salaries and benefits, transportation, and educational materials have placed a heavy burden on local school districts. Declining enrollments in many areas point to a reduced tax base and consequent funding shortages. In addition, the unequal tax base between rich and poor school districts has led to a perceived lack of equal educational opportunity, and has resulted in several court cases around the country. Pressure is being placed on state legislatures by local education agencies to remedy the problem of disproportionate funds for education. And school districts are finding that bond issues to raise the tax base are being defeated at the polls; citizens do not want to pay more taxes at the local level either.

Implications

It appears that the prevailing philosophy is one of "pass the buck." However, whether state and local governments can raise sufficient funds to address adequately their obligations to their citizens has yet to be determined. There is no doubt that the total number of programs and comprehensiveness of services will be affected. If there is to be an *increase* in services to young handicapped children, we as professionals will have to develop new alternatives.

DEVELOPING ALTERNATIVES

The dilemma of how to attain necessary funds for early intervention programs is not easily solved. Both imagination and creativity are necessary. In all likelihood, single funding sources will be a rarity, and program coordinators will need to develop a multiple source funding base. By diversifying the funding sources, programs will not be as vulnerable to fluctuations in the level of funds from each source.

For the program coordinator newly planning a program or for the coordinator who has just lost funding, it is time to reexamine the alternatives. First, a critical analysis of the budget is required. The purposes of the program should not be compromised, but any "frills" may need to be eliminated. All possible funding sources should be identified. At the local level, the county commissioners, local agencies, businesses, and special interest groups may be approached. State agencies other than the state education agency may be able to reimburse or provide certain services. For example, new provisions under Title XIX of Medicaid may permit allocation of funds to reduce institutional placements. Another option is that proposals may be written to federal agencies or foundations requesting grants for specific aspects of the program (see Chapter 11).

In addition to seeking alternative funds, it may be necessary to develop ways of supplementing personnel or services. Volunteers may be recruited and trained or personnel may be "shared" with another agency. Coordination with other agencies providing similar services may result in the development of a more comprehensive program with fewer duplicated services (see Chapter 4).

The program coordinator may find it helpful to develop two parallel lists, one a breakdown of program expenses and the other a list of possible resources. Table 2 offers a format for solving funding problems. The general areas of the

Table 2. Problem-solving funding alternatives

Budget items[a]	Resources[b]

Salaries and Wages
    Administrators
    Educators
    Therapists
    Maintenance
    Support staff
	Funds
	    Local revenue
	    State revenue
	    Special education reim-
	        bursement
	    Entitlement funds

Contracts and Consultants
    Ongoing
    Specific need
	Competitive grant funds
	    Federal/state
	    Foundations
	    Corporations

Travel
    For children
    For staff
        local
        state
        national
	Tuition/fees
	
	State and Local Agencies
	    Health related
	    Social service related
	    Education related

Space
    Administrative
    Program
	People
	    Specialists
	    Volunteers
	    Advocates

Consumable Supplies
    Administrative
    Program
	Individuals in commu-
	        nity

Equipment
    Office
    Program
	Clubs or Organizations
	    Business
	    Special interest
	    Advocacy
	Other

[a]Substitute specific details relevant to your program.
[b]Substitute actual resources of your community.

budget are indicated in the left-hand column, with common resources in the right. (Specific budget items and actual resources can be substituted at left and right so that the chart reflects your own particular program.) The coordinator can then analyze all the combinations and permutations that might contribute to solving the funding dilemma.

Moreau (1980) stated that $40 billion was awarded to nonprofit organizations in the United States in 1978. Of that amount, 82.9% came from individuals, 5% from corporations, 5.5% from private foundations, and 6.6% from bequests. The recipients of this money included 46.5% religiously affiliated organizations, 13.8% health and hospitals, 14% education agencies, 10% social welfare agencies, 6.3% arts and humanities organizations, 2.9% civic and public agencies and 6.5% other affiliations. These figures should be kept in mind when seeking additional funding sources.

Given the current funding fluctuations, it is advisable to consider backup strategies. Contingency plans to enable program continuation may include the reallocation of existing programs, substitution of staff or services from other agencies, and flexibility in utilizing funding mechanisms.

ON A LARGER SCALE

Advocacy

It is not enough to be concerned about a specific early childhood special education program. Although the survival instinct is strong in all of us, if programs are to succeed over time, it is necessary to build a strong national advocacy base. Such a base implies, first, that persons from a wide variety of backgrounds and professions need to become aware of the importance of early intervention; and second, that such persons become *vocal* advocates of early intervention. Building a vocal support base will take coordination, time, and energy. There is now a tremendous body of data supporting the benefits of quality early intervention, and vigorous supporters can contribute greatly to disseminating this information.

Level One—Parents and Colleagues   The first step that needs to take place is for professionals to reach out to parents in the program and to colleagues in education and public administration. Their knowledge and support is paramount to successful continuation of programs. Parents are the first and most potent advocacy force for early childhood special education. As consumers, parents have insight into the "human" impact of programs in terms of their child's development and the support that early intervention programs give to their families. Armed with facts and figures, local, state, and national parent groups can become the foundation and strength of an advocacy movement, effecting change through persuasion, litigation, and legislation.

In coalition with parents, professionals can work to establish a communication network. Organizations such as the Association for the Education of Young Children and the Division on Early Childhood of The Council for Exceptional Children (CEC) are both interested in early education and handicapped children. An exchange of ideas between members of these two groups on how to publicize information on the benefits of early childhood intervention would benefit both. Other special education and parent organizations such as the American Association on Mental Deficiency (AAMD) and the Association for Retarded Citizens (ARC), who are already involved in programs and research, can become stronger advocates.

It is time, too, to reach out to other groups who are not as knowledgeable, so that they may become more informed. The observation that administrators and regular education teachers have at times been "reluctant" hosts to early intervention programs attests to the fact that they do not always fully understand the purposes and far-reaching benefits of this highly specialized segment of education. It is, thus, the responsibility of professionals in the field of early intervention to better educate administrative colleagues and teachers. Administrators will increasingly be making tough decisions regarding which programs to fund with limited dollars. Early intervention programs will survive only if the decision makers are persuaded of the facts on the benefits of such programs to children, families, educators, and society. Discussions with and presentations to administrators, teachers, and others in education are imperative. Whenever possible, professionals must speak to groups such as the American Society for Public Administration (ASPA), the National Association of Elementary School Principals, the American Association of School Administrators (AASA) and state associations for school administrators. As administrators' knowledge levels increase, so too will their support.

Level Two—Related Fields Persons in related fields can add a powerful force to the advocacy base. The areas of psychology, social work, speech and audiology, vision, physical and occupational therapy, nursing, and pediatrics are all involved or have an interest in early intervention programs. Sharing information and coordinating with their respective local and state agencies and professional organizations will promote a second broader level of advocacy.

Level Three—Business The role of business in supporting social programs and in affecting social legislation is becoming increasingly evident. It therefore becomes expedient to inform the corporate and business sector of the economic benefits of early intervention. Cost benefits and accountability are factors to which business and industry can relate. Not only can businesspersons influence legislators in how tax dollars will be spent, but they can also influence their own companies to make charitable contributions and sponsor grants and contracts. It is wise to include representatives from business on local advisory boards. Such board members can often become strong promoters within the business community of the early intervention program. Parents, professionals, and concerned business representatives can also work to develop ties with community groups such as local "jaycees," Kiwanis, Lions, Elks, and other service oriented business clubs. Presentations to other corporate and business organizations can also make a difference.

Level Four—Legislators State and federal legislators obviously have a substantial impact on legislation authorizing program development and funding. In order for legislators to understand and espouse the human and economic benefits of early intervention programs, it will be necessary to mobilize all of the previously mentioned—parents, educators, public administrators, professionals from related fields, and persons from the business and corporate sector to voice their support of early intervention. This is a formidable task that will require coordination and the commitment of time, effort, and resources. A systematic approach can, however, reap considerable benefits.

Interagency Coordination

Discussion with other professionals should not be limited to dissemination of information. It is also important that dialogue center on ways to coordinate services and maximize the use of service dollars. If programs can point to careful planning of service delivery and prudent financial management, their case for continued funding is that much stronger. For example, if a single agency can assume primary responsibility for a certain service, such as screening, then dollars can be freed for other needed services. By examining which agencies can be responsible for specific aspects of the continuum of services, costly duplication can be avoided and gaps in service can be filled. Agencies with expertise in one area (for example, evaluation) can negotiate with another agency to obtain their expertise in another area (for example, counseling).

With the projected shift to block grants, it will also become critical for state agencies to develop corresponding state level interagency cooperative agreements. Maximum utilization of resources will be encouraged by coordinated efforts.

Needed Legislation

At the state level, but particularly at the federal level, legislation is needed to strengthen the mandates for early childhood special education. Although mandates for preschool education are included in PL 94-142, the law contains loopholes that enable states to avoid serving handicapped preschool children (see Chapter 1). Furthermore, it will be difficult to realize these mandates, given the administration's resistance to new federal programs. The only hope for such legislation will be through the effects of a forceful advocacy-based coalition as previously described. Even if this legislation were to be passed, a diversity of funding sources would still be needed. The establishment of a dynamic and extensive advocacy base, the coordination of resources, and the creation of multiple funding sources will go far toward ensuring the longevity of early intervention programs.

REFERENCES

Mayer, C.L. *Educational administration and special education: A handbook for school administrators*. Boston: Allyn and Bacon, 1982.

Moreau, A.J. The private sector. In: B.A. McNulty & A.J. Moreau (eds.), *Public and private funding alternatives*. Seattle: WESTAR, 1980. (Address: 215 University District Bldg., JD-06, 1107 NE 45th, Seattle, WA 98105.)

Sugarman, J.M. *A citizen's guide to changes in human service programs*. Human Services Information Center, 1981. (Address: 1408 N. Fillmore Street, Suite 7, Arlington, VA 22201.)

U.S. Department of Health, Education and Welfare. *Progress toward a free appropriate education: A report to Congress on the implementation of Public Law 94-142: The Education for All Handicapped Children's Act*. Washington, DC: 1979.

chapter

11

Proposal
Writing

As mentioned in Chapter 1, many of the initial models and much of the existing research in early childhood special education have their beginnings in federal grants. The ability to write a convincing proposal to obtain subsidies for programs or research is a necessary and important skill for any one dependent on outside funding. This chapter provides general guidelines to assist project coordinators or investigators in developing proposals.

Throughout this book are found examples of exemplary program practices that would be helpful to persons developing early childhood special education program proposals. Many of the tables and figures would also be useful to refer to or incorporate into a proposal. Rather than repeat those examples here, the reader is referred to the appropriate chapter for further explanation. By placing this chapter at the end of the book, it is hoped that readers will bring to it a substantial amount of information absorbed in earlier chapters.

IDENTIFICATION OF FUNDING SOURCES

Once a program need has been established and it has been determined that outside funds will be sought, it is necessary to identify the most logical funding sources. The three main sources of grant funds in the United States are governmental agencies, foundations, and corporate organizations, with the federal government the largest single source of grants in the world. Moreau (1980) discusses five types of foundations that provide funding: 1) *national foundations*, which do not limit their awards to geographic areas, and are most likely to fund programs with national implications; 2) *special interest foundations*, which are primarily interested in funding projects related to a particular problem; 3) *corporate foundations*, which usually fund programs compatible with the corporation's major interests; 4) *family foundations*, which are run more informally, generally favor local awards, and may be more subject to personal influence; and 5) *community foundations*, which receive their funds from and direct their grants to their own community.

Grants from corporations may be in the form of direct grants. Usually these grants are for a cause that is felt to benefit the employees or the company in some way. Corporations generally are more responsive to local and personal appeals.

Specific information on funding alternatives may be obtained from libraries, institutional grants offices, subscriber information services, workshops, and the news media. A list of publications and centers that specialize in providing grant information is provided at the end of this chapter.

In examining potential funding sources, it is necessary to study the program areas in which the agency, foundation, or corporation has special interest. Agencies or organizations whose interests, requirements, or limitations are inappropriate to your program needs can be eliminated. (Many more may be eliminated by checking the deadline dates, though many foundations do not list deadlines.) Up-to-date information should always be requested and thoroughly studied prior to submitting a proposal. Moreau (1980) has stated that "the more you know about an organization or individual, the better you can tailor your request to meet its interests and/or financial capabilities" (p. 11).

After selecting an agency or organization to submit the proposal to, an outline of the project should be developed. Usually the organization or agency will provide guidelines of what needs to be included. While the federal government provides quite specific instructions, some foundation or corporate guidelines may be fairly general. The initial outline should address several important questions:

What is the purpose of the proposal?
What are the proposed activities?
Why is the project needed?
Who will be responsible for administering and conducting the activities?
Where will the project be conducted?
How long will the project last?
How much will it cost?

Time spent at this stage in careful conceptualization of the project is important, not only as ground work for discussions with potential funders but in developing ties with cooperating institutions.

After the initial planning has taken place, an appropriate institution needs to be located to house the project. Frequently this is not a problem, as the person conceptualizing the proposal is involved in some capacity with a desired site. If this is not the case, however, a sponsoring institution must be found. (Most agencies or organizations will not fund isolated individuals but, rather, fund only not-for-profit agencies.) The institution agreeing to sponsor the project must have both something to contribute and something to gain from involvement in the proposed project. Consideration should be given to 1) the adequacy of facilities that would be made available; 2) clarification of roles and responsibilities, including the contribution of staff; 3) equipment and property allocation; 4) financial arrangements; and 5) institutional policies relevant to project activities (White, 1979). It is recommended that these issues be discussed and agreed upon prior to the submission of a proposal, so that any modifications can be incorporated into it. Many problems may be avoided by careful planning and coordination prior to submission of the proposal or the awarding of a grant.

Determining the costs of the project is also important. Both direct and indirect costs must be examined. Direct costs are those expenses directly attributable to the proposed activities—salaries, fringe benefits, supplies, and so on. Indirect costs are those shared by other services or projects housed at the same site, and include such things as general administrative expenses, research administrative expenses, and maintenance expenses. Indirect costs rates are either predetermined or negotiated with either the sponsoring site or funding agency. The proposal writer needs to investigate the funding agency's policy regarding indirect costs as well as any other specific guidelines on cost.

Other areas that need to be examined include funding policies relating to copyrights and patents, allowable costs for equipment acquisition, and mandated cost-sharing and matching funds. As a condition for eligibility for some federal programs, the agency requesting funds may need to contribute matching funds or a certain percentage of "in-kind" goods and services. Proposal writers must be aware of such requirements to insure eligibility.

To this point, communication with a funding sponsor has been in writing or through brief telephone calls. Once the above initial information is obtained, White (1979) recommends that, if possible, a more formal, personal interview or telephone call be arranged with the most appropriate representative from the organization for the purpose of further clarifying issues for both parties. Questions may be raised by the funding organization in relation to other possible funding sources, cost justification, and benefits to their organization. Corporations are particularly concerned about the potential cost benefit to their organization. The need for adequate preparation and documentation on the part of the proposal writer is readily apparent. For the proposal writer, the interview may provide insight into the funding organization's degree of interest in the proposed project, the possible level of financial support, special requirements or restrictions, and what elements of the proposal should be emphasized. If the interview is conducted with sufficient lead time, modifications can be made prior to the deadline for submission.

WRITING THE PROPOSAL

Depending on the agency or organization to which the proposal is submitted, formal application forms may or may not be available. The federal government, for example, has different application forms for its various agencies. An agency will announce a "Request for Proposals" (RFP) in certain program areas and application forms may be requested. The RFP will usually outline specific purposes, deadlines, and evaluation criteria that apply to the proposals. Foundations and corporations may simply state general requirements upon request.

The general proposal format described in this chapter will assist in the preparation of the narrative section of any proposal. Guidelines specific to a particular type of project should of course be followed.

Careful organization is a critical element of a good proposal. It is standard practice that proposals submitted for funding are read by several reviewers, who may be reading many other proposals simultaneously. Reviewers are often under time constraints and other stresses; thus a clearly organized proposal will facilitate quick understanding of what is proposed and will be viewed more positively. Explicit organization that highlights important points in a specific and concise manner is a great asset.

Proposal writers also need to be aware that some reviewers may not be expert in the aspects of early childhood special education presented, although they may have sophisticated knowledge of programs and research in education or special education. Under these circumstances, it is important that the information be stated in precise, understandable terms. Any jargon necessary to include in the proposal should be defined. The first explanatory paragraphs of the proposal are crucial, and can influence the reader's entire attitude toward the proposal. The cautions of clarity and conciseness also apply to the title of the proposal. The title should convey some of the intent of the project, but should not be overly wordy. In fact, some federal programs limit the number of words that can be used in a title.

COMPONENTS OF THE PROPOSAL

Although the format will vary depending on the requirements of the funding agency or organization, proposals will usually include:

1. The program or project abstract
2. The statement of need
3. The statement of purpose or goals
4. The statement of project objectives
5. Activities that will accomplish the stated objectives
6. The plan for evaluation of accomplishment of objectives
7. The plan for dissemination of successful accomplishments

In the discussion following, each of the above areas will be addressed further. Again, it is emphasized that the proposal writer should adhere to the sponsoring agency's guidelines. Research proposals may follow a similar, but slightly different approach (see Figure 1).

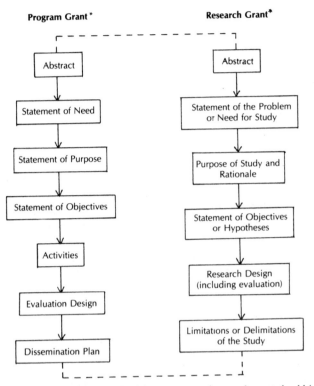

Figure 1. Overview of grant formats. (*A joint program and research grant should include elements of both models.)

The Abstract

The abstract may not be a stated requirement, but it is recommended. The abstract is a summary of the proposal and gives the reader a quick overview of the project. It is thus helpful to a reviewer who has read many proposals, as it can refresh his or her memory without the need to re-read the whole proposal. Key words or terminology should also be explained in the abstract. A length of 100 to 300 words is suggested.

The Statement of Need

"A need is said to exist when there is a discrepancy between what is happening and what one believes ought to be happening" (Bourgeois, 1971). A proposal is usually written in order to meet a specific unmet need. In the section containing the statement of need, the writer indicates the significance of the project. The statement will serve as a justification for the entire project and, thus, should be convincingly, yet objectively, stated. Problems, gaps, or deficiencies related to services, methodology, and areas of knowledge may be identified as needs, which may themselves relate to an individual, a specific group of individuals, or to aspects of a system. If research is to be conducted, the significance of the results should be addressed. Whenever possible, needs should be supported by objective data. The needs may be documented by information from a needs assessment, a review of the literature, or both.

Needs Assessment A needs assessment may be conducted in a variety of ways. One method involves surveying professionals in the field by questionnaire or interview. Information may be gathered from these persons on their perceptions of the state of the art and current needs for programs or research in a specific area of early childhood special education. Another significant type of needs assessment involves collecting data on a certain population or topic. The data may include numbers of children or families, types of programs or problems, availability of services, demographic information, and other information relevant to the project proposal. A third type of needs assessment might use information from pilot studies or evaluation data from existing programs to document a need. A fourth type of needs assessment may be identified through a review of current literature.

Review of the Literature The proposal writer needs to be extremely knowledgeable about the area in which he or she wishes to establish a program or conduct research. First, the idea that is proposed should be new in some aspect or innovative and, as previously indicated, should address a need. The review of the literature demonstrates the project director's or investigator's knowledge of existing and current information relevant to the project. It illustrates the way(s) in which the project is innovative in comparison to what has previously been done. The literature review also may help validate the identified need by providing "expert testimony," so to speak, that further investigation or program development in the designated area is important. If readers of the proposal are experts in the area being proposed, they will quickly spot a poorly conceived or inadequately researched proposal.

If, for example, a proposal is being written for the development of an innovative approach to the treatment of behaviorally disordered preschool children, this need might be documented by: 1) a community-wide needs assessment that asks professionals to identify areas of need in services to preschool handicapped children; 2) a tabulation of the actual number of identified emotionally disturbed children of preschool age plus the projected number of children based on statistical and demographic data; 3) an accounting of the actual number of children being served; 4) the approaches being used to serve these children; 5) a review of the literature citing the importance of early intervention with young emotionally disturbed children; and 6) a review of the literature supporting aspects of the innovative approach that is proposed. Needs statements should not be so general that they apply to all situations (for example, "a need for early intervention programs"). Rather, the writer should relate the needs statement to the specifics of the proposal. One of the reasons for this is that the purpose and the objectives of the proposal should derive from the needs statement. By indicating the need in measurable and observable terms, the writer provides continuity to the proposal and a justification for what is to follow. The goals of the project should be implied by the need.

Statement of Purpose

Following the statement of the need should be a statement of the purpose(s) or goal(s) of the project. For example, "As a result of the previously identified need, it is the purpose of this project to demonstrate the effectiveness of the medium of play for helping parents to facilitate growth in their developmentally delayed preschool child."

Objectives

The project objectives flow from both the need and the purpose, and indicate the project outcomes or expected results. A common error in proposal writing is the failure to establish a clear relationship between a need and the project objectives. In stating an objective, it is necessary to identify what changes will occur in relation to certain variables. The way objectives are written will vary depending on the type of project and the funding agency being addressed. Federal agencies tend to prefer objectives that can be measured (see Chapter 5 for instructions on writing behavioral objectives). An example of an objective that might be found in a program proposal for developmentally delayed children would be: "Given four half-days of play intervention per week, 80% of program children will demonstrate 6 months' growth in cognitive and social development within 9 months, as measured by normed and criterion-referenced tests." Both process oriented and performance-based objectives can be written in measurable terms.

The number of objectives should be kept to a minimum (Bourgeois, 1971). Many writers make the mistake of confusing objectives and activities by including activities in the form of objectives. Chapter 3 outlines a number of objectives and activities for a program. Although the number of objectives presented is excessive for a proposal, the distinction between objectives and activities can be seen. The evaluation component of the proposal will evolve from the objectives, so it makes sense to keep the objectives to a manageable number.

Activities and Proposal Narrative

The methods or procedures that will be used to accomplish the stated objectives need to be discussed in detail. The rationale for specific approaches should be clarified. The proposal writer should indicate all the activities that will be performed for each objective and the relationship between activities. For example, a program may intend to do individual child assessment and family assessments and then develop individual child and parent program plans to meet their needs. The proposal writer needs to designate exactly what methods and instruments will be used for each assessment and how they interrelate.

Time-lines and flowcharts may help to illustrate the overall course of the project (see Figure 2). Examination of the flowchart reveals that the child's program and the parents' program diverge after assessment, yet they also share a

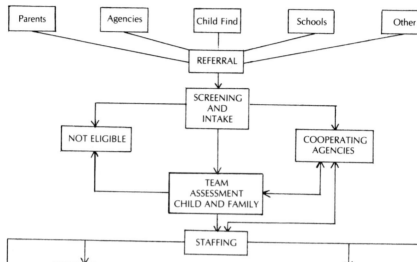

Figure 2. Flowchart of a general program plan.

common parent-child component. The relationship of each aspect of the program to cooperating agencies can also be seen.

Activities presented need to be practical and administratively and economically feasible. Proposal readers will critically examine activities to determine whether the pieces comprise a cohesive whole. Are the activities consistent with the overall conceptualization of the project? Is each aspect of the design accounted for in the activities? The activities area should be the most detailed area of the proposal.

Narrative for Program Development Proposals In proposals that seek to develop a program for young handicapped children and their families, additional elements need to be described clearly in the narrative. Many of these factors will be

	Narrative Discussion	Charts or Figures
Need	Needs Assessment Review of Literature	
Purpose	Goals of Program Relation to Need	
Objectives	Objectives of Program	Objectives Activities to Meet Objectives
Activities	Target Population —identification Proposed Model —theoretical approach —setting —staffing pattern —details of program —daily schedule Coordination with Other Agencies —services —referral —consultation Parent-Family Involvement Facilities Advisory Council Inservices Training	Budget Program Task Matrix Time-line
Evaluation Design	Evaluation Methods —elements to be evaluated —formative evaluation —summary evaluation	Evaluation —what —who —how —when —how analyzed
Dissemination	Dissemination Plan —local —state —national	

Figure 3. Critical elements in a program grant.

included in descriptions of specific activities, while others will require separate explanation. In addition, charts delineating the objectives and activities and indicating related evaluations that will be conducted are helpful to the reviewer. Figure 3 describes those aspects of the proposal that need to be addressed in the body of the narrative and those that may also be included in figures or charts.

Target Population The criteria for eligibility for the project's services should be clearly delineated. How the children will be identified and the validity of identification procedures for the target population should be discussed.

Curriculum Design If a particular model of a program is being proposed, the justification for this model needs to be presented, with an explanation of why these services are appropriate for the population. All of the elements of developing a program philosophy discussed in Chapter 2 should be addressed. For example, a program proposal might be designed with a home-based setting, a transdisciplinary staffing pattern, a cognitive developmental intervention approach, and staff in the role as home consultants to parents and facilitators of play interactions. The rationale for this program design would need to be explained in terms of the identified needs of the target population, the geographic determinants, and the philosophical and practical purposes of the program. The details of the services to be offered, the staff-child ratio, the amount of time children will receive services (i.e., hours per day, per week) all need to be explained. A sample daily schedule should be included to clarify how the program will operate. Specific instruments, curricula, equipment, or materials that will be incorporated also should be examined.

Facilities If special facilities are important to the programs, these should be discussed. It may be helpful to include a diagram of classroom, therapy, or outdoor areas that are relevant to the program design. Explanation of the cooperative arrangements made with agencies in relation to these facilities may also be included.

Parent-Family Participation The importance of the role of the family in a handicapped child's program has been well substantiated. Many funding agencies, in particular the federal government, prefer the inclusion of options for meaningful family participation in the proposed program. It is wise to delineate in detail the alternatives that will be available to parents to obtain guidance, information, and to participate in program implementation and decision making (see Chapter 7).

Inservice Training The training that will be conducted for staff prior to and during the implementation of the proposal also needs to be discussed in the narrative. Areas of projected inservice needs should be outlined.

Coordination with Other Agencies Sponsoring agencies usually like some assurance that projects can continue after the initial grant terminates. For this reason it is advisable, and in some cases mandatory, that coordination efforts with other agencies be spelled out. These efforts should also be reflected in both the objectives and activities.

Chapter 4 provides details on planning local program coordination. It should be noted that in the case of research grants from some corporations, however, the profit motive and interest in controlling various aspects of the research may be important; interagency coordination in this case may be contraindicated. The agency guidelines should always be consulted.

Advisory Councils Agency guidelines may also require that an advisory council be established to advise and monitor the project implementation and evaluation. A broadly based council with representatives from diverse elements of the community is recommended. The general categories of persons (for example, parent of handicapped infant, local pediatrician) should be listed. In some cases, names of prominent persons who have agreed to serve in an advisory capacity can and should be identified in the proposal. The responsibilities that the council will undertake should also be listed. It is recommended that the tasks of the committee be meaningful rather than perfunctory.

Projected Activities*	1st Quarter			2nd Quarter			3rd Quarter			4th Quarter		
	June	July	Aug.	Sept.	Oct.	Nov.	Dec.	Jan.	Feb.	Mar.	Apr.	May
Objective 1												
Activity 1a												
Activity 1b												
Activity 1c												
Activity 1d												
Activity 1e												
Objective 2												
Activity 2a												
Activity 2b												
Activity 2c												
Activity 2d												
Objective 3												
Activity 3a												
Activity 3b												
Activity 3c												
Activity 3d												
Activity 3e												

Figure 4. A sample time-line format. Horizontal lines indicate when a projected activity is to begin and when it will end. (*In an actual time-line, the activities would be named, e.g., "screening of target population.")

Timetable The size, scope, and duration of the project should be presented in the narrative. In addition, a time-line or graphic representation of when each of the activities and evaluations will be undertaken and completed is also necessary. The time-line may also delineate staff time for each objective or activity. The timetable for implementation may be incorporated at the end of the narrative section (see Figure 4).

Personnel Detailed descriptions of the roles and responsibilities of each of the project staff need to be presented, along with the qualifications for each staff position. Vitae of the project director and others who will be involved in the project should be included. Since all staff may not work full time on the project, this section should also identify the percentage of time for each staff member (for example, .25 FTE [Full Time Equivalent] Project Director, .50 FTE Physical Therapist, 1.5 FTE Speech and Language Pathologists). The narrative should also discuss the justification for personnel. A Program Task Matrix (see Figure 5) can relate personnel needs to identified program activities. (See also discussion below, under Budget Building.)

Budget Building When grant money was more abundant, it was common practice to pad a budget with excess costs. Budget building now requires a close accounting of project activities and costs. Detailed budget information is typically required, with a rationale for each expenditure. Proposal reviewers are usually experienced proposal writers and know when a budget is excessive. It is best to ask for what is needed to conduct the project activities, while keeping the budget within the guidelines of the granting agency. Most funding sources will provide a range of total acceptable grant costs and a mean amount of their grants in the RFP. If it is impossible to conduct the project activities within the agency cost guidelines, it is best not to apply unless prior approval for a larger amount is obtained.

Although grant writers have often overstated their budget costs, the opposite is also true. Many will promise extensive activities for too little money. Such proposals are often rejected by reviewers as being unrealistic (Seeley, 1982). It should therefore be the rule of budget building to project honest costs tied closely to project activities and project objectives.

As stated, internal consistency is an important aspect of grant writing. The budget must display the same consistency. Budget costs should flow directly from the objectives and activities so that it is clear who will be hired to do what, at what salary, and what related expenses (for example, travel, supplies, equipment, contracted services) will be incurred. The largest expense in any budget is usually personnel and the attendant fringe benefits. It is, therefore, essential to describe time, tasks and costs. A Program Task Matrix, mentioned earlier, is helpful as a budget supplement. Figure 5 provides an example of this format. Accounting for time can be accomplished by the use of Full Time Equivalent (FTE), which is a percentage of a 12-month full-time position spread over a variety of tasks. Another approach is to use "man hours" or "man months" to account for time on the task; this is described in actual hours or a 40-hour work week to calculate man-months.

Personnel	Project Activities								
	1.1 Develop Identification Screening	1.2 Administer Testing	1.3 Hold Parent Conference	2.1 Develop IEP	2.2 Implement Treatment and Program Plan	2.3 Evaluate IEP Progress	3.1 Supervise Project Staff	3.2 Administer Budget	3.3 Evaluate Project
Project Director 0.6 FTE	0.1		0.2				0.1	0.1	0.1
Psychologist 0.3 FTE		0.3							
Educational Diagnostician 1.0 FTE	0.1	0.3	0.3	0.2		0.1			
Teacher 1.0 FTE			0.2	0.2	0.4	0.2			
Secretary 0.5 FTE	0.2		0.1					0.2	

Figure 5. Excerpt from a program task matrix. (FTE = Full Time Equivalent.)

The total amount of time spent in all activities should not exceed the percentage of FTE designated for the position.

Other budget expenses should be listed and justified. Different granting agencies have different restrictions and definitions of items. For instance, if a filing cabinet is purchased for $99, it may be charged to supplies (software), but if it costs $210, it becomes equipment (hardware). There are often restrictions on equipment purchases, particularly items that are normally found in offices. Granting agencies typically expect institutional support for space, utilities, office equipment, and accounting services. These may be charged as "indirect costs" or "overhead" in the grant budget. Budget items for travel supplies, contracted services, consultants or other items need to be explained in some detail. Figure 6 is an example of a budget description. More detailed information is usually appended as may be required for justification of expenditures.

In budget negotiations after the grant has been reviewed, certain expenses may be required to be eliminated or the total budget reduced. In such situations, remember that money is tied to activities. Thus, a reduction in budget should eliminate certain activities. The question becomes "can we accomplish some of our objectives with the reduced budget or should we not undertake the project?" These are difficult decisions and require careful study. It is better to delay or scale down a project than to promise to deliver the same project for less money (Seeley, 1982).

Budget Items	Grant Funds	State Resources	Local Resources and In-Kind Matching

Personnel Salaries
  Program Coordinator   0.5 FTE
  Developmental Specialist   2.0 FTE
  Speech/Language Therapist   1.0 FTE
  Occupational Therapist   1.0 FTE
  Social Worker   1.0 FTE
  Instructional Aide   1.0 FTE
  Secretary 1.0 FTE			

Employee Benefits			

Supplies
  Instructional Materials
  Instructional Supplies
  Office Supplies			

Contracted Services
  Psychologist
  Program development and
    evaluation consultants
  Inservice consultants			

Equipment			
Travel Staff			

Figure 6.   Sample budget format. (In an actual budget, specific line items would be listed along with actual cost or in-kind value in the corresponding columns.) (FTE = Full Time Equivalent.)

Evaluation

Several points should be kept in mind in planning evaluation. The evaluation design indicates what evidence is to be submitted to demonstrate that the objectives have been obtained, how the evidence is to be collected, the instrumentation and data collection procedures to be used, and the proposed methods of analyzing the data. In order to address adequately these concerns, the evaluation plan *must* be designed as the proposal is being developed, not after-the-fact (White, 1979).

The evaluation design should follow logically from the stated objectives. It should be internally consistent; that is, the measures used for evaluating various aspects of the project need to be related to identified activities. The specific procedures for data collection need to be carefully outlined, and the methods for data analysis discussed (Bourgeois, 1971). The instruments used for evaluation should be valid and reliable. The evaluation design should address the changes that occurred as a result of the project and the results of research that was conducted. Chapter 9 addresses program evaluation in further detail, outlining considerations in developing formative and summative evaluation. For specific guidance in developing evaluation and research designs, the reader is referred to the following references:

Bloom, B.S., Hasting, T.J., & Madaus, G.F. *Handbook of formative and summative evaluation of student learning.* New York: McGraw-Hill Book Co., 1971.

Goodwin, W.L., & Driscoll, L.A. *Handbook for measurement and evaluation in early childhood special education.* San Francisco: Jossey-Bass, 1980.

Isaac, S., & Michael, W.B. *Handbook in research and evaluation* (2nd ed.). San Diego: EDITS, 1981. (EDITS, P.O. Box 7234, San Diego, CA 92107)

Evaluation Process   The evaluation plan should be fully developed in the proposal. Questions that need to be addressed include: What is to be evaluated? What instruments will be used? Who will be responsible for the various aspects of evaluation? When will each element of evaluation begin? How often will each element of evaluation occur? When will data be analyzed? How will data analysis be done? The charts on pages 232–240 in Chapter 9 illustrate a general program evaluation plan. Specific instruments and statistical information would need to be included.

Evaluation Instruments   The evaluation instruments that will be used in the project must be identified and discussed in relation to their purpose, standardization, validity, and reliability. If instruments are yet to be determined or new ones developed, the writer should be specific in detailing exactly how the instruments will be chosen or developed and validated. Measurements that will incorporate other than standardized instruments should be identified, described, and justified. Such methods might include questionnaires, surveys, observational ration scales, time samples, anecdotal records, and developmental scales. Sample pages of various instruments may be appended to the proposal.

Dissemination

One of the reasons agencies and organizations fund proposals is to enable innovative ideas and approaches to be developed and verified so that resulting useful information may be provided for other program developers and researchers in the field. Knowledge of successful, as well as unsuccessful, models, practices, and procedures can benefit other practitioners.

A dissemination plan is often, therefore, requested. The dissemination plan should outline a variety of methods by which information will be shared, including 1) articles in local, regional, or national publications; 2) media or press releases; 3) presentations to organizations; and 4) workshops at conferences or inservice meetings. The purpose of each of these methods is to raise the communal and professional level of awareness concerning successful programs and practices. Reviewers will often want to see a "packaged" product developed that can be disseminated and replicated in other sites.

REVIEWING THE PROPOSAL

After the proposal has been completed, it is a good idea to have several other persons read it. Often terminology or processes that are clear to the writer are vague or confusing to someone else. The objective "outsider" may be able to identify aspects of the proposal that need clarification or modification.

Proposal readers' review guidelines may also be helpful. The federal Handicapped Children's Early Education Program (HCEEP) in the office of Special Education Programs has been one of the most significant funding programs for early childhood special education. Field reviewers of projects proposals are provided a checklist to enable them to review all the pertinent aspects of the proposals. At the end of this review form is another checklist that summarizes reasons proposals are *not* funded. This checklist is reproduced in Table 1. Proposal writers who are submitting proposals for the purpose of obtaining funding for program development are advised to review this list.

Writing a good, strong proposal is not easy. It demands knowledge, skill and perseverance. The proposal may need to be modified and resubmitted numerous times before funding becomes a reality. But the effort is small compared to the benefits that result for handicapped children, their families, and society as a whole. Much dedication and tenacity are required to persist when the funding odds are greatly against us. Yet, without research, programs, and services the odds against our young handicapped children grow larger every day. It is an effort well worth making.

SOURCES OF INFORMATION ON FUNDING SOURCES

Publications

Catalogue of Federal
Domestic Assistance
Superintendent of Documents
U.S. Government Printing Office
Washington, DC 20402

The Annual Register of Grant Support
Marquis Who's Who
4300 West 62nd St.
Indianapolis, IN 46202

Table 1.   Reasons for not funding proposals

_____ 1.   It failed to show sufficient need for the proposed activity in the area to be served or justify the significance of the proposed approach.

_____ 2.   It did not indicate the relevance to the priority areas that are contained in applicable Federal statutes and regulations.

_____ 3.   The expected potential for using the results of the proposed project in other projects or programs for similar education purposes was not sufficient to make the proposal competitive as a demonstration program.

_____ 4.   The size and scope of the project were not sufficient to secure enough productive results to make the project a competitive one.

_____ 5.   The objectives were not sufficiently or sharply defined, clearly stated, or capable of being measured by the proposed procedures.

_____ 6.   Objectives of the project are not capable of being attained by the proposed procedures.

_____ 7.   The qualifications and experience of personnel designated to carry out the proposed project were not considered adequate or appropriate for a HCEEP demonstration project.

_____ 8.   The facilities and other resources were not adequate for the proposed demonstration activities.

_____ 9.   The plans for evaluation of the effectiveness of the project and for determining the extent to which the objectives would be accomplished were not sufficiently developed.

_____ 10.   Eligibility criteria to determine a child's acceptance into the program and the severity of the handicap(s) are not indicated.

_____ 11.   The children designated to be served did not meet the requirements of the definition in the Federal regulations.

_____ 12.   The curriculum did not appear to be appropriate for the age and handicapping condition(s) of the children.

_____ 13.   A sample of the daily schedule of activities and the program content are not provided.

(continued)

The Grantsmanship Center News
The Grantsmanship Center
1015 West Olympic Boulevard
Los Angeles, CA 90015

ORYX Press Grant Information System
The Oryx Press
7632 East Edgemont Avenue
Scottsdale, AZ 85257

Funding Sources Clearinghouse, Inc.
2600 Bancroft Way
Berkeley, CA 94704

Educational Resources Newsletter
Educational Resource Systems, Inc.
1200 Pennsylvania Avenue, NW
Box 6180
Washington, DC 20044

Standard & Poor Register of Corporations, Directors, and Executives
Standard & Poor
345 Hudson St.
New York, NY 10014

Aid to Education: Programs of Some Leading Business Concerns
Council for Financial Aid to Education, Inc.
680 Fifth Avenue
New York, NY 10019

Handicapped Funding Directory: 1980–81 Edition
B.J. Eckstein, Editor
Research Grant Guides
P.O. Box 357
Oceanside, NY 11572

Table 1. *(continued)*

____ 14.	The plans for assessing the functioning of the children and evaluating their progress on an ongoing basis did not appear to be adequately developed.
____ 15.	Needed supplementary services (e.g., health, social, psychological, etc.) do not appear to be available.
____ 16.	It did not adequately discuss the active involvement of parents.
____ 17.	No provision was made for inservice training connected with project services.
____ 18.	Plans for inservice training did not appear to be comprehensive.
____ 19.	Coordination with the public school did not appear to be highly developed.
____ 20.	The proposed approach does not appear to have promise or potential for developing improved or increased services for young handicapped children and/or families.
____ 21.	Coordination with other appropriate agencies did not appear extensive.
____ 22.	The Advisory Council did not appear to be broadly based or its role clearly defined.
____ 23.	It did not adequately discuss the establishment of an Advisory Council.
____ 24.	It did not contain adequate discussion of the plans for demonstrating and disseminating the results of the project.
____ 25.	The plans for demonstration and dissemination were not highly rated.
____ 26.	Plans for replication activities were not adequately developed.
____ 27.	A timetable was not provided.
____ 28.	The timetable did not appear realistic to allow for accomplishment of the project objectives.
____ 29.	The estimated cost was considered high in relation to the anticipated results.
____ 30.	The estimated cost was considered low in relation to the anticipated results.
____ 31.	Plans for continuation after the period of Federal funding for demonstration are not indicated.

This list is reproduced from the checklist provided to reviewers by the U.S. Department of Education for review of Application for Grants under the Handicapped Children's Early Education Program, CFDA Number 13.444A, Special Education Programs, U.S. Department of Education.

The Foundation Directory
Columbia University Press
136 South Broadway
Irvington-on-Hudson, NY 10533

Foundation News
P.O. Box 783
Chelsea Station, NY 10011

Centers

The Foundation Center
888 Seventh Avenue
New York, NY 10019

The Foundation Center
1001 Connecticut Avenue, NW
Washington, DC 20036

The Donors Forum
208 South La Salle St.
Chicago, IL 60604

REFERENCES

Bourgeois, M.M. *Grantsmanship: How to develop and write proposals.* Wyoming State Department of Education: Cheyenne, WY, 1971.

Moreau, A.J. The private sector. In: B.E. McNulty & A.J. Moreau, *Public and private funding alternatives* (Position paper). Seattle, WA: WESTAR, 1980.

Seeley, K. *Grantsmanship in special education.* Unpublished position paper, University of Denver, Denver, CO, 1982.

White, V.P. *Grants: How to find out about them and what to do next* (6th ed.). New York: Plenum Publishing Corp., 1979.

Appendix

Sample Program Plan for Early Childhood Special Education

The sample plan that follows provides a basic outline of important concerns in program development. Although specifically addressing early childhood, the process and content are appropriate for various age levels. The reader is referred to Chapter 2, Conceptualizing and Developing a Program, and Chapter 3, Leadership and Administration, for a more detailed discussion of the planning process. The chart offers fundamental program objectives, activities projected in order to accomplish the objectives, and policies and procedures needed to administer the plan effectively.

The objectives are organized into five basic areas: 1) services to children, including child find, assessment, and program; 2) services to parents, including due process, parent support, parent involvement, and parent education; 3) staff development, including preservice/inservice and staff evaluation; 4) coordination of community resources; and 5) demonstration/dissemination. Each of the activities listed in the chart is discussed in further depth in Chapters 4–9. The construction of such a plan is useful to both program administrators and to persons writing grant proposals (see Chapter 11). The content can be modified depending on the purpose of the plan.

Sample Program Plan for
Early Childhood Special Education

Objectives	Activities	Policies and Procedures
I. Services to Children **A. Child Find** *Goal:* To identify and serve handicapped children from birth to 6 years old. 1. To implement semi-annual screening in three locations, screening at least 60% of the estimated population from birth to 6 within 1 year.	1.1. Contact a minimum of 15 agencies in the school district and coordinate a meeting to discuss screening. 1.2. Coordinate screening efforts with other agencies, including social services, health, institutions. 1.3. Conduct a community awareness campaign to include: —presentations to 10 service clubs and organizations —5 articles in local newspapers —10 air spots on local radio stations —distribution of 1,000 fliers through grocery stores, food stamp stations, doctors' offices, schools 1.4. Conduct developmental screenings at three different locations in the school district twice a year in cooperation with other community services and agencies. 1.5. Refer children with significant developmental delays in one or more developmental areas for further evaluation.	Write a policy statement to indicate Child Find compliance with PL 94-142. Document step-by-step procedures for identification, screening, and referral.

274

B. Assessment

Goal: To identify and serve handicapped children from birth to 6 years old.

Objective	Activity
2. Within 60 days of referral, 100% of children will be assessed, determination of handicapping condition will be made, service provisions will be planned, and IEPs written.	
2.1. Establish due process procedures and develop written documents for informing parents of due process rights.	Write a policy statement regarding assessment. Procedures include: —due process procedures —nondiscriminatory testing —placement in least restrictive environment —free appropriate education —individualized education program —annual review of IEP and placement
2.2. Develop guidelines for assessment and staffing.	
2.3. Conduct inservice training concerning due process, assessment, IEPs, staffing procedures, and parent counseling.	Delineate procedures for: —pre-assessment planning —assessment —staffing —classroom follow-up —evaluation
2.4. Conduct appropriate evaluation and care review for all children referred for assessment. Refer children to appropriate placements if a handicap is determined to exist.	
2.5. Conduct classroom assessments to determine exact program needs, style of learning, and appropriate intervention techniques.	Fiscal policy should be written to reflect money allocation on a service needs basis.

C. Program

Goal: To identify and serve handicapped children from birth to 6 years old.

Objective	Activity
3. Within 30 days of assessment, 100% of children will be receiving appropriate services.	
3.1. Develop a full continuum of service alternatives to meet the needs of handicapped children and their families.	Develop policy regarding a continuum of services and noncategorical placement. Staff personnel policies are needed, including procedures for: —hiring —job descriptions —salary determination —termination
3.2. Hire staff with competencies needed to provide a full range of services.	
4. 90% of all handicapped children served will demonstrate continuous growth, as demonstrated through ongoing evaluation.	
4.1. Develop maximally effective learning environments to meet individual needs of children.	Develop policy regarding program and staff evaluation. Delineate procedures for: —evaluating children

(continued)

Sample Program Plan for
Early Childhood Special Education
(continued)

Objectives	Activities	Policies and Procedures
	4.2. Select a variety of curricula to be used in program planning.	—evaluating environments —evaluating staff —evaluating curricula and materials —team coordination —planning and evaluation
	4.3. Have a transdisciplinary team meet at least weekly to plan child activities, evaluate progress, and modify program intervention strategies to ensure continued growth.	Write fiscal policy regarding expenditure of funds.
	4.4. Provide ongoing inservice training and professional development activities, based on needs assessed by the ECSE coordinator to increase staff knowledge and skills.	Develop procedures for processing equipment and materials. —determining per-child expenditures. Determine policy regarding staff development. Delineate procedures for: —assessing needs
	4.5. Involve parents in a range of activities to ensure follow-through at home.	—alternative methods for professional growth —evaluation
	4.6. Develop methods for integrating handicapped with nonhandicapped children.	Write a policy statement regarding mainstreaming.
	4.7. Develop a system for transition between services on a continuum with follow-up for the child and family.	Delineate procedures for: —integration with nonpublic school programs
II. Services to Parents **A. Due Process** *Goal:* To provide parents with needed services.		
5. 100% of parents of handicapped children will receive notification of their due process rights and have these rights explained.	5.1. Provide all parents with due process information and have it explained by a staff member.	Write a policy statement regarding due process. Develop procedures for due process: —notification —explanation
	5.2. Encourage parents to contribute in staffings and in the development of the IEP.	

B. Parent Support

Goal: To provide parents with needed services.

6. 75% of parents of children in the early intervention program will indicate that support services have helped them to cope with having a handicapped child.

5.3. Give parents ongoing notification of their child's progress and methods of measuring progress.

6.1. Make counseling services available to parents through the parent/family worker at staffings and regularly during the year.

6.2. Form parent support groups and make available to parents.

6.3. Notify parents of the parent support program.

6.4. Devise a method for pairing parents with each other to provide parent-to-parent support.

6.5. Make materials available to parents concerning:
   —books, journals, etc.
   —parent organizations
   —advocacy groups

Write policy regarding support services to parents.
Develop procedures for:
   —getting services
   —evaluating services

C. Parent Involvement

Goal: To provide parents with needed services.

7. 80% of parents will participate in various activities offered by the early intervention program.

7.1. Develop alternative parent involvement activities, including:
   —classroom participation
   —advisory board participation
   —program participation with children

7.2. Develop means by which parents can participate in decision making regarding their child's program:

Develop policy regarding parent involvement and its importance to child growth.
Develop procedures regarding due process rights.

(continued)

**Sample Program Plan for
Early Childhood Special Education**
(continued)

Objectives	Activities	Policies and Procedures
	—staffings/IEPs —conferences —program modifications —child/program evaluation 7.3. Develop evaluation measures.	
D. Parent Education *Goal:* To provide parents with needed services. 8. 80% of parents will demonstrate increased knowledge regarding issues related to their handicapped child.	8.1. Develop program options for individualized parent education: —classes —demonstration workshops —parent library —toy library —videotapes —counseling sessions —home demonstration —parent pairing —manuals	Develop policy regarding parent education.
9. 80% of parents will demonstrate increased skill in interacting with their handicapped child.	9.1. Develop means of getting input from parents regarding their concerns about parent-child interactions. 9.2. Develop means of helping parents develop interaction skills that take into consideration their child's strengths and weaknesses: —direct teaching —modeling	

| | —demonstration
—observation
—reinforcement | |
| | 9.3. Develop evaluation measures. | |

III. Staff Development
A. Preservice/Inservice

Goal: To increase staff skills in working with handicapped children.

10. 100% of staff hired will have appropriate credentials and will demonstrate competence in their work.	10.1. Write job descriptions that indicate needed qualifications, background and experience. Delineate job responsibilities and philosophy of the program.	Document staff/personnel policies. Develop procedures for hiring.
	10.2. Develop methods for interviewing to involve all team members and parents.	
11. 100% of staff will acquire a minimum of two needed skills and practice them with children and families.	11.1. Develop means by which to ascertain staff needs for staff development activities: —pretests —questionnaires —observation —interviews	Write a policy statement regarding inservice education.
	11.2. Establish systematic methods for inservice education: —classes —workshops —journals —consultation —materials center —demonstration teaching —instructional guides —institutes —intervisitations	
	11.3. Develop evaluation measures.	

(continued)

Sample Program Plan for
Early Childhood Special Education
(continued)

Objectives	Activities	Policies and Procedures
B. Staff Evaluation		
Goal: To increase staff skills in working with handicapped children.		
12. 100% of staff will be effectively evaluated on a regular basis.	12.1. Develop staff utilization and evaluation measures: —peer ratings —interviews —observation scales —forms for time/scheduling, staff/child ratios, meetings, planning times	Delineate staff evaluation procedures.
	12.2. Develop means for determining the effectiveness of staff evaluation procedures.	
IV. Coordination of Community Resources		
Goal: To increase services to handicapped children.		
13. Services to children will be provided in the most effective and efficient method 75% of the time.	13.1. Develop a system for coordination of services and funding among community agencies to include: —initial contacts —planning meetings —ongoing interaction around specific children —evaluation efforts	Develop procedures for development of interagency agreements.

V. Demonstration/Dissemination*

Goal: To increase awareness of effective programs.

14. Information concerning effective intervention practices will be demonstrated or disseminated to 10 other programs in the city or state.

14.1. Develop a plan for demonstration and dissemination to include:
   —timeliness
   —projected presentations
   —projected products
   —evaluation measures

---

*Demonstration/dissemination objectives and activities may not be needed in non-grant-funded projects.

Index